SAINT PETER

Professor and Mrs. Hengel at their home in Tübingen, spring 2007.
Photograph by Thomas Trapp.

SAINT PETER

The Underestimated Apostle

Martin Hengel

Translated by

Thomas H. Trapp

William B. Eerdmans Publishing Company

Grand Rapids, Michigan / Cambridge, U.K.

First published 2006 in German by Mohr Siebeck as
Der unterschätzte Petrus. Zwei Studien
© 2006 Mohr Siebeck, Tübingen

English translation © 2010 Wm. B. Eerdmans Publishing Co.

Published 2010 by
Wm. B. Eerdmans Publishing Co.
2140 Oak Industrial Drive N.E., Grand Rapids, Michigan 49505 /
P.O. Box 163, Cambridge CB3 9PU U.K.

Printed in the United States of America

16 15 14 13 12 11 10   7 6 5 4 3 2 1

Library of Congress Cataloging-in-Publication Data

Hengel, Martin.
[Unterschätzte Petrus. English]
Saint Peter: the underestimated Apostle / Martin Hengel;
translated by Thomas Trapp.
p.   cm.
Includes indexes.
ISBN 978-0-8028-2718-0 (pbk.: alk. paper)
1. Peter, the Apostle, Saint. 2. Apostles — Family relationships.   I. Title.

BS2515.H3813   2010

225.9'2 — dc22

2010009230

www.eerdmans.com

Contents

Translator's Preface		vii
Preface		ix
Abbreviations		x
	I. Peter the Rock, Paul, and the Gospel Tradition	1
1.	Three Questions for Matthew 16:17-19	1
2.	The Message of the "Man of Rock"	14
3.	Peter as the "Apostolic Foundational Figure of the Church" in the Time before Matthew	28
4.	Mark, the Disciple of Peter	36
5.	The Later Role of Peter and His Conflict with Paul	48
	5.1. Peter's Activity outside of Judea	48
	5.2. The Conflict with Paul in Antioch	57
	5.3. Peter in Corinth	66
6.	The Unknown Years for Peter and His Theological and Missionary Importance	79
	6.1. Concerning Peter's Theology	79
	6.2. The Organizer and Mission Strategist	89
	6.3. Reconciliation with Paul?	97
7.	Summation: Ten Points	100

II. The Family of Peter and Other Apostolic Families 103

1. Mark and the Other Evangelists 103

2. Paul and the Other Apostles 111

3. Later Information about Apostolic Families 116

4. Clement of Alexandria and Encratism 123

5. Concluding Considerations 133

    Chronology 135

    Index of Ancient Works 139

    Index of Modern Authors 150

    Index of Subjects 153

    Greek Terms 161

Translator's Preface

What a joy to have been able to translate this book about the apostle Peter for Professor Hengel! I am honored that Eerdmans Publishing Company asked me to do this project.

Professor Hengel is certainly a most respected scholar. He was a humble man as well. My wife, Kathy, and I were privileged to meet Professor and Mrs. Hengel at their home in Tübingen in the spring of 2007. They received us most graciously. I was stunned by the personal library that he had, with books filling almost every space, floor to ceiling, and then going around the corner into his personal study and beyond that into the anteroom, which was filled with virtually all the Greek and Latin works of the Loeb Classical Library. His wife shared with Kathy that he frequently worked late into the evening, even though he had recently celebrated his eightieth birthday. He was proud to tell me that this book was given as a gift to Pope Benedict XVI, who, like Hengel, had taught in Tübingen, when the pope paid an official visit to the country of his birth.

Professor Hengel was able to see this translation before it was edited. He and Prof. Christoph Schaefer, his assistant at the time, were both most helpful in answering all the questions that I posed about technical matters and how to render certain terms. We even discussed the best way to translate the title, and I of course followed his suggestion.

I also want to thank Craig Noll, who has been a wonderful, detail-oriented editor for this volume. He has improved the flow of the translation throughout. We enjoyed detailed discussions about concepts behind words, and I am most appreciative.

I am grateful for the support given to me by Concordia University and by Emmaus Lutheran Church, both in St. Paul, Minnesota, the settings for my teaching and pastoring ministries, where I can share the fruits of the labor.

Professor Hengel calls for a reevaluation of the role played by Peter in the early church. He analyzes Peter's relationship with James (Jerusalem) and Paul (the Gentile world) and suggests a much more central role for Peter in the history of the early church than he is usually given. He calls into question those who see the early church as formed primarily by unknowns in a Gentile setting. He observes that those who question what Papias says about Peter and John Mark never explain why they call the tradition into question. He offers a "Petrine" side of the story about the confrontation at Antioch and Peter's role in Corinth.

I have sought to translate so that the reader will forget that it is a translation. My fervent hope is that you will hear Professor Hengel as if you too had the privilege of sitting with him in his study, listening to him share his passion for the New Testament era and beyond. I mourn his passing, in June 2009, but I rejoice that this work can see the light of day in English.

I have often made my own translations of biblical and other ancient quotations. Some of the published translations sound very old, some do not render the text in such a way as to make the argument flow, and some use different technical terms at crucial junctures. Wherever possible, English translations are noted for comparison.

THOMAS H. TRAPP
Professor of Religion and Theology,
Concordia University
Pastor of Emmaus Lutheran Church,
St. Paul, Minnesota

Preface

The first of the two studies published here originates in a lecture that was presented in November 2005 at a joint meeting of the Collegium Germanicum et Hungaricum and the Melanchthon Center in Rome, and subsequently on various other occasions. I have expanded that presentation considerably in this published format. The second study appeared with the title "Apostolische Ehen und Familien" in the *INTAMS Review* 3, 1 (1997): 62-74. I essentially reworked and considerbly expanded this study as well, more intentionally placing the person of Peter thereby into the central position.

I chose the title *Saint Peter: The Underestimated Apostle* because I believe that the historical and theological importance of the fisherman from Bethsaida has been generally underestimated within both evangelical and Catholic exegetical circles. Furthermore, he is generally studied in order to harmonize him in his relationship with Paul. Both studies in this volume are ancillary studies that were done in connection with a history of Jesus and the early church that is a present work in progress.[1]

I offer thanks to Frau Dr. theol. Anne Käfer for putting the manuscript into computer format and to Frau Prof. Dr. theol. Anna Maria Schwemer and Frau Monika Merkle for a critical examination of the manuscript. My hearty thanks also to Herr Dipl. theol. Christoph Schaefer, who read the corrected page proofs and prepared the indexes.

Tübingen, during Advent 2005   MARTIN HENGEL

---

1. *Translator's note:* Professor Hengel planned a four-part work, *Geschichte des frühen Christentums*, the first volume of which has appeared: M. Hengel and A. M. Schwemer, *Jesus und das Judentum* (Tübingen, 2007). The following three volumes will cover (1) the time up to the Apostolic Council, (2) Paul's era and his missionary activity to the end of the first century, and (3) the era of the Apostolic Fathers.

Abbreviations

Ancient Literature

ActVerc	*Actus Vercellenses*
b. Ḥag.	Babylonian Talmud, tractate *Ḥagigah*

Clement of Alexandria

Hypot.	*Hypotyposes*
Paed.	*Paedagogus*
Strom.	*Stromata*

Epiphanius

Pan.	*Panarion (Adversus haereses)*

Eusebius

Hier.	*Hieronymi chronicon*
Hist. eccl.	*Historia ecclesiastica*

Hermas

Sim.	Shepherd of Hermas, *Similitude*

Ign. [Ignatius]

Eph.	*Letter to the Ephesians*
Pol.	*Letter to Polycarp*
Rom.	*Letter to the Romans*
Smyrn.	*Letter to the Smyrnaeans*

Irenaeus

Haer.	*Adversus haereses*

Jerome

Vir. ill.	*De viris illustribus*

Abbreviations

Josephus

Ant.	*Antiquitates judaicae*
B.J.	*Bellum judaicum*

Justin

Apol.	*Apologia*
Dial.	*Dialogus cum Tryphone*

Origen

Cels.	*Contra Celsum*
Comm. Matt.	*Commentarium in evangelium Matthaei*
Hom. Luc.	*Homiliae in Lucam*

Polycarp

Phil.	*Letter to the Philippians*

Pseudo-Clementines

Hom.	*Homiliae*
Recog.	*Recognitiones*

Suetonius

Claud.	*Divus Claudius*
Nero	*Nero*

Tacitus

Ann.	*Annales*

Tertullian

Bapt.	*De baptismo*
Marc.	*Adversus Marcionem*
Praescr.	*De praescriptione haereticorum*
Pud.	*De pudicitia*
Scorp.	*Scorpiace*

Modern Literature

AAAp	*Acta apostolorum apocrypha*, ed. R. A. Lipsius and M. Bonnet, 2 parts in 3 vols. (1891-1903; repr., Darmstadt, 1959)
AGJU	Arbeiten zur Geschichte des antiken Judentums und des Urchristentums
AGLB	Aus der Geschichte der lateinischen Bibel
AGSU	Arbeiten zur Geschichte des Spätjudentums und Urchristentums
AKG	Arbeiten zur Kirchengeschichte (Berlin)

ANF	*The Ante-Nicene Fathers: Translations of the Writings of the Fathers down to A.D. 325,* ed. Alexander Roberts and James Donaldson (Edinburgh, 1868-72; repr. Grand Rapids, 1975, 10 vols.)
ANRW	*Aufstieg und Niedergang der römischen Welt. Geschichte und Kultur Roms im Spiegel der neueren Forschung,* ed. H. Temporini and W. Haase (Berlin, 1972-)
ANTZ	Arbeiten zur neutestamentlichen Theologie und Zeitgeschichte
APAW	Abhandlungen der Preußischen Akademie der Wissenschaften
ARGU	Arbeiten zur Religion und Geschichte des Urchristentums
BAR	*Biblical Archaeology Review*
BBKL	*Biographisch-bibliographisches Kirchenlexikon*
BBR	*Bulletin for Biblical Research*
BDAG	F. W. Danker, W. Bauer, W. F. Arndt, and F. W. Gingrich, *A Greek-English Lexicon of the New Testament and Other Early Christian Literature,* 3d ed. (Chicago 2000)
BDR	F. Blass, A. Debrunner, and F. Rehkopf, *Grammatik des neutestamentlichen Griechisch,* 18th ed. (Göttingen, 2001)
BG	Berlin Gnostic Codex
BHT	Beiträge zur historischen Theologie
BKV	Bibliothek der Kirchenväter
BThSt	Biblisch-theologische Studien
BZ	*Biblische Zeitschrift*
BZNW	Beihefte zur Zeitschrift für die neutestamentlichen Wissenschaft
CCSA	Corpus Christianorum. Series apocryphorum
CSEL	Corpus scriptorum ecclesiasticorum Latinorum
DACL	*Dictionnaire d'archéologie chrétienne et de liturgie,* ed. F. Cabrol, 15 vols. (Paris, 1907-53)
EBib	Études bibliques
EHPR	Études d'histoire et de philosophie religieuses
EKKNT	Evangelisch-katholischer Kommentar zum Neuen Testament
FAZ	*Frankfurter Allgemeine Zeitung*
FC	Fathers of the Church
FGNK	*Forschungen zur Geschichte des neutestamentlichen Kanons und der altchristlichen Literatur,* T. Zahn, 10 vols. in 11 (Erlangen, 1881-1929)
FRLANT	Forschungen zur Religion und Literatur des Alten und Neuen Testaments
FS	Festschrift
GCS	Die griechischen christlichen Schriftsteller der ersten [drei] Jahrhunderte
HAL	*The Hebrew and Aramaic Lexicon of the Old Testament,*

Abbreviations

	L. Koehler, W. Baumgartner, and J. J. Stamm; trans. and ed.
	M. E. J. Richardson; 5 vols. (Leiden. 1994-2000)
HNT	Handbuch zum Neuen Testament
HSem	Horae Semiticae
ICC	International Critical Commentary
ILCV	*Inscriptiones latinae christianae veteres,* ed. E. Diehl, 2d ed.
	(Berlin, 1985)
INTAMS	International Academy for Marital Spirituality
JBL	*Journal of Biblical Literature*
JJS	*Journal of Jewish Studies*
JSNT	*Journal for the Study of the New Testament*
KNT	Kommentar zum Neuen Testament
LCC	Library of Christian Classics
LCI	*Lexikon der christlichen Ikonographie*
LTK	*Lexikon für Theologie und Kirche,* ed. W. Kasper, 3d ed., 11 vols.
	(Freiburg, 1993-2001)
NHC	Nag Hammadi Codices
NHS	Nag Hammadi Studies
NKZ	*Neue kirchliche Zeitschrift*
NovTSup	Supplements to Novum Testamentum
n.s.	new series
NTAbh	Neutestamentliche Abhandlungen
NTApocr	*Neutestamentliche Apokryphen in deutscher Übersetzung,* E. Hennecke, ed. W. Schneemelcher, 2 vols., 3d ed. (Tübingen, 1959-64), English trans. *New Testament Apocrypha,* 2 vols., trans. R. McL. Wilson (Philadelphia, 1963-65); German 5th ed. (Tübingen, 1987-89), rev. English ed. (Cambridge, 1991-92)
NTS	*New Testament Studies*
ÖTK	Ökumenischer Taschenbuchkommentar zum Neuen Testament
PG	Patrologia graeca, ed. J.-P. Migne
PuP	Päpste und Papsttum
QD	Quaestiones disputatae
RAC	*Reallexikon für Antike und Christentum,* ed. T. Klauser et al. (Stuttgart, 1950-)
RGG	*Religion in Geschichte und Gegenwart,* 3d ed., ed. K. Galling, 7 vols. (Tübingen, 1957-65); 4th ed., ed. H. D. Betz et al., 9 vols. (Tübingen, 1998-2007)
RHPR	*Revue d'histoire et de philosophie religieuses*
SBS	Stuttgarter Bibelstudien
SchLBA	Schweich Lectures on Biblical Archaeology
SHAW.PH	Sitzungsberichte der Heidelberger Akademie der Wissenschaften, Philosophisch-Historische Klasse

SPAW	Sitzungsberichte der Preußischen Akademie der Wissenschaften
STAC	Studien und Texte zu Antike und Christentum
Str-B	H. L. Strack and P. Billerbeck, *Kommentar zom Neuen Testament aus Talmud und Midrasch,* 6 vols. (Munich, 1922-61)
TANZ	Texte und Arbeiten zum neutestamentlichen Zeitalter
TB	Theologische Bücherei. Neudrucke und Berichte aus dem 20. Jahrhundert
TDNT	*Theological Dictionary of the New Testament,* ed. G. Kittel and G. Friedrich, trans. G. W. Bromiley, 10 vols. (Grand Rapids, 1964-76)
TRE	*Theologische Realenzyklopädie,* ed. G. Krause and G. Müller, 36 vols. (Berlin, 1977-2004)
TSAJ	Texte und Studien zum antiken Judentum
TU	Texte und Untersuchungen zur Geschichte der altchristlichen Literatur
TWNT	*Theologische Wörterbuch zum Neuen Testament,* ed. G. Kittel and G. Friedrich, 10 vols. (Stuttgart, 1932-79)
UTB	Uni-Taschenbücher
WMANT	Wissenschaftlichen Monographien zum Alten und Neuen Testament
WUNT	Wissenschaftliche Untersuchungen zum Neuen Testament
ZDPV	*Zeitschrift des Deutschen Palästina-Vereins*
ZNW	*Zeitschrift für die neutestamentliche Wissenschaft*
ZWT	*Zeitschrift für Wissenschaftliche Theologie*

I. Peter the Rock, Paul, and the Gospel Tradition

1. Three Questions for Matthew 16:17-19

"Tu es Petrus, et super hanc petram aedificabo ecclesiam meam et portae inferi non praevalebunt adversum eam. . . ." The Protestant who visits Rome is impressed when reading an excerpt from this text in a circular inscription in the dome of St. Peter's Basilica, even if he or she cannot give assent to the interpretation of this text that lies behind it, applying it to the bishop of Rome. In any case, it is worthwhile to reflect upon these texts and others that discuss Peter, and in fact to go further still to consider the unique person of this disciple. The majestic passage in Matt. 16:18, within its wider context in 16:17-19,[1] has posed certain puzzling questions since the time of Tertullian, Origen, and Cyprian. The entire passage reads:

1. Concerning the overabundance of the literature, see the extensive commentary by U. Luz, *Das Evangelium nach Matthäus. Mt 8–17*, EKKNT 1/2 (Zurich, 1990), 450-83 (with a summary of how the text has been interpreted over time) [Engl: *Matthew 8–20*, Hermeneia (Minneapolis, 2001), 354-77]; on the topic, idem, "Das Primatwort Matthäus 16,17-19 aus wirkungsgeschichtlicher Sicht," *NTS* 37 (1991): 415-33 [Engl: "The Primacy Saying of Matthew 16:17-19 from the Perspective of Its Effective History," in *Studies in Matthew* (Grand Rapids, 2005), 165-82]; in addition, W. D. Davies and D. C. Allison, *The Gospel according to Saint Matthew*, vol. 2, *Commentary on Matthew 8–18*, ICC (Edinburgh, 1991), 602-52; see also A. Schlatter, *Der Evangelist Matthäus* (Stuttgart, 1948³), 504-13; P. M.-J. Lagrange, *Évangile selon Saint Matthieu* (Paris, 1922; 1941⁷), 322-28. Among the monographs, the foundational work remains O. Cullmann, *Petrus: Jünger — Apostel — Märtyrer. Das historische und das theologische Petrusproblem* (Zurich, 1960²), 183-243; in addition, C. Grappe, *D'un temple à l'autre. Pierre et l'église primitive de Jérusalem*, EHPR 71 (Paris, 1992), 110-11, 148-49, 227-31; idem, *Images de Pierre aux deux premiers siècles*, EHPR 75 (Paris, 1996); see, in addition, O. Böcher, "Petrus," *TRE* 26:263-73, bibl. 265-66; R. Pesch, *Simon-Petrus. Geschichte und*

ἀποκριθεὶς δὲ ὁ 'Ιησοῦς εἶπεν αὐτῷ·
μακάριος εἶ, Σίμων Βαριωνᾶ,
ὅτι σὰρξ καὶ αἷμα οὐκ ἀπεκάλυψέν σοι
ἀλλ' ὁ πατήρ μου ὁ ἐν τοῖς οὐρανοῖς.
κἀγὼ δέ σοι λέγω
ὅτι σὺ εἶ Πέτρος,
καὶ ἐπὶ ταύτῃ τῇ πέτρᾳ οἰκοδομήσω μου τὴν ἐκκλησίαν
καὶ πύλαι ᾅδου οὐ κατισχύσουσιν αὐτῆς.
δώσω σοι τὰς κλεῖδας τῆς βασιλείας τῶν οὐρανῶν,
καὶ ὃ ἐὰν δήσῃς ἐπὶ τῆς γῆς
ἔσται δεδεμένον ἐν τοῖς οὐρανοῖς,
καὶ ὃ ἐὰν λύσῃς ἐπὶ τῆς γῆς
ἔσται λελυμένον ἐν τοῖς οὐρανοῖς.

But Jesus answered and said to him:
"Blessed are you, Simon son of Jona;
For flesh and blood has not revealed this to you,
but my Father, who is in heaven.
And I tell you,
you are Peter,
and on this rock I will build my community,
and the gates of the realm of the dead will not overpower it.
I desire to give you the keys of the realm of heaven,
and whatever you bind on earth,
that will be bound in heaven;
and whatever you loose on earth,
that will be loosed in heaven."

Few verses in the New Testament have caused such disagreement with respect to their interpretation, especially since the Reformation; at the same

---

geschichtliche Bedeutung des ersten Jüngers Jesu Christi, PuP 15 (Stuttgart, 1980), 96-104;
idem, Die biblischen Grundlagen des Primats, QD 187 (Freiburg, 2001), 31-39, bibl. 62-63;
G. Claudel, La confession de Pierre. Trajectoire d'une péricope évangélique, EBib, n.s., 10 (Paris,
1988); A. J. Nau, Peter in Matthew (Collegeville, Minn., 1992), 49-56; P. Dschulnigg, Petrus im
Neuen Testament (Stuttgart, 1996), 40-43; L. Wehr, Petrus und Paulus — Kontrahenten und
Partner, NTAbh, n.s., 30 (Münster, 1996); idem, "Petrus, Apostel I," LTK 8:90-94; T. Wiarda,
Peter in the Gospels, WUNT 2/127 (Tübingen, 2000), 96-99; J. Gnilka, Petrus und Rom. Das
Petrusbild in den ersten zwei Jahrhunderten (Freiburg, 2002), 10-11, 152-60, 253, 259.
    The text is astonishingly well transmitted. With respect to the decisive verse 18, Nestle/
Aland, 27th rev. ed. (2001), lists no variants.

time, few have been so important within history as these. At this point we cannot proceed further in considering the many-faceted effect their interpretation has had within history. Instead, in view of our basic theme, we will direct only three questions to the Matthean text at this time:

1. Who is responsible for this textual unit?
2. When did it come into existence?
3. Why did the evangelist insert it as a "special unit" into his writing, or else conceptualize it on his own?

The last question can also be formulated: Why does Peter hold such a position for the evangelist, which one might even say is unique? This question will give direction to the study that follows.

1. The promise to Peter, following right after his confession about the Messiah, does not go back directly to Jesus himself but presents itself as an artfully constructed compositional unit in the *manuscript of the evangelist,* who is reworking older tradition, though there is no way any longer to distinguish sharply between his redaction and the sources he had available. His is the only one of the four gospels that uses the term ἐκκλησία (community), and twice at that: in 16:18 he uses it for the universal community in Christ, and in 18:17 for the concrete individual community — the two senses in which it was used in early Christianity. The evangelist thus assumes thereby that Jesus himself established a "unique community" within and in addition to Israel, even though during his ministry he concentrated his efforts on the people of the twelve tribes.[2] When looking to what was ahead for him at this point, he was not concentrating on events that would lead to the onset of the history of the church after Easter but was speaking of his suffering as the servant of God and looking forward to the inbreaking of the reign of God, for all to see, when the Son of Man would be revealed.

---

2. U. Luz, *Matthäus,* 456 [Engl: *Matthew 8-20,* 357-58]; L. Wehr, "Petrus," 91. I am skeptical of the possibility of the literary separation of redaction from tradition, as suggested by U. Luz, "Primatwort," 423 [Engl: "Primacy Saying," 173], who himself admits that "the marks of redactional language in vv. 17 and 19a are not unambiguous." With respect to operations of this type, we know far too little about the relationships between the gospels during the time they came into existence. In my opinion, there were years of oral teaching that preceded the writing of Matthew. One might suppose that there is more of what is "traditional" in the Matthean composition than is commonly acknowledged. This begins already with the enigmatic Βαριωνᾶ (son of Jonah); see n. 58 below.

"Binding" and "loosing" are rabbinic technical terms for halakic and disciplinary decisions that "forbid" or "permit"; said another way, they indicate that one imposes or removes a ban.[3] We do not know how broadly such terms were in use in this sense before A.D. 70. The evangelist, who himself was an unknown Jewish Christian scribe and, one might assume, an experienced congregational leader toward the end of the first century,[4] takes this terminology from his opponents, the Pharisaic scribes who reformulated Palestinian Judaism anew after the catastrophe of A.D. 70. He thus uses 16:19 to articulate the fullness of the power of Peter with respect to proclamation and church leadership, in teaching and in organization, which would have validity on "earth" and in "heaven."[5] By contrast, in the parallel passage that is directed in general to the (twelve) disciples in 18:18, within the framework about discussion of the church, their full authority to carry out discipline is more heavily accentuated.[6] The "keys of the reign of heaven" (16:19a) are mentioned, with respect to Peter, in the message entrusted to him after Easter, which has as its central point the confession to Jesus that he is "the Messiah, the son of the living God" (16:16) and the one who brings the reign of God. Whoever takes hold of this message in faithful obedience and lives out his or her life in a way that corresponds to it, for that person the entrance to the reign of God will open itself, whereas the Pharisaic scribes had closed off access for themselves and for others at the time of the evangelist because of their enmity against Jesus in Jewish

3. Str-B 1:738-47 (739); see also W. D. Davies and D. C. Allison, *Matthew*, 635-41; on this specific topic, 639: "Peter is the authoritative teacher without peer."

4. Cf. Matt. 13:52 (unique to Matthew), certainly a circumspect reference to himself as a Christian scribe, and 23:34. Just as divine wisdom does (see Luke 11:49), the glorified Christ sends "prophets, wise men, and scribes." The author counts himself among the last group.

5. P. Vielhauer, *Oikodome. Aufsätze zum Neuen Testament*, ed. G. Klein, vol. 2, TB 65 (Munich, 1979), 66: "The power of the keys identifies the power to teach; in the same way, the power to teach and to discipline binds and loosens. . . . The *ecclesia*, in which binding and loosing take place, [is] in fact not in heaven but on the earth; but there is a correspondence between community and heaven in the sense that what applies to the community on earth applies also in heaven. . . . To this extent, the power to teach and to discipline that is given to Peter is the 'keys of the kingdom of heaven.'" See pp. 27-28 below.

6. In Matt. 19:28 (cf. Luke 22:30) they appear as judges over the twelve tribes; cf. Dan. 7:9-10, 22, 26; 1 Cor. 6:2-3; Rev. 20:4. The Old Latin manuscript c (Colbertinus, twelfth/thirteenth century) resolves the tension in that it has the plural *ligaveritis* and *solveritis* (you will have bound/loosed) in both 16:19 and 18:18. The influence of Western exegesis may be at work here. See A. Jülicher, *Itala. Das Neue Testament in altlateinischer Überlieferung*, vol. 1, *Matthäusevangelium* (Berlin, 1972²), 116.

Palestine.[7] By analogy, the same admittedly holds true for the (only seemingly) Christian "antinomians" and "libertines" who say "Lord, Lord" but who spurn "the will of my Father in heaven."[8] For those living at the end of the first century, the evangelist wants to restate this message once again in his work, which is addressed to the entire church in the critical situation that was confronting them.

2. These comments provide us with an answer to our second question, which deals with the *time of origin* for the passage. The text as a whole reflects the unique situation and the theology of the evangelist, who is cognizant of the tradition and who composed his gospel relatively late, approximately between A.D. 90 and 100, either in southern Syria or at the border between Palestine and Syria. As is demonstrated by Matthew 23, he assumes the existence of the decisions of the house of teaching established by R. Gamaliel II, which reconstituted Palestinian Judaism at Yavneh.[9] The historical situation of the First Gospel allows itself to be determined rather specifically. It is considerably younger than Mark and Luke, and it shows an awareness of both. An analysis of its historical situation shows that it could not have come into existence at an early time. Its theological vocabulary is the most developed of the three Synoptics and gives the most evidence of having been carefully thought through. The evangelist was an impressive theological thinker, whose effect on the ancient church compares favorably with that of Paul and of John. All of this leads to the conclusion that the anonymous author looks back upon Peter as someone who was, for him, a unique authority from the past, one who had died a martyr's death in Rome approximately one generation earlier, presumably within the context of Nero's persecution.[10] According to Tacitus, there was a

---

7. Matt. 23:13; on this, see the text available to him in Luke 11:52, where the scribes (νομικοί) have set aside the key of knowledge (κλεῖδα τῆς γνώσεως), which means the correct explication of the Scriptures. Cf. *Gospel of Thomas* 39.1-2, which, in my opinion, is dependent upon Luke and Matthew.

8. Matt. 7:21-22; cf. 7:13-14, 24ff., etc.; see n. 85 below.

9. For a thorough discussion, see H.-J. Becker, *Auf der Kathedra des Mose. Rabbinisch-theologisches Denken und antirabbinische Polemik in Matthäus 23,1-12*, ANTZ 4 (Berlin, 1990), 45-51; M. Hengel, *The Four Gospels and the One Gospel of Jesus Christ* (London, 2000), 196ff., 318, nn. 770-73.

10. On this, see 1 Peter (5:1, 13) and 2 Peter (1:13-15) as pseudepigraphic testaments of Peter; *1 Clement* 5 and 6, after A.D. 96; Dionysius of Corinth in Eusebius, *Hist. eccl.* 2.25.8, about 160; *ActVerc* 37-41 = *NTApocr*[5] 2:287-88 [Engl: 2:315-17]; cf. *Ascen. Isa.* 4:2-3 = *NTApocr*[5] 2:552 [Engl: 2:609]; see also the Greek fragment of an *Apocalypse of Peter*, ibid., 2:575, n. 43 [Engl: 2:637, n. 43], and John 21:18-19; cf. 13:36. All of them testify to his death as a witness to the

multitudo ingens (great multitude) who received a gruesome execution at that time.[11] This bit of information might be somewhat overstated, but it was in any case the greatest mass execution of Christians in the first century. The "gates of the realm of death"[12] "would not be stronger" than the church of Christ that was built upon Peter the rock,[13] even though the

---

faith. On Peter as a martyr, see the extensive work of O. Cullmann, *Petrus*, 78-178; in addition, see C. Grappe, *Images*, 49-81, and R. Bauckham, "The Martyrdom of Peter in Early Christian Literature," *ANRW* 2.26/1:539-95; a short assemblage of the evidence is provided by W. Bauer in *NTApocr³* 2:21 [Engl: 2:48]. On this, see also pp. 98-99 below.

11. Tacitus, *Ann.* 15.44.2-5(4): "Deinde indicio eorum [which means, the first ones arrested] *multitudo ingens* haud proinde in crimine incendii quam odio humani generis convicti sunt." (Next, on their disclosures, vast numbers were convicted, not so much on the count of arson as for hatred of the human race.) The report includes a literary play on the Bacchanal scandal in Rome in 186 B.C. Concerning *multitudo ingens*, see Livy 39.13.14; cf. *1 Clem.* 6:1: A πολὺ πλῆθος ἐκλεκτῶν (great multitude of the elect) were joined to the martyrs Peter and Paul, who were put to death under torment. There is no reason, in opposition to Tacitus, to deny the connection between the burning of Rome and the persecution of Christians, speaking here against H. G. Thümmel, *Die Memorien für Petrus und Paulus in Rom*, AKG 76 (Berlin, 1999), 10-14; idem, "Petrustradition," *RGG⁴* 6:1165. That Suetonius, in *Nero* 16.2.38, separates the two means nothing, since he does not keep to any chronological order, and since he discusses the persecution only at the beginning and then only briefly. Eusebius, *Chronik des Hieronymous* (GCS 47, ed. R. Helm, 185), places the persecution as the highpoint of the wicked deeds of Nero, at the very end of the ruler's reign; he committed suicide on June 9, 68. If this is the case, the just punishment follows right after the transgression. After the outbreak of the Jewish War in the summer of A.D. 66, it is unlikely that there would have been a persecution of loyal Christians (see Romans 13 and 1 Pet. 2:13ff.). At this point one would more likely expect there to be some action taken against the Jews in Rome. There is just as little evidence that Paul was executed in Rome sometime close to A.D. 62, after being imprisoned for two years (Acts 28:30). The last word of Acts, ἀκωλύτως (without hindrance), would more likely speak against that conclusion. Cf. *1 Clem.* 5:7 as well: His further travels "reaching to the limits of the West [ἐπὶ τὸ τέρμα τῆς δύσεως ἐλθών]" is to be taken seriously. It would only make sense that this refers to Spain (Rom. 15:24, 28; *ActVerc* 1:1 = *NTApocr⁵* 2:259 [Engl: 2:288]; *Muratori Canon* 37ff. = *NTApocr⁵* 1:28 [Engl: 1:35]). On the basis of *1 Clement* 5 and 6 (on this, Polycarp, *Phil.* 9:1-2), Dionysius of Corinth in Eusebius, *Hist. eccl.* 2.25.8, and Irenaeus, *Haer.* 3.1.1 (concerning the Gospel of Mark coming into existence after the death of both apostles), one can proceed from the assumption that their death came in connection with the same persecution. This will have been drawn out for a considerable time. The time of execution for Peter and Paul did not necessarily take place at the same time. But early on, still in the first century, the martyrdom of both was seen as having happened concurrently; see p. 99 below.

12. Cf. *Pss. Sol.* 16:2: πύλαι ᾅδου (gates of Hades); Wis. 16:13; 3 Macc. 5:51.

13. Concerning the translation of κατισχύσουσιν (prevail), see H. Hommel, "Die Tore des Hades," *ZNW* 80 (1989): 124-25, in agreement with A. v. Harnack, "Der Spruch über Petrus als den Felsen der Kirche," in *SPAW* 32 (Berlin, 1918), 637-54 = *Kleine Schriften zur Alten Kirche*, vol. 2, *1908-30* (Leipzig, 1980²), 511-24.

"Man of Rock" himself had been offered up as a martyr. This incident reminds one concretely of this persecution that brought death, but also of the present and even more severe future persecutions that one expected would accompany the arrival of the Antichrist.[14] Because the architect of the church, as the Resurrected One, was the one who broke the power of death, his church, which is built upon Peter the Rock, is also stronger than all the powers of death. The situation of the church during the late period of Domitian had gotten considerably worse than it was during the earlier reign of the Flavians.[15] Even the message about bearing the cross, which Matt. 16:24 takes from Mark 8:34, could point indirectly to Nero's persecution, which is the first time that we hear about Christians being crucified. Even Peter is said to have been crucified at that time.[16] The Lord, who erected his church upon Peter the Rock, which was invincible in spite of all future suffering, is the same one who assures the community of the disciples at the end of the gospel: "I am with you to the end of the world" — that is, until the parousia.[17]

3. Jesus' word about the "Man of Rock," which presents the climax within the Gospel of Matthew, along with the first prediction of suffering, which is set forth in stark contrast to it by design,[18] is unique in the entire

---

14. Matt. 24:9ff., 21-29 par.

15. Cf. the sixfold use of the verb διώκειν (persecute, pursue) in Matt. 5:10-12, 44; 10:23; 23:34. In the last passage he even speaks about crucifixion of Christians; see M. Hengel, *Four Gospels*, 323, n. 807. Concerning eschatological persecution, see Mark 13:19-20 = Matt. 24:21-22. Even the Apocalypse of John anticipates mass executions of Christians when the Antichrist comes, using Nero's persecution as a way to frame what would happen, but that would not be able to preclude the victory of Christ, accompanied by those who would stay true to the faith. In the end, the devil, death, and Hades would be thrown into the "sea of fire": Rev. 20:10, 14.

16. Tacitus, *Ann.* 15.44.4: "aut crucibus adfixi atque flammati, ubi defecisset dies, in usum nocturni luminis urerentur " (or they were fastened on crosses and, when daylight failed, were burned to serve as lamps by night); cf. John 21:18 and its interpretation in Tertullian, *Scorp.* 15.3; *Acta Andreae*, ed. J.-M. Prieur, CCSA 5-6, 2 vols. (Turnhout, 1989), 1:615, lines 9-10; on this, see C. Grappe, *Images*, 51-52, 55, n. 43; R. Bauckham, "Martyrdom," 546-50. According to *ActVerc* 37-38 = NTApocr[5] 2:287-88 [Engl: 2:315-16] and Origen in Eusebius, *Hist. eccl.* 3.1.2, Peter, by his own request, was crucified head downward; Matt. 23:34 provides the only evidence in the gospels that speaks clearly about the crucifixion of Christians. At this point, about whom would Matthew have been thinking?

17. Matt. 28:20. Matthew is the only evangelist even to mention the parousia of Jesus or of the Son of Man, doing so four times: 24:3, 27, 37, 39.

18. Matt. 16:21-23 = Mark 8:31-33; cf. Luke 9:22. Matthew sharpens the shocked reaction of Peter (16:22b), as well as Jesus' rejection of the response (23b: σκάνδαλον εἶ ἐμοῦ, you are a

New Testament. In no other passage is any particular disciple of Jesus se-
lected for particular emphasis in any comparable way. That is true simply
with respect to the beatitude that is directed uniquely toward him. The
closest one can come to a comparable passage would be that of the puzzling Beloved Disciple in the Gospel of John, who is presented in a way that
competes with Peter because of his closeness to Jesus. But even this ideal
disciple does not play the unique, salvation-historical role that the Matthean Christ promises to the Man of Rock. In fact, it is not to that Beloved
Disciple but to Peter that Jesus gives the directive in John 21:15-17, to "feed
my sheep," three times, which means that, even in John, the Resurrected
One confers a leadership role that is higher and of lasting duration, which
will come to an end only with his martyrdom.[19] Thus one cannot fail to see
that such special authority is attributed to Peter, even in the Fourth Gospel
itself.

The closest parallel to this remarkable promise from Jesus to Peter in
the middle of the First Gospel appears in an apocryphal gospel from the
second century, from the "hidden words" of Jesus "that Didymus Judas
Thomas wrote." There, in logion 12, it says: "The disciples said to Jesus: 'We
know that you will depart from us. Who [then] will rule over us?' Jesus
said to them: 'No matter wherever you have come from, you should go to
James the Just, for whose sake heaven and earth came into being.'"[20]

Here Jesus' brother James, who has been given the epithet "the Just," is
promised the position of leadership among the community of the disciples. The reason behind this is admittedly very different. In contrast with
the address to Peter, the grounds are not Christological or eschatological
but cosmological; it corresponds to the Jewish ideal of one who is perfectly

---

stumbling block to me). This stands in conscious contrast to 16:17, μακάριος εἶ, Σίμων
Βαριωνᾶ (blessed are you, Simon, son of Jonah), whereas Luke shortens it to harmonize it.
He does not wish to impute this false step of Peter before the distinguished Theophilus.

19. See John 21:15-19; on this, see U. Heckel, *Hirtenamt und Herrschaftskritik*, BThSt 65
(Neukirchen, 2004), 43-46, 139-58, and often elsewhere. On Matt. 16:18-19, see pp. 166-69.
Within the context of a crisis within the community of the disciples, Peter uttered the deci-
sive confession (John 6:66-69), which was superseded only by Thomas's statement after
Easter, in 20:28.

20. See the text and translation in K. Aland, *Synopsis* (Stuttgart, 1996[15]), 522. That the
world "was created for the sake of *the* elect" is accentuated in *2 Bar. (Syriac Apocalypse)* 15:7;
21:24; according to 14:18 and *4 Ezra* 8:44, it is for the sake of human beings; according to 6:55-
59, it is for the sake of Israel; and according to *As. Mos.* 1:12, it is created for the sake of the
law. See also Prov. 10:25: "The righteous one is the foundation [*yĕsôd*] of the earth," and its
cosmological interpretation in *b. Ḥag.* 12b.

righteous. As stated in the monograph by R. Mach that is still the standard: "The entire creation . . . is placed under the Zaddik [Righteous One] and stands ready to serve him."[21] The role here ascribed to James clearly competes with the unique position of Peter for the early church. This competitive relationship is also seen in the fact that James, not Peter, is promised in the *Gospel of the Hebrews* that the first appearance of the Resurrected One will be to him.[22] Later church tradition, from the time of Clement of Alexandria and afterward, in opposition to this claim, which originated from within a staunch Jewish Christian framework, sought to find a compromise, in which James was installed as bishop by all the apostles in Jerusalem.[23] But James can also appear for Clement as the leading recipient of revelation, being named first among those who receive "gnosis" from Jesus.[24] With respect to the institution itself, the "monarchical episcopate" in

---

21. R. Mach, *Die Zaddik in Talmud und Midrasch* (Leiden, 1957), 113; see especially 108-33: "The Works of the Righteous"; individual parallels are also in W. Pratscher, *Der Herrenbruder Jakobus und die Jakobustradition,* FRLANT 139 (Göttingen, 1987), 151-57, which admittedly misses the connection with the ideal righteous person. See also M. Hengel, "Paulus und Jakobus," in *Kleine Schriften III,* WUNT 141 (Tübingen, 2002), 557ff., and P.-A. Bernheim, *Jacques, frère de Jésus* (Paris, 1996), 132ff., 260ff., 278ff. Bernheim attributes the leadership role in Jerusalem to James from the very beginning.

22. *Gospel of the Hebrews,* frg. 7, according to Jerome, *Vir. ill.* 2, TU 14/1.7-8: The appearance takes place in Jerusalem on the day of the resurrection. See W. Pratscher, *Jakobus,* 46-48: the Resurrected One celebrates the Eucharist with him. The plural of Jesus' summons permits one to assume that James is surrounded by a circle of disciples.

23. Eusebius, *Hist. eccl.* 2.1.3, according to Clement of Alexandria, *Hypot.* 6; cf. Hegesippus in Eusebius, *Hist. eccl.* 2.23.4: "The [leadership of] the church was taken over, [together] with the apostles [διαδέχεται τὴν ἐκκλησίαν μετὰ τῶν ἀποστόλων], by James, the brother of the Lord." The Syriac translation takes this to mean "after the apostles"; cf. Irenaeus, *Haer.* 3.12.15: "circa Iacobum apostoli [the apostles [who were] with James]." According to Jerome, *Vir. ill.* 2, he was "installed [*ordinatur*] immediately [*statim*] after the passion of the Lord as bishop in Jerusalem by the apostles"; see also pp. 51ff. below.

24. Eusebius, *Hist. eccl.* 2.1.4, according to Clement of Alexandria, *Hypot.* 7, according to whom "the Lord, after the ascension, [gave] Gnosis to James the Just, John, and Peter," and these then "to the rest of the apostles," and these "to the Seven, among whom was also Barnabas"; as in Gal. 2:9, James stands in the first position as the greatest authority. Concerning the development of the tradition, see W. Pratscher, *Jacobus,* 178-86. Also in the original version of the Pseudo-Clementines, Peter and the other disciples are subordinated to James. See also the *Ep. Petri* at the beginning of the Pseudo-Clementines, *Hom.* (GCS 42, ed. B. Rehm, 1-2): Πέτρος Ἰακώβῳ τῷ κυρίῳ καὶ ἐπισκόπῳ τῆς ἁγίας ἐκκλησίας (Peter, to James, the lord and bishop of the holy community). In this way James appears as bishop of the entire church. In the last sentence he is addressed once more as κύριέ μου (my lord). Cf., in addition, the *Ep. Clementis* 1:1 (ibid., 5): ἐπισκόπων ἐπισκόπῳ (bishop of bishops), and

the church might actually have its roots in James being the leader of the community in Jerusalem, who is at the head of the "elders," and it might have spread to the West from there. Already at the so-called Apostolic Council James is mentioned as the first of the three pillars according to Gal. 2:9, before Peter and John. And according to Acts 15:13-21 James's suggestion resolves the dispute in Jerusalem, which means that he has the final, decisive word. The brother of the Lord apparently functioned as the leading authority figure for the original community in Jerusalem for approximately twenty years — from the time of persecution by Agrippa, roughly A.D. 42/43,[25] until he was stoned in about 62.[26]

It is thus all the more surprising that James appears in the Gospels only in Mark and Matthew, and then in a merely cursory role each time, as the first-named of the four brothers of Jesus, who lived in Nazareth and who are mentioned in the entire New Testament a mere 11 times, including 3 times in Acts and 4 times in Paul.[27] That is certainly also because he (and his brothers) still had an estranged relationship with their strange brother during Jesus' lifetime.[28] By contrast, Peter, when one counts the variety of ways he is named (Peter, Simon, Cephas), is mentioned 75 times in the Synoptics alone and 35 times in John.[29] His person is referred to in the New

---

now also the texts from Nag Hammadi, the *Apocryphon of James* (NHC I, 2), in which he is consistently placed ahead of Peter as the receiver of revelation.

25. Concerning the decisive importance of the persecution by Agrippa and its consequences, see A. M. Schwemer, "Verfolger und Verfolgte bei Paulus. Die Auswirkungen der Verfolgung durch Agrippa I. auf die paulinische Mission," in *Biographie und Persönlichkeit des Paulus,* ed. E. M. Becker and P. Pilhofer, WUNT 187 (Tübingen, 2005), 169-91 (182ff.). See also n. 254 below.

26. Surprisingly, it is mentioned only by Josephus, *Ant.* 20.200ff., as the earliest witness, then in a legendary, glamorized form reported by Hegesippus, in Eusebius, *Hist. eccl.* 2.23.4-18, then in a brief mention by Clement of Alexandria, *Hypot.,* according to Eusebius, *Hist. eccl.* 2.1.5, in the *(Second) Apocalypse of James* from Nag Hammadi (NHC V, 4; see *Nag Hammadi Deutsch,* GCS, n.s., 12, 2:431-32), and by Epiphanius, *Pan.* 78.14, but by no Christian text before 160 (Hegesippus), which means it is first mentioned roughly one hundred years after his death; see M. Hengel, *Kleine Schriften III,* 553-57.

27. Mark 6:3 = Matt. 13:55: "the brother of James, Joses/Joseph, Judas, Simon"; cf. Acts 12:17; 15:13; 21:18; 1 Cor. 15:7; Gal. 1:19; 2:9, 12; Jam. 1:1; Jude 1.

28. See the critical notations in Mark 3:21 and John 7:5: "For even his brothers did not believe in him," and, in addition, Jesus' criticism of his family in Mark 3:31-35 = Luke 8:19-21 and Matt. 12:46-50, as well as the fact that Luke is silent about James being the brother of Jesus.

29. Mark: 19 (Peter) + 5 (another name); Luke: 18 + 8; Matthew: 23 + 2. The compound name Simon Peter is counted as one individual. John has it 34x as (Simon) Peter, twice as Simon, and once as Cephas. Acts has it 56x as (Simon) Peter and once as Simeon; Paul refers to

Testament 181 times altogether; he is mentioned even more often than Paul/Saul, who appears 177 times. Both of them thus appear for us more often than the collective terminology that refers to οἱ μαθηταί (the disciples), οἱ ἀπόστολοι (the apostles), or οἱ δώδεκα (the Twelve). This radical difference in the number of times that James is mentioned, over against Peter and Paul, shows, among other things, that there was significant inner conflict within early Christianity. The result of this was that later, in the decades following 70, James and the relatives of Jesus stood on the Jewish Christian side, and that Peter and Paul — discounting for the moment observable theological and personal differences between them — stand on the stronger, expanding, and primarily Gentile Christian side.[30] This means that the traditions passed on by the church at-large, preserved for us in the canonical Scriptures of the New Testament after the catastrophe of the destruction of Jerusalem, are clearly one-sidedly representative of this latter view.[31] After this deep blow, Palestinian (-Syrian) Jewish Christianity, which remained faithful to the law, had less and less influence. During the second century, it was expelled from the church altogether, just as it had previously been expelled from the synagogue.[32]

In any case, we see from this cursory statistical comparison of names that — at least in retrospect — the two "apostolic princes" obviously played a transcendent role within earliest Christianity that almost completely marginalized the role played by the Lord's brother. This observation is particularly apt with respect to Peter in the gospel traditions and in the Acts of the Apostles. His unique position of importance can be

---

him 8x as Cephas and twice as Peter; thus, along with 1 Pet. 1:1 and 2 Pet. 1:1, the total is 181 references.

30. In spite of Gal. 2:11-12; see pp. 57-65 below. An exception is found in the Pseudo-Clementines, with their anti-Pauline, Jewish Christian sources, from the second half of the second century, which seek to position Peter under James and which make Paul into an opponent.

31. On this, see P.-A. Bernheim, *Jacques.*

32. Justin, *Dial.* 47, differentiates between the tolerant and the radical Jewish Christian groups and seeks to maintain church fellowship with the first group, if they do not demand that the non-Jewish Christians must keep the law. By contrast, Irenaeus, *Haer.* 1.26.2, judges the Jewish Christians the opposite way, calling them Ebionites (from 'ebyônîm; cf. the πτωχοί [poor] in Jerusalem in Gal. 2:10 and in Rom. 15:26), since they use only the Gospel of Matthew and reject Paul, considering him to be an apostate ("apostatam legis dicentes eum"). On this, see J. Carleton Paget, "Jewish Christianity," in *Cambridge History of Judaism,* vol. 3, ed. W. Horbury (Cambridge, 1999), 731-75 (756ff.), and S. C. Mimouni, *Le Judéo-Christianisme ancien* (Paris, 1998).

seen already by the very fact that, in a way that is similar to Jesus himself, but in contrast to Paul, we have no genuine written testimony from him. The two letters of Peter are pseudepigraphic, prepared by those who wanted to do something about the lack of written materials when compared to Paul. First Peter probably came into existence about A.D. 95-100, possibly as an answer to the publication of the collection of eleven "Letters of Paul"[33] and at the same time as a way to strengthen the faith when increasing oppression of the church came late in Domitian's reign and early in the reign of Trajan.[34] Second Peter comes from approximately one generation later and laments the misuse of the Letters of Paul, plus addresses doubts that have arisen about the apocalyptic expectation of the parousia. Both writings have the character of testaments of the apostle just before his martyrdom. In this sense they can be compared with the pseudepigraphic Pastoral Epistles. In reality, we do not even know whether we can say for sure that Peter, who was once a Galilean fisherman, even knew how to write decently. The ability to read, already on the level of being able to know the Holy Scriptures, was more important and more widespread.

According to Acts 4:13, the leading high priests (4:6) expressed wonder about the fearless speech of Peter and John, since they were "uneducated laity."[35] Even Peter's knowledge of Greek would have had its faults, since information furnished by Papias says that Mark was the "interpreter" of Peter,[36] which means that the priests' remark cannot be simply rejected out of hand. The Greeks placed great importance on having a grasp of the grammar of their language, about which no one should be able to find mistakes, and they emphasized good rhetoric. So where would a simple

33. Still without the Pastoral Epistles, but with Hebrews; see U. Schnelle, *Einleitung in das Neue Testament*, UTB 1830 (Göttingen, 2002⁴), 397ff.; G. Zuntz, *The Text of the Epistles*, SchLBA (London, 1953), 263-83 (278-79). He dates the collection of the ten letters and Hebrews, though without the Pastorals, to about A.D. 100. The use of individual letters (1 Corinthians, Romans, Philippians) by Clement of Rome permits one to conclude that there were smaller collections in the archives of the communities that were earlier still.

34. The Gospel of Matthew and the Gospel of John, which is written a bit later, both assume a similar situation; cf. John 16:2; 10:12; on Matthew, see n. 15 above.

35. Acts 4:13: ἄνθρωποι ἀγράμματοί [literally "uninformed about writing"] εἰσιν καὶ ἰδιῶται. On this, see BDAG, 15. On the problem, see the extensive examination by C. Hezser, *Jewish Literacy in Roman Palestine*, TSAJ 81 (Tübingen, 2001). On Acts 4:13, see 186, n. 96. She assumes that the "literacy rate" in Judean Palestine in the first century after Christ was relatively low (496ff.).

36. Eusebius, *Hist. eccl.* 3.39.15; see pp. 38ff. below.

fisherman from Bethsaida/Capernaum[37] have learned grammatically and rhetorically correct Greek? It is not just by chance that, once again as reported by Papias, the oldest written collection of sayings of Jesus is attributed to the disciple Matthew and not to Peter: a tax farmer ought to be able to write without mistakes.[38] With respect to the art of expressing oneself in a manner that is rhetorical and literary, Saul/Paul, who was at one time a Pharisaic scribe, would have far exceeded the abilities of someone who was once a fisherman and who came from a Galilean village. Furthermore, Paul came from the world-class town of Tarsus,[39] which would have provided rich educational opportunities, and he also studied in Jerusalem. When simply giving a speech, however, Peter must also have been one who was empowered by the Spirit, but certainly in his mother tongue, Aramaic.[40] His Greek would thus possibly have been sprinkled with some errors, "exotic" to the extent that it was influenced by Semitic thinking. Only in this way can we explain his unique authority, which is accentuated in such a special way by Matthew in 16:17-19 — first, as the spokesman for the disciples in Jerusalem, and later also as a missionary beyond Palestine.

According to Matthew, the three verses apply directly to Peter alone, as

37. John 1:44 identifies Bethsaida as the home town of the pair of brothers Andrew and Peter. Mark 1:21, 29 par. identifies Capernaum as the place of residence for the married man Peter; see pp. 104ff. below. Concerning the transfer of the small town Bethsaida to become the city of Julia, through Philip, one ought not to use that to explain the Greek construction of Peter's name. On the one hand, there is no uncontested identification of either of the places; on the other hand, questions about their establishment and dating, on the basis of Josephus, exist as well. The renaming certainly did not take place to honor the daughter of Augustus, Julia, who was banished in 3 B.C., but because of his wife Livia (= Julia Augusta), who was taken into the royal Julian family in A.D. 14 and who at that time received the title "Augusta." The change in the town name certainly took place only after her death, in 29. The Greek construction of Peter's name cannot be evaluated on the basis of this unclear establishment as a city. Julia never had any type of greater meaning. On the entire topic, see M. Bockmuehl, "Simon Peter and Bethsaida," in *The Missions of James, Peter, and Paul: Tensions in Early Christianity,* ed. B. Chilton and C. Evans, NovTSup 115 (Leiden, 2005), 54-91.

38. According to Eusebius, *Hist. eccl.* 3.39.16. The information, as does the notation in Mark, goes back to the presbyter John. It is not based on our Greek Gospel of Matthew but goes back to one of his sources. One might forgive me the purely hypothetical speculation about whether Peter, as the head of the Twelve, might have commissioned Matthew, who had writing skills, with the task of collecting the logia of Jesus. A significant addition such as this would explain the attribution of the later gospel to Matthew.

39. M. Hengel, "Der vorchristliche Paulus," in *Kleine Schriften III,* 71-84.

40. With a Galilean accent; see Matt. 26:73 and Str-B 1:157.

the confessor who is singled out by God, and not just to the confession itself; it makes no reference to the collective group of the disciples. *He* is the
foundation stone, for Matthew, upon which Christ as the master builder
builds his church. With respect to Matthew, the question about Peter's person and activity is at the same time the question about this individual's
lasting authority.

2. The Message of the "Man of Rock"

We have considered the overarching importance of Simon Peter for the
early church during the entire time of the first three generations, which
means before and after Peter's martyrdom all the way to *First Clement* and
the letters of Ignatius.[41] In doing so, we have thus answered the third question that was posed above, regarding why the evangelist redactionally inserted the text of Matt. 16:17-19, a specially fashioned unit of material, into
his work in connection with Peter's confession. He employs this text because, for him — corresponding to the name that the Lord himself gave
Peter — Peter functions as the ruling head of the circle of disciples and in
the growing church. Peter's authority, as the one who was conveying the
traditions about Jesus, found its expression in the work of the evangelist.[42]
Matthew says this in the three verses in 16:17-19 in many ways more clearly
than is the case with the other evangelists.

First, by means of his confession that Jesus is the Messiah and the Son
of God, Peter shows himself to be in a unique position as one who receives

41. *1 Clem.* 5:4; Ign., *Rom.* 4:3; *Smyrn.* 3:1ff.; the last passage is certainly dependent on
Luke 24:37, 39 and Acts 10:41 (cf. John 20:20, 27; 21:5, 12; 1 John 1:1), or else on the traditions
that stand behind them. Concerning Ignatius and Peter, see M. Bockmuehl, "Syrian Memories of Peter: Ignatius, Justin, and Serapion," in *The Image of the Judaeo-Christians in Ancient Jewish and Christian Literature*, ed. P. J. Tomson and D. Lambers-Petry, WUNT 158
(Tübingen, 2003), 124-46. The effect of Peter extends into the second century. Once again,
this has to do with the particular effect that the First Gospel had in the second century. On
this, see W.-D. Köhler, *Die Rezeption des Matthäusevangeliums in der Zeit vor Irenäus*,
WUNT 2/24 (Tübingen, 1987). Concerning the number of apocryphal works of Peter, see
n. 80 below.

42. On this, see U. Luz, "Primatwort," 426 [Engl: "Primacy Saying," 175-76]: Peter "more
than all others represents tradition continuity with Jesus." Admittedly, the question immediately arises: Why Peter alone, and not the other disciples? I cannot understand why Luz
passes over the role of Peter in Mark. In my opinion, Matthew bases what he writes very
clearly on Mark, because it is the gospel of the student of Peter; see pp. 36-48 below.

a revelation from the heavenly Father.[43] His confession and the prediction of suffering that follows immediately thereafter are presented already in Mark as the climax of his gospel, which is narrated as a drama. In Matthew this is strengthened still more with Jesus' promise to Peter, which directs this promise on into the history of the church and all the way to the time of the evangelist — in fact, all the way to the parousia.[44] To be sure, already in Matt. 14:33, in the setting of the miracle of the storm being stilled, which also accentuates the role of Peter, the disciples confess in the boat that Jesus is "God's Son." This took place, however, as a spontaneous impression left by this miracle, whereas Peter now answers the question that Jesus addressed to the disciples by going beyond the original Markan material to articulate the worthiness of Jesus for the entire salvation history in a complete and in an ongoing sense: "You are the Anointed, the Son of the living God."[45] This confession does not come because of the will of a sinful man who is of "flesh and blood."[46] It thus cannot come because of one's own human insight, but only from the heavenly Father of the Messiah and from Jesus, the Son of God — and Peter alone can give it utterance. The beatitude also clearly elevates the one who receives this revelation above and beyond the collective blessing upon the disciples as those who witness with their eyes and ears in 13:16-17. It gives expression to a very special election.[47] The closest parallel to this *revelatio specialissima* to Peter is the autobiographical witness that Paul himself gives of the most personal revela-

43. On this, cf. also Luke 10:21 and Matt. 11:25: ὅτι . . . ἀπεκάλυψας αὐτὰ νηπίοις (because . . . you have revealed them to infants); see, in addition, 1 Cor. 2:10; Gal. 1:16; Eph. 3:5; 1 Pet. 1:5.

44. The voice of God in Matt. 17:5 = Mark 9:7 and Luke 9:35 underscores this high point. Concerning the parousia, see Matt. 16:27-28.

45. The confessions in Mark and Luke are not sufficient for Matthew. Mark 8:29 has simply σὺ εἶ ὁ χριστός (you are the Christ); Luke 9:20, based on the Old Testament pattern, reads τὸν χριστὸν τοῦ θεοῦ (the Christ of God). In addition, the masculine χριστός (Christ), with reference to a person, would not have made sense to Greek ears. We find it used only as a translation of *māšiaḥ* (anointed) in the LXX and in a few Jewish-Hellenistic texts that had been translated. The complete dignity of Jesus is seen in Mark for the first time in the legal proceedings before the Sanhedrin, 14:61-62; but see already 1:1 and John 20:31: The title χριστός by itself, without the additional υἱὸς θεοῦ (Son of God), did not express this dignity in its entirety.

46. Cf. Matt. 11:27 = Luke 10:22. On σὰρξ καὶ αἷμα (flesh and blood) as a paraphrase to refer to a human being as a creature, focusing on one's temporary existence, see 1 Cor. 15:50; Str-B 1:730-31.

47. The language and imagery in Matt. 16:17-19 both point to roots in Palestinian Judaism, from which the evangelist himself comes. He himself is making use of older traditions.

tion of the Son of God, ἐν ἐμοί (in me), from God himself and because of the act of election that stands behind it (Gal. 1:15-16), when in Gal. 1:12 Paul speaks of the revelation of his gospel from Christ without human mediation. Here one encounters two revelatory experiences, which could lead to conflicts about who has the more ultimate authority.

Second, Peter appears as the *Rock*, that is, as the foundation upon which the Resurrected One will build his community for the end times. The metaphors of a foundation stone and of construction hang closely together with the concept of the community as the city of God or even as the temple of the end times; we find both motifs at Qumran,[48] the second also being used by Jesus himself, in the context of the proceedings that took place before the Sanhedrin.[49] Even the death of the Man of Rock through martyrdom in Rome, and the many members of the community who were also put to death, cannot affect this *building of Christ*.

The most important and earliest parallel text, which additionally deals with the conflict between Peter and Paul, is 1 Cor. 3:10-15. In this passage the metaphoric language is admittedly opposite to that used in Matt. 16:18, since, for Paul, Christ is the one foundation: "For no one can lay any foundation stone other than the one that has been laid, which is Jesus Christ."[50] In fact, that is the same stone that Paul himself sets in place, which, according to the grace of God that is given to him "as a wise master builder,"[51] ap-

---

48. See O. Betz, "Felsenmann und Felsengemeinde," in *Jesus, der Messias Israels. Aufsätze zur biblischen Theologie*, WUNT 42 (Tübingen, 1987), 99-126. Cf. already Isa. 28:16 and Zech. 6:12: Starting there, the building of the temple could be understood as a task for the Messiah. Concerning the imagery of the construction of a fortress against the powers of evil in the Qumran community, see 1QH14:26ff., Martínez and Tigchelaar, *The Dead Sea Scrolls* 1:176: "My God, I support myself on your truth, since you set a foundation on rock [*tsym swd 'l sl*'] . . . to build a fortress, which is immovable, and all who go in there will not totter." It speaks earlier of the threat posed by the "gates of death," from which the one who prays "escapes into a fortified city and finds protection behind a high wall" (14:23-24); cf. the very similar metaphoric language in 15:8-9. A historical connection between the metaphoric language used in Qumran and the analogous concepts that describe the community as the eschatological temple is pointed out by C. Grappe, *Temple*, 51-115; see further parallels with Qumran there, on pp. 93-101.

49. See now J. Ådna, *Jesu Stellung zum Tempel*, WUNT 2/119 (Tübingen, 2000), 25-153; see p. 144, n. 184, on Matt. 16:18.

50. First Cor. 3:11: θεμέλιον γὰρ ἄλλον οὐδεὶς δύναται θεῖναι παρὰ τὸν κείμενον, ὅς ἐστιν ᾽Ιησοῦς Χριστός. Cf. Rom. 15:20; Eph. 2:20; Heb. 6:1; Hermas, *Sim.* 9.14.6: The Son of God is the θεμέλιος (foundation), who supports the church. On 1 Cor. 3:10-15 and the motive for building the temple, see C. Grappe, *Tempel*, 88-93.

51. First Cor. 3:10: ὡς σοφὸς ἀρχιτέκτων.

propriately serves as the basis for the community in Corinth. Immediately thereafter he offers his interpretation that this community is the holy temple of God, in which the Spirit of God dwells (1 Cor. 3:16-17). This means that, by means of his missionary activity, Paul appears as the only "establisher" of that community.[52] The self-confidence that the apostle shows here is remarkable. Others can do nothing but build further on top of the foundation stone he has laid, and the quality of their work will become manifest at the Last Judgment. *The indirect polemic against Peter the missionary is thus unmistakable.* This might, at the same time, be directed against the understanding of community that was held by the Jerusalem community. One might suppose that Peter was already seen as the "foundation" of the church.

In Clement's letter to James from the Pseudo-Clementine literature,[53] with specific reference to Matt. 16:17-18, Peter is identified not only as "the first of the apostles," "the first one to whom the Father revealed the Son," and "the one who blessed the Christ" but also as the one "who, on the basis of true faith and trustworthy content of his teaching, was designated to be the foundation stone of the church" (τῆς ἐκκλησίας θεμέλιος εἶναι ὁρισθείς), and who "thus, from Jesus himself, . . . received the name Peter." Even Tertullian reflects within his writing against Marcion on whether the name was given "because Christ is both stone and also rock [quia petra et lapis est Christus]." For that reason he would have "given a name to the most beloved of his disciples [carissimo discipulorum] that is connected closely with the metaphors that are linked to Christ himself [de figuris suis], [an indication] that this one stood closer to him than did others." Since Tertullian also lays particular emphasis on the designation of Christ as the Rock elsewhere, his interpretation of Matt. 16:18 is to be considered primarily because of its relationship to Christ as the Rock *(petra)* in connection with 1 Cor. 10:4, a passage that he cites on six different occasions in *Adversus Marcionem.* Christ himself transfers his function as the "foundation stone" to that disciple with whom he is particularly connected. The connection between Christ as foundation (θεμέλιος) in 1 Cor. 3:11, or as "the Rock" in 1 Cor. 10:4, and the meaning of the name Cephas/Peter

52. Cf. already the change of metaphor in 1 Cor. 3:9: θεοῦ γάρ ἐσμεν συνεργοί, . . . θεοῦ οἰκοδομή ἐστε (for we are God's servants, working together; you are . . . God's building), which prepares for 3:10-17.

53. *Letter of Clement to James* 1.2-3, in Pseudo-Clementines, *Hom.* (GCS 42, ed. B. Rehm, 5); Tertullian, *Marc.* 4.13.6; cf. *Praescr.* 22.44 and *Pud.* 22.9. On 1 Cor. 3:10ff., see C. Grappe, *Tempel,* 97ff.

(Πέτρος) as "foundation stone" was seen clearly already in the earliest references to Matt. 16:18, in texts from the beginning of the third century; in my opinion, Paul himself knew it as well.

In the Deutero-Pauline text Eph. 2:20-21, which presents a further development of this metaphor, the community, by contrast, is "built" by God "upon the foundation stone [θεμέλιος] of the apostles and prophets, with Christ Jesus as the cornerstone.[54] In him the entire building is joined together and grows into a holy temple in the Lord." In this passage, the entire group of those who are sent out in this early period by Christ, who are gifted with the Spirit, are the foundation of the church, along with their message; through him, the cornerstone, they are held together to grow to become the place of the presence of God.[55] Schlier is correct when he notes the "closeness" of this text to Matt. 16:18 and to Rev. 21:14, where the twelve gates of the end-time Jerusalem have inscribed, on their foundation stones (θεμέλιοι), the names of "the twelve apostles of the Lamb."

And yet there are significant differences over against the Matthean word of Jesus. Matthew refers to a future construction; in Ephesians it is about a present structure that is in fact completed already, and Christ does not appear there as the chief builder (in addition, he is not the θεμέλιος, as in 1 Cor. 3:10ff.);[56] instead, he is the cornerstone who guarantees the survival of the structure. Also in the text of 1 Pet. 2:4-8, which is roughly contemporary with Matthew and Ephesians, Christ is identified as the living "chosen, precious (corner-) stone," which is rejected by mortals, whereas at the same time the believers are called "living stones," which as a "spiritual house" are being built into a "holy priesthood." The reason for saying this is provided by an extensive citation from the most important passage on the subject in the Old Testament: Isa. 28:16. As in Ephesians, the motif of the temple comes to the fore here as well. The individual members of the

---

54. ἀκρογωνιαῖον; cf. 1 Pet. 2:4, 6 and the citation from Isa. 28:16: see n. 48 above.

55. On the text and translation, see M. Dibelius, *Kolosser, Epheser, Philipper*, HNT 12 (Tübingen, 1927²), 54-55; cf. also H. Schlier, *Der Brief an die Epheser. Ein Kommentar* (Düsseldorf, 1963⁴), 140-45; P. Vielhauer, *Oikodome*, 117ff. The Letter to the Ephesians came into existence about the same time as Matthew, between A.D. 90 and 100; in my opinion, it is connected with the collection of the Letters of Paul; see n. 33 above.

56. According to Rev. 21:2 the preexistent holy city comes "from the heaven," which means, from God himself; cf. already Gal. 4:26. H. Schlier, *Epheser*, 142-43, tries to smooth out this apparent contradiction. But Col. 2:7 (ἐποικοδομούμενοι ἐν αὐτῷ, built up in him), which he cites in support, is not a mediating position; in terms of content, it stands closer to 1 Cor. 3:10ff.

community appear at the same time as individual stones within the sanctuary's structure, in addition to being members of the priesthood. In conjunction with Exod. 19:6, 1 Pet. 2:9 thus speaks of a "royal priesthood" and of a "holy people." Instead of using ἐκκλησία, a word that 1 Peter never uses, the royal and priestly people of God appear, a connection that is missing in Matt. 16:18, which also does not mention the temple motif. In that passage, in contrast to Eph. 2:20, the foundation is not a collective group of apostles and charismatics; it is an individual person, who is thereby placed in an elevated position with respect to all the others. In this form, such a description is unique in the New Testament. In the very first comment of the Fathers that deals with Matt. 16:17-19 in detail, Tertullian (*Pud.* 22.9) noted this very clearly when he emphasized the fact that the Lord had directed this text *personaliter* (uniquely) to Peter and had not given the power of the keys to someone such as a bishop or to a church.

Concerning Matt. 16:17-18, one must assume historically that Jesus himself gave Simon, the fisherman whom he called, the Aramaic nickname Kêphā', which was later translated into Greek as Πέτρος. We can admittedly only hazard a guess at the original sense of what happened here. The gospels all report on the fact that the name was given, but admittedly not in exactly the same way. John 1:42-43 connects it with the beginning of Jesus' public ministry and the selection of the first disciples, in which case Simon is only the third one called, after an unknown disciple (one would guess the Beloved Disciple) and after his own brother Andrew.[57] Mark 3:16 and Luke 6:14, which is dependent upon it, initially mention the name as being given at the time when the "twelve apostles" are appointed. Matthew is the only one who draws a connection between the confession of Christ as Messiah and the nickname Πέτρος; in contrast to the Markan text that he was following, he uses it as well, at the outset, as an addition to the name Simon.[58] This means that he places great emphasis on this nick-

---

57. John 1:35-40; on this, see M. Hengel, *Die johanneische Frage. Ein Lösungsversuch*, WUNT 67 (Tübingen, 1993), 216-17, 314.

58. On this, see already the call narrative in Matt. 4:18: εἶδεν . . . Σίμωνα τὸν λεγόμενον Πέτρον (he saw . . . Simon, who is called Peter); cf. 10:2, where this one, as the πρῶτος (first), leads the list of the disciples, and 16:13-16: Simon Peter as spokesman of the disciples who are being addressed. The name Peter, by itself, appears already in 8:14 and is common usage for Matthew. It is the actual name by which the evangelist knows him. The only exceptions are 17:25, the question of Jesus: τί σοι δοκεῖ, Σίμων (what do you think, Simon), and 16:17: "Simon Bar-Yona." The Aramaic name of the father is an Aramaic "archaism" of the evangelist (cf. Matt. 27:16; Mark 3:18; 10:46; Acts 1:23; 4:36; 13:6); it is very difficult to reconcile it with

name, which at the same time accords honor to the one who bears it. At this point he is certainly indebted to a widely practiced ancient tradition.

In and of itself, with respect to Palestinian Judaism, the use of nicknames is common among the relatively small number of examples available from the turn of the era.[59] Since Shim'ôn/Simon was the most commonly used personal name during the century before and after the turn of the era,[60] it would make sense that a nickname could be used as well, especially since there was a second Simon among the circle of the Twelve who had the nickname the Cananaean (ὁ Καναναῖος), which Luke renders "who was called the Zealot" (ὁ λεγόμενος ζηλωτής).[61] But with Kêphā'/Πέτρος, the bestowal of the name must have had special significance even from the outset; otherwise this name would not have so quickly become the more common, having largely pushed the name Simon out of the picture.

Certain problems are caused when trying to translate the nickname Kêphā', since the Aramaic word means "stone" or "rock," whereas the Greek Πέτρος, by contrast, normally means only "stone."[62] The Greek

---

John 1:42; 21:15-17, since Yônâ' as an abbreviation for the common name Yôhānān is not to be found in contemporary Judaism. On this, see T. Ilan, *Lexicon of Jewish Names in Late Antiquity*, TSAJ 91 (Tübingen, 2002), 134ff.: it is mentioned 129x. Since the name of the prophet Yônâ (Jonah) is equally rare (p. 143), this suggests in any case that it is an abbreviation. On the names of Peter, see M. Bockmuehl, "Simon Peter's Names in Jewish Sources," *JJS* 55 (2004): 58-80.

59. Rabbinic examples are in Str-B 2:5-6. See also the numerous nicknames on ossuaries and in inscriptions; cf. T. Ilan, *Lexicon*, 43-44, and L. Y. Rahmani, *A Catalogue of Jewish Ossuaries* (Jerusalem, 1994), index, 283, see under "nicknames" etc.

60. T. Ilan, *Lexicon*, 218-26, counts 257 individuals who had this name and notes: "This was the most popular name for Jewish Palestinian males in this period" (226), since this was a patriarchal name that was also linked to the most successful of the Maccabean rulers, and the Hebrew and Greek forms of the name were almost identical. L. Rahmani, *Catalogue*, 294, 296, mentions that there are eighteen inscriptions with the name Shim'ôn and eight with the name Σίμων. It is possible that the differences between the names were no longer even noticed. See also M. Bockmuehl, "Simon Peter's Names," 60ff.: "A Name of the Hasmonean Revival." It is thus possible that Simon, as well as his brother Andrew and the disciple Philip from Bethsaida (John 1:44; cf. 12:20ff.), always had the Greek forms for their names. Against this view would be the archaizing LXX-form Συμεών (Simeon) in the mouth of James in Acts 15:14 and in 2 Pet. 1:1. See also M. Hengel, *Judentum und Hellenismus*, WUNT 10 (Tübingen, 1988³), 120 [Engl: *Judaism and Hellenism* (Philadelphia, 1981), 105].

61. Mark 3:18 = Matt. 10:4; Luke 6:15; on this, see M. Hengel, *Die Zeloten*, AGSU 1 (Leiden, 1976²), 72-73.

62. See H. Stephanus and W. Dindorf, *Thesaurus* 7:1020: "Lapis, Saxum"; F. Passow, *Wörterbuch* (1852) 2/1:901: "seldom = πέτρα, rock." H. G. Liddell and R. Scott, *A Greek-English Lexicon* (Oxford, 1996⁹), 1398, still reads only "stone" and, as a special case, "boulder"

2. The Message of the "Man of Rock"

hearers could thus have heard the sense of the name Πέτρος[63] in the sense of a stone, since it would not have been known in the pre-Christian era. It is only with the Greek play on words πέτρος/πέτρα in Matt. 16:18 that this is clearly shown to be the "foundation stone." A. Dell, and in more recent times P. Lampe, R. Pesch, U. Luz, and others, have thus argued that the only possible meaning for Kêphā' and Πέτρος is "stone," and this suggestion has met with general agreement. But already in 1979 Fitzmyer pointed out that twice in the *Targum of Job*, from Qumran Cave 11, *kêph* means "rock," and that it can also mean "rock" in the Aramaic Enoch fragments.[64]

= rock fragment. In terms that use πετρο-, this part of the word means equally often "rock-" or "stone-."

63. C. C. Caragounis, *Peter the Rock*, BZNW 58 (Berlin, 1990), 17-25, assembles the various examples together. The earliest evidence is a tax receipt from the fourth year of Trajan (100/101) in Egypt (p. 23). The Latin examples for Petronius and similar names ought not to be cited here, however. Their derivation remains questionable. See part II, n. 108, on Petronilla, the supposed daughter of Peter according to later Roman tradition.

64. A. Dell, "Matthäus 16,17-19," *ZNW* 15 (1914): 1-49 (14-27); P. Lampe, "Das Spiel mit dem Petrusnamen — Mat XVI.18," *NTS* 25 (1979): 227-45; cf. idem, "Petrus," *RGG*[4] 6:1160; agreeing with this, among others, are R. Pesch, *Simon-Petrus*, 30-31; he considers especially the meaning "stone = precious stone" by accepting the suggestion of J. M. Ford, "Jewel of Discernment: A Study of Stone Symbolism," *BZ*, n.s., 11 (1967): 109-16; in addition, U. Luz, *Matthäus*, 457-58 [Engl: *Matthew 8-20*, 358-59]; C. Böttrich, *Petrus. Fischer, Fels und Funktionär* (Leipzig, 2001), 42-46; L. Wehr, "Petrus," 91, and many others. For another view, however, see already A. F. J. Klijn, "Die Wörter 'Stein' und 'Felsen' in der syrischen Übersetzung des Neuen Testaments," *ZNW* 50 (1959): 99-105, and especially J. A. Fitzmyer, *To Advance the Gospel: New Testament Studies* (New York, 1981), 112-24 (114ff.), who also calls attention to an Aramaic patronym *kp'* in Elephantine (fifth century B.C.) (117). Concerning the Aramaic meaning of Kêph as "rock," see already 11QtgJob 39:1, 29 (= 11Q10, col. 32.1 and 33.9): Martínez and Tigchelaar, *The Dead Sea Scrolls* 2:196/98, admittedly as a translation of *sela'*, as is also common in the later Targums. The meaning "higher rock" also seems correct for 4QEn[e] ar (= 4Q206) frg. 5, col. III.19 (see Martínez and Tigchelaar, 1:428); cf. 4Q205, frg. 2, col. II.27 (1:422) and 4Q204, frgs. 4, 5 (1:418). In 4QEn[a] ar (= 4Q201), col. II.8, it is possible that the translation could be either "stone" (Martínez and Tigchelaar) or "rock" (thus J. T. Milik and K. Beyer). For Job 30:6, the LXX translates *ḥorê . . . kēpîm* (holes in rocks) with τρῶγλαι πετρῶν; cf. Jer. 4:29, the rocks (*kēpîm*; LXX: πέτρας) as a place to flee; see also Sir. 40:15 and, on this, see W. Gesenius, *Hebräisches und Aramäisches Handwörterbuch*, ed. H. Donner and J. Renz (Berlin, 2005[18]), 565, and *HAL* (Leiden, 1974[3]), 2:468. The pre-Christian Aramaic (and Hebrew) language usage is certainly less clear than what is assumed by Dell, Lampe, and others; see also M. Sokoloff, *A Dictionary of the Jewish Palestinian Aramaic of the Byzantine Period* (Jerusalem, 2002[2]), 256: כִּיפ, "stone, rock." In contrast, πέτρα can be used by someone such as Josephus for the huge stones in the towers in Herod's fortress or for the wall of the temple; see *B.J.* 6.410 and 5.189, and, on this, see A. Schlatter, *Matthäus*, 506.

Kêph also appears in Old Testament Hebrew texts, as a loanword from the Aramaic, with the connotation "rock." The overlap in meaning is fluid. The designation "stone" can easily transition to mean "rock," and vice versa. It is thus not improbable that Jesus' characterization[65] of Simon with the word "Kêphā'" carried the meaning "rock (fragment)," especially since, as can be seen in the *Targum of Job, sela'* (rock) was commonly translated with *kêph*. This applies especially for the later, post-Christian Targums, in which we find many other examples. The step that led to "foundation stone" was close at hand in any case.[66] "Since . . . כֵּיף as πέτρος can be used to refer both to the block of stone that is inserted into the wall as well as to the rocky foundation on which the building stands, it remains unclear which aspect of the comparison is being used."[67] Its "foundational" meaning is essential, in addition, because the disciples and the early community understood the nickname Kêphā' in a completely positive sense from the very beginning. Also, the original name Shim'ôn/Simon was quickly pushed off to the side, so that in the ancient "summary of the gospel" in 1 Cor. 15:5, which goes back to the Jerusalem tradition, Κηφᾶς, which is the form the Aramaic name assumed in the Greek, had already replaced Simon's own personal name.[68]

The translation of Kêphā' to Πέτρος[69] must have taken place early on as well, possibly among the Hellenists in Jerusalem, who had reason to articulate the theological terminology for the new messianic movement in the Greek language.[70] Apparently the effort started at the very beginning,

---

65. Concerning the characterization of the disciples, see also Mark 3:17, where the two sons of Zebedee are called Βοανηργές, which means "thunder sons"; on this, see H.-P. Rüger, "Die lexikalischen Aramaismen im Markusevangelium," in *Markus-Philologie*, ed. H. Cancik, WUNT 33 (Tübingen, 1984), 73-84 (76-77).

66. So, for example, *Tg. Onq.* and *Tg. Yer. I* on Num. 20:8-10 and the *Tg. Neb.* on Judg. 6:20; 15:13; 1 Sam. 13:6; 23:25; 1 Kgs. 19:11; Jer. 23:29; 48:28; Amos 6:12. R. Pesch, *Simon-Petrus*, sees a close connection between the two terms.

67. A. Schlatter, *Matthäus*, 507.

68. καὶ ὅτι ὤφθη Κηφᾷ (and that he appeared to Cephas). In 24:34 Luke still reads καὶ ὤφθη Σίμωνι (and he has appeared to Simon); cf. also the archaizing form of the name as Συμεών in the mouth of James in Acts 15:14, and in 2 Pet. 1:1. It is striking that, even though the name Peter is already used much more than any other, Jesus himself addresses the disciple only as Simon: Mark 14:37; Luke 22:31; Matt. 16:17; 17:25; John 21:15, 17. One can detect here a fine, narrative tracking point concerning the original situation.

69. John 1:42: σὺ κληθήσῃ Κηφᾶς, ὃ ἑρμηνεύεται Πέτρος (you are to be called Cephas, which is translated Peter).

70. On this, see M. Hengel, *Kleine Schriften III*, 49ff.

since Aramaic nicknames such as this, which were incomprehensible to the Greeks, were understood to be a type of honorific name. For this reason I would also like to maintain that the new name for the leading disciple could not have been rendered in Greek as a noun with a feminine ending, that is, as πέτρα (foundation stone). It would have come to mind that one could use the related but admittedly rare form with the masculine ending, πέτρος. If the meaning was clearly "stone" or even "precious stone," it would have seemed appropriate that the much more common word λίθος would have been used.[71] The play on words with πέτρος/πέτρα, which means the understanding of the nickname in the sense of "foundation stone" in Matt. 16:18, itself already goes back to an ancient tradition and is certainly not an invention by Matthew. It comes from the double meaning in the Hebrew and Aramaic for *kêph-kêphā'*. The evangelist made use of this same interplay and made it function as the center of his own unique promise of Jesus in 16:17-19. It is also not just by chance that, specifically for Matthew, the nickname Πέτρος, which carried such great meaning for him, had almost completely replaced the original name Simon. In the ten places where Paul mentions this disciple of Jesus, he uses the Aramaic

---

71. The common term for stone was indeed ὁ λίθος; Liddell and Scott, on πέτρος: "The usual Prose word is λίθος" (1398). In addition, one also finds the feminine ἡ λίθος, Liddell and Scott: "mostly of *some special stone*" (1049). Also πέτρος could "in the later poets" of the *Anthologia Palatina* be feminine. The very common λίθος appears in the LXX roughly 240x, πέτρος only twice, in 2 Macc. 1:16 and 4:41, with the meaning of ballistic stones that could kill. Josephus uses λίθος about 130x, πέτρος 4x (among which are two of uncertain reading). For Philo the relationship is 90 to 2. In the Jewish Pseudepigrapha (according to the concordance by Denis), we find λίθος over 100x, πέτρος not even once. Also in the entire early Christian literature of the second century, including Clement of Alexandria, I do not find a single example of the noun πέτρος = stone. In comparison with λίθος, it was clearly a rare word that appeared only when purposely chosen. In my opinion, this was chosen as a translation because it was close to πέτρα. Because of Old Testament examples (Ps. 118:22; Isa. 8:14; 28:16, and other passages), λίθος (along with θεμέλιος) is used more frequently with reference to Christ; on this, see J. Jeremias, "λίθος," *TWNT* 4:275-83 [Engl: *TDNT* 4:268-80]. A selection of these "stone-(rock) utterances" were chosen in Judaism "to refer to the Messiah" (276 [Engl: 272-73]). Πέτρος, by contrast, was kept solely as a referent to the unique disciple. L. Wehr, *Petrus und Paulus* (83, 252, 255, 258ff.), supposes, because of a questionable, exclusive translation of *kêphā'* = πέτρος = stone, that the play on words πέτρος-πέτρα in Matt. 16:18 develops within "the Matthean-Community." In his opinion, the same would not have been true for the earliest community. He is too dependent here upon the secondary literature, and he has paid too little attention to the linguistic problem. There were many Jews in both Galilee and Jerusalem who spoke Greek, so that for them this play on words would have come to mind easily, particularly since *kêphā'* could mean both "stone" and "rock."

form of the name eight times, even though his community would not have understood it, and the Greek name only two times, both in connection with the formulation of the clearly stated decision of the Apostolic Council.[72] This usage could point to his desire to distance himself from the claim that was made by that name.[73] The reference to the only "foundation stone," Jesus Christ, which Paul himself laid,[74] permits one to suppose,

72. See n. 94 below.

73. Only Gal. 2:7-8; both earlier, in Gal. 1:18, and later, in 2:9, 11, 14, he uses "Cephas." Apparently he cites 2:7-8 from an agreement with the Christians in Jerusalem, in which the Greek form of the name was preserved. H.-C. Kammler, *Kreuz und Weisheit. Eine exegetische Untersuchung zu 1 Kor 1,10–3,4*, WUNT 159 (Tübingen, 2003), 10, bases his denial of a relationship between 1 Cor. 3:11 and Matt. 16:18 on the fact that Paul identifies Peter in 1 Corinthians "throughout as 'Cephas,' and thus with his title of honor." He does not notice that this name would make no sense to the Greeks and that the customary name "Simon" for Peter would not have been useful in the church outside of Palestine. The question is whether Paul avoids using the name Πέτρος, which could be understood. It is also doubtful when he suggests that one would have trouble detecting in 1 Corinthians "any hesitations on the side of Paul" against Peter. Is there no connection between the ἄλλοι (others) and ἀνακρίνοντες ([those] wanting to examine [me]), who have called the full authority of Paul into question (1 Cor. 9:2-3), with what is stated in v. 5? And why does he place special emphasis on Cephas at the end? First Corinthians was written just a few years after the incident described in Gal. 2:11ff. Is it possible that this conflict, which deals with more than simple "public criticism" (one could speak more accurately of a deeply hurtful frontal assault), would go without further consequences? The Cephas people in Corinth would have been informed about these events. The situation there was completely different from that in Galatia. Paul would have no reason to attack Peter directly in Corinth. He reprimands the community. He refers to the conflict in Antioch in Gal. 2:11ff. only because untruths were being spread in Galatia and his personal trustworthiness was being challenged. One must call into question the assertion that the historical issues concerning a textual block, such as 1 Cor. 1:10–3:4, which is clearly based on historical events, "are of no value in determining the precise understanding of the sense of Pauline statements." That is demonstrated by the disagreement that has not yet come to an end with respect to ἐγὼ δὲ Χριστοῦ (and I [belong] to Christ), to which this scholar gives five pages of discussion. On Gal. 2:11ff., see pp. 57ff. below.

74. First Cor. 3:11: θεμέλιον γὰρ ἄλλον οὐδεὶς δύναται θεῖναι παρὰ τὸν κείμενον ὅς ἐστιν Ἰησοῦς Χριστός (for no one can lay any foundation other than the one that has been laid; that foundation is Jesus Christ); cf. Rom. 15:20. By means of his proclamation of the gospel, Paul set in place this foundation stone, which later missionaries, such as Apollos (he passes by the name of Peter), could build upon (ἐποικοδομεῖν) only with their preaching, whatever that quality might be, whether gold and silver, or down to hay and straw. About whom might he have been thinking with these last references? Should that not be taken as directed against Peter (or his associates)? The assortment of traveling missionaries, who would have visited Corinth just a few years after the congregation was founded, cannot have been all that great. See also 1 Cor. 10:4, about Christ as the πνευματικὴ . . . πέτρα (spiritual rock), who accompanied the people of God during the period of Israel's wandering in the wilderness.

within the larger framework of 1 Corinthians 1–3, that Paul wants to reject other "foundation"-claims. The picture of Peter the Rock, on which Christ builds his church, reminds one also of Isa. 51:1-2, where Abraham is identified as the rock from whom the people of God issued.[75]

The Matthean Peter is not simply the "typical disciple,"[76] neither as "rock" nor as the one who carries the keys of the reign of God by being provided with the complete power of binding or loosing. He appears instead as *the only authoritative disciple figure,* with all of the other disciples disappearing completely behind him, generally being dealt with only as a collective group and appearing as walk-ons. Admittedly, one ought not to conclude too quickly that this name, which carries such importance for Matthew, is given because of psychological reasons.

Instead, one must follow Schlatter and emphasize that for Matthew the nickname Πέτρος "describes the function of the disciple, not his character, nor his unique spiritual qualities that would purportedly show him to be special above the others and would make him particularly suited for his calling. For Matthew, σὰρξ καὶ αἷμα [flesh and blood] is never a 'rock.'

75. Isa. 51:1-2 (MT): "Look to the rock [ṣûr; LXX: στερεὰν πέτραν], from which you were hewn. . . . Look to Abraham, your father. . . . For it was as *a single person* that I called him, blessed and multiplied him." Here it is clearly a matter of being progeny, not a matter of what one is made of. Concerning Abraham as a rock *foundation* (pîṭra = πέτρα), according to Isa. 51:1, see *Yalqut Shimoni* I §766, from Yelamedenu, a very late text, which could have been influenced by Matt. 16:18. M. Bockmuehl, "Simon Peter's Names," 73-74, suggests that this is a reference to the name Peter. Even Matthew, the chief gospel for the Jewish Christians, was not unknown to rabbinic scholars. On Isa. 51:1-2 and Peter as a rock, see also P. Stuhlmacher, *Theologie des Neuen Testaments,* vol. 1 (Göttingen, 1992), 115, and W. D. Davies and D. C. Allison, *Matthew,* 642-63: "Peter is, like Abraham, a rock (cf. Isa. 51:1-2), and the change in his name denotes his function."

76. This is emphasized most especially by U. Luz, "Primatwort," 422-23 [Engl: "Primacy Saying," 172]: for him "Peter is the typical disciple." Also, in Matthew 16, "there seems to be nothing about Peter . . . which is not true of all the disciples." But this can be shown to be wrong just by the unique beatitude, the word about the rock, and the one about the keys. Luz himself admits, at that point, that "in the composition of the Gospel, Peter is given prominence as the apostle for the church." Here one simply needs to expand: in a way that is without parallel in early Christian literature, which places him in a unique position over against all the other disciples. Using contradictory language, L. Wehr, "Petrus," 92, says: He becomes, "on the one hand, the 'typical' disciple; on the other hand, he has his unique and foundational function." The two, however, are mutually exclusive. Even his denial is his own specific action and accentuates him uniquely over against the rest of the disciples. He alone confesses Jesus' messianic nature as Son of God; he alone denies his Lord. Instead of being a "typical" disciple, one ought rather to speak of Peter as a unique example, which — in the dual sense of what is positive and what is negative — elevates him far above the other disciples.

For him, the Father was the creator and the human being was placed into the world by divine action without synergistic activity."[77] This means that, for the scribes and evangelists within the Jewish Christian community, giving such a name is not because of a characteristic that has a psychological basis. Instead, it is an act of divine election and promise; one could even say it was an act of overflowing free grace.

Particularly for Matthew, other than Peter, the rest of the individuals within the circle of the Twelve do not play even a marginally similar role. Even the two sons of Zebedee, James and John, are mentioned only three other times, and that comes only within the group of three, with Peter always being the most important. Even Mark, which is a good one-third shorter, mentions them another ten times and gives John a chance to speak alone with Jesus.[78] Peter's brother Andrew appears only two other times in Matthew, though in Mark there are four other instances.[79] Only when one gets to John does one see a change from this typical Synoptic reduction, which is strongest in Matthew. In John one notes that the Beloved Disciple is closer to Jesus than is Peter, and Philip, Thomas, and some other individuals are mentioned as well. This tendency to magnify the importance of Peter is chiefly detected in the apocryphal literature of the second and third centuries. It is only with the later Acts literature that the other apostolic names appear more commonly as well.[80]

---

77. A. Schlatter, *Matthäus*, 507.

78. Mark 9:38. In order to clear the sons of Zebedee of responsibility in the situation in 20:20 (against Mark 10:35), Matthew has their mother request for them places of honor in the future, and he also inserts her name in 27:56, in place of Salome, who is mentioned in Mark 15:40. References of this type point to disagreements concerning the way ranking took place among the community of disciples.

79. Matt. 4:18, at the call; 10:2, when the disciples are listed; by contrast, cf. Mark 1:16, 29; 3:18; 13:3. Even Luke mentions Andrew in the gospel (6:14) and in Acts (1:13), only once in each volume. John, by contrast, mentions him five more times, in 1:40, 44; 6:8; 12:22 (2x). Concerning Andrew as a person, see also pp. 49-50 below.

80. Even among the texts that are attributed to the apostles among the Nag Hammadi texts, the name of Peter is the most frequent, with four texts being attributed to him: *Acts of Peter and the Twelve Apostles* (NHC VI, 1), *Apocalypse of Peter* (VII, 3), *Letter of Peter to Philip* (VIII, 2), and *Acts of Peter* (BG 8502, 4); James has three, Paul has two, Thomas has two, and John, one — the *Apocryphon of John*, admittedly preserved in four copies; see *The Nag Hammadi Library in English* (1988³). In the index of *Nag Hammadi Deutsch* (GCS, n.s., 12, *Koptisch-gnostische Schriften*, vol. 3 [Berlin, 2003], 2.905), which includes the number of times mention is made in the introduction and in the notes, Peter appears more frequently than Paul, John, James (both the Zebedee brother and the brother of Jesus), and Thomas. Even the total number of the rest of the Petrine apocryphal texts, as well as the times his

2. The Message of the "Man of Rock"

For this reason, one also cannot take the words of Jesus to the disciples in Matt. 18:18, despite the content that sounds somewhat similar, to be on the same level with the promise concerning the office of the keys that is accorded to Peter. For the evangelist, this promise encompasses the *unrestricted power of teaching and order* for the one being addressed. The short message to all the disciples in 18:18, in contrast to 16:19, is set within the more restricted context of organization within the community and deals primarily with the matter of discipline. With respect to tradition-history, it hardly furnishes the model for understanding 16:19;[81] at least as far as Matthew is concerned, its character is much more that of an echo of the preceding word of address from Jesus to Peter. In order to accentuate Peter in this connection as well, Matthew closes his "address to the community" in chapter 18 with a question by Peter concerning forgiveness and Jesus' answer, which is illustrated by the parable of the servant who was a scoundrel.[82] He is the leading spokesman for the disciples and is the only real discussion partner with Jesus.

The word about the keys for the βασιλεία (realm, reign) sets Peter forth as the proclaimer and teacher who is truly authorized, in stark contrast to the scribes and Pharisees, who close off the reign of God to those

---

name is mentioned, is more than those of the other apostles. See the table of contents of *NTApocr*⁵, vols. 1 and 2, and the indexes, for the names of the apostles. See, in addition, the impressive list by K. Berger, *LTK* 8:98ff., concerning the Petrine apocryphal texts, which belong to radically different types of literature, as well as his extensive analysis of apocryphal texts of Peter that stretch into the Middle Ages, with the title "Unfehlbare Offenbarung. Petrus in der gnostischen und apokalyptischen Offenbarungsliteratur," in *Kontinuität und Einheit*, FS Franz Mußner, ed. P.-G. Müller and W. Stenger (Freiburg, 1981), 261-326. It is striking, in that article, that the largest number of texts are preserved in Coptic, Ethiopic, and Arabic, from lands that are situated along the margins of the Eastern Church, whereas the apocryphal literature about Peter in Latin becomes less common. To be noted is the consideration of "Title(s) of Honor and Attribute(s) of Peter" (315-16). Matthew 16:17-19 gave decisive impetus to this apocryphal Petrine literature. An overview of these "Acts of Peter" is provided by H.-J. Klauck, *Apokryphe Apostelakten* (Stuttgart, 2005), 93-124 and 203-38, with reference to the Pseudo-Clementines. Only in the later acts do names appear such as Philip, Bartholomew, Matthew, etc.; see pp. 239ff. A student of Klauck, M. C. Baldwin, *Whose Acts of Peter?* WUNT 2/196 (Tübingen, 2005), presents a detailed study of the *Actus Vercellenses* and dates this to the late fourth century. Concerning the development of the legends about Peter from Clement of Alexandria to Eusebius, see especially pp. 64-94.

81. See n. 5 above. John 20:23 is hardly an older, more original parallel to Matt. 18:18 and 16:19. It is more likely that the opposite is the case, with the Johannine text being dependent upon the tradition from Matt. 16:19.

82. Matt. 18:21-35.

who are taught by them,[83] but also in opposition to all the "antinomians" and "libertines" who despise the new Torah of the Messiah and the righteousness that is required thereby.[84] This points to the front lines of a bitter struggle in which the First Evangelist was engaged toward the end of the first century. The door to the reign of God would be unlocked only through a proclamation about Christ that would awaken faith and obedience to follow in the tracks of the Man of Rock. This proclamation would serve to open "the narrow gate."[85]

3. Peter as the "Apostolic Foundational Figure of the Church" in the Time before Matthew

In a most remarkable way, Matthew expands, sharpens, and makes more precise the references to Peter in his gospel, both positively and negatively,[86] but he certainly did not fabricate what he wrote. In terms of the relative frequency of the mention of Peter, his 25 instances show restraint. He tends, rather, to shorten the text that he had at hand, omitting Peter's name 9 of the times that it occurs in the Markan text with which he works; he adds Peter's name only 3 times. The name appears 6 times in the material unique to Matthew's text, in which we cannot clearly separate traditional and redactional material.[87] John, who writes somewhat later — in spite of a certain distance, which one can in some way identify as critical — mentions Peter the most: 39 times (admittedly 12 of these are in the appended chapter 21); Luke, which comes earlier, mentions his name 30

83. Cf. Matt. 23:13. Matthew has taken a word of Jesus (Luke 11:52) that is directed against the νομικοί (lawyers), who have taken away the "key of knowledge," that is, the correct interpretation of Scripture, and has recast it in his own sense; see also pp. 4-5 above.

84. On this, see R. Deines, *Die Gerechtigkeit der Tora im Reich des Messias. Mt 5,13-20 als Schlüsseltext der matthäischen Theologie*, WUNT 177 (Tübingen, 2004).

85. Concerning the "narrow gate," see Matt. 7:13-14; Luke 13:24.

86. On this, see the chart in A. J. Nau, *Peter*: 25 times for Matthew and 41 for Luke; in general, Matthew follows the presentation of Mark, though he strengthens it and dramatizes it. See passages such as πρῶτος Σίμων ὁ λεγόμενος Πέτρος (first, Simon, known as Peter, Matt. 10:2); walking on water, 14:28-29 (unique there); 15:15; the temple tax, 17:24ff. (unique there); and 18:21-22 (unique there). He sharpens the scene in 16:23 (see n. 18 above), 26:33-35 and 75c (dependent here on Luke 22:62). See also R. Feldmeier, "Die Darstellung des Petrus in den synoptischen Evangelien," in *Das Evangelium und die Evangelien. Vorträge vom Tübinger Symposium 1982*, ed. P. Stuhlmacher, WUNT 28 (Tübingen, 1983), 267-71.

87. R. Feldmeier, "Darstellung," 268.

times, and the still older Mark, though considerably shorter, also mentions him 25 times. If one takes the length of each gospel into account, Mark clearly mentions him most often.[88]

The numerous times the Galilean fisherman and disciple of Jesus is mentioned is without parallel in early Christianity. It cannot be explained simply as the typical portrayal of a disciple, with his strengths and weaknesses, which still survives as a literary topos for the postapostolic age, and which is intended to depict an authoritative ideal. That is not sufficient with respect to the reference to his call as the first disciple according to the Synoptics, which is admittedly contradicted by John,[89] nor with his being the recipient of the first appearance (protophany) of the Resurrected One in 1 Cor. 15:5, which is mentioned in the gospels only in Luke 24:34. Even his role as the spokesman for the disciples in the gospels is not expansive. It could indeed be possible that his later role as a leader in the post-Easter age further strengthened his original importance as a follower and disciple of Jesus and suppressed the mention of the names of the other apostles. One can suppose that the other eleven who were called by Jesus did more originally than simply play the role of walk-ons, which is all that is now attributed to them in the gospels. Instead, we must *examine the activity of Peter altogether and seek to explain why he and only he was given this role.* The same holds true for his function as the leader of the original community in Luke, which survived intact for only the first twelve years or so, to the time of the persecution by Agrippa in A.D. 42/43, after which the Lord's brother James comes to the fore with an increasingly important role as leader in Jerusalem.[90] At the same time, it is striking that all four gospels, which make such a generous amount of space available for Peter, are either silent about Jesus' brothers or report about them in negative terms.[91]

This means that we need to explain, in a satisfactory way historically,

---

88. R. Feldmeier, ibid., 267: "Based on a total of 11,078 words in Mark, 18,298 in Matthew, and 19,448 in Luke, the frequency with which he is named in Mark is 1:443, for Luke it is 1:648, and for Matthew it is 1:772." The numbers are extracted from the statistical synopsis of R. Morgenthaler.

89. John 1:35-42: The unknown disciple, presumably to be equated with the Beloved Disciple, and Andrew were called before him. Simon comes to Jesus by means of the witness to the Messiah by his brother Andrew; cf. Papias in Eusebius, *Hist. eccl.* 3.39.4, and M. Hengel, *Johanneische Frage*, 80ff.

90. On this, see A. M. Schwemer, "Verfolger."

91. Mark 3:21, 31, 35 par.; John 7:3-10. See n. 28 above.

why Peter could have achieved such an important position, not only within the circle of the disciples and within Jewish Palestine or later within the adjacent country of Syria, with its large Jewish Diaspora population,[92] but *within the entire church at large, even as far as Rome,* a position of importance that continued during the following centuries as well. This is evidenced not only in the gospels, Acts, *1 Clement,* Ignatius, and the rich pseudepigraphic material that begins with 1 Peter,[93] but also with Paul, our earliest author, who, among those who were not part of his community of coworkers, names Cephas/Peter as often as all the other figures of the earliest community combined, that is, ten times in all.[94]

U. Luz rightly poses the question: "Why was it specifically Peter who became *the apostolic foundational figure for the church?*"[95] His answer is that, for the postapostolic era, it happened "because of his connection to Jesus."[96] This is certainly not wrong, but does the explanation go far enough? Were there not other disciples who were called by Jesus in the same way and who were just as closely connected with him? Does not the corrective offered by the Fourth Evangelist come into play here, who links the Beloved Disciple even more closely to Jesus, but who still cannot deny the special authority of Peter? It is not the anonymous Beloved Disciple but the one who had earlier denied him who is commissioned three times by the Resurrected One: "Feed my sheep."[97] It is Peter who overcomes the

---

92. According to Josephus, *B.J.* 7.43, in comparison to their presence in other foreign countries, the Jews "were most intensively spread into Syria, because of its nearness [to the mother country]," and most especially here in Antioch. See E. Schürer et al., *History of the Jewish People in the Age of Jesus Christ,* 3 vols. (Edinburgh, 1973-87), 3:13ff.; M. Hengel and A. M. Schwemer, *Paul between Damascus and Antioch: The Unknown Years* (Louisville, Ky., 1997), 52-53, 189ff. For this reason Palestinian Judaism could view Syria as a portion of the messianic kingdom; see M. Hengel, "'Ιουδαία in der geographischen Liste Apg 2,9-11 und Syrien als 'Grossjudäa,'" *RHPR* 80 (2000): 51-68 [expanded Engl ed.: "'Ιουδαία in the Geographical List of Acts 2:9-11 and Syria as 'Greater Judea,'" *BBR* 10 (2000): 161-80]; concerning the special relationship between Syria and Eretz Israel, see also M. Bockmuehl, "Antioch and James the Just," in *James the Just and Christian Origins,* ed. B. Chilton and C. A. Evans (Leiden, 1999), 158-98.

93. See n. 80 above, and O. Knoch, "Petrus und Paulus in den Schriften der Apostolischen Väter," in *Kontinuität und Einheit,* FS Franz Mußner, ed. P.-G. Müller and W. Stenger (Freiburg, 1981), 240-60.

94. Cephas: 1 Cor. 1:12; 3:22; 9:5; 15:5; Gal. 1:18; 2:9, 11, 14; Peter: Gal. 2:7, 8. He names Barnabas (including Col. 4:10) five times, James four times, John once.

95. U. Luz, *Matthäus,* 469 [Engl: *Matthew 8-20,* 367], italics by M.H.

96. Ibid., 470 [Engl: 368].

97. John 21:15-17. The motif was strengthened later through his martyrdom; see M. C. Baldwin, *Whose Acts?* 313: "For Eusebius, as for his contemporaries and those following him,

crisis among the circle of the disciples with his confession,[98] and it is pre-
dicted about him alone that he will undergo martyrdom by crucifixion,
just as it had happened to Jesus.[99] The question remains open: Why was
Peter placed into such an important role at the side of Jesus precisely in the
postapostolic age, and why was he given such a position of importance
over against the other disciples?

P. Lampe also takes up this phraseology about the "apostolic foundational figure": "*For Matthew,* P[eter] is *the* apostolic foundational figure
for the church."[100] One can heartily agree with this assessment. This can be
explicated, along with other elements, by the theological situation of the
author of the First Gospel, who presents himself as a Jewish Christian
scribe, as one who is obligated by the tradition and authority of Peter,
which is decisively opened to him in the decades following A.D. 70 with respect to the mission to the Gentiles. For this reason Matthew both rejects a
narrow Jewish Christianity that obligates itself to a literal observation of
the Torah and, at the same time, uses the commandments of Jesus to reject
the Gentile Christianity that mistakes God's will by advocating freedom
from the law.[101] When one looks at the persons who are mentioned by
Paul about forty years earlier, in Gal. 2:9 — James, Peter, and John — the
Jewish Christian author of the First Gospel, this Christian scribe, had to

---

Peter was not only the symbolic head of the church, he was the symbolic head of the martyrs," with reference to Eusebius, *Hist. eccl.* 8.6.1-4. See pp. 5-7 above, and pp. 98-99 below.

98. John 6:60-61, 66-69.

99. John 21:18-19; cf. 13:36; 16:2.

100. P. Lampe, "Petrus,"*RGG*⁴ 6:1162 (emphasis by the author and M.H.); cf. 1163-64: In
John 21, in spite of the Johannine "tendency to relativize the acknowledged authority of
P[eter], . . . analogously to Matt. 16:18 he is recognized as the foundational figure of the entire church also in his role as martyr." The threefold summons in 21:15-17 points, in my opinion, in the direction of an ongoing function right up to the point of his martyrdom; it is not
minimized simply to the level of being a foundational event. W. Schenk, "Das
Matthäusevangelium als Petrusevangelium," *BZ,* n.s., 27 (1983): 58-80, wants to see in Matthew an actual "Gospel of Peter." But why then does it have the title εὐαγγέλιον κατὰ
Μαθθαῖον (gospel according to Matthew)? An earlier εὐαγγέλιον κατὰ Πέτρον would have
been more successful. The apocryphal *Gospel of Peter,* from the middle of the second century, which assumes knowledge of the four gospels and in which Peter speaks in the first person, appeared too late and — for which we can rejoice! — it specifically came too late, with
respect to the four "canonical" gospels, to be able to supplant them. On this, see M. Hengel,
Four Gospels, 12-15.

101. On the text Matt. 5:17-19, which is misinterpreted so often, see now the foundational work of R. Deines, *Gerechtigkeit;* on Matt. 5:18, see especially pp. 289-370. Typical of
Matthew is 28:20.

make a choice. Not James, the brother of the Lord in Jerusalem, not Paul and his Gentile Christian missionary communities, and not the aged John and his circle of disciples in Ephesus[102] is "foundational" for the extended future history of the church. Instead, for him — using the vocabulary from Paul in Gal. 2:9 — Cephas/Peter is the only "pillar" who is deserving of this designation. The success of his gospel, which he had composed from the outset for the church at large,[103] speaks for the fact that he was not alone in holding this view.

Peter, though, had not arrived at this special level of importance initially only in the postapostolic age and "for Matthew," which, if true, would significantly underestimate the importance of Peter for the early church. He *is* the "foundational figure" already in the "early apostolic" age, in the first generation — in fact, in retrospect already before Easter. And he remains in that position from that time on, in essence, even after the time of his martyrdom — along with his "rival" Paul — throughout the entire history of the church and right up to the present. His overarching importance is evidenced in *all* the gospels and, one might even say, for the entire

---

102. I assume that the presbyter John, in Ephesus, was a student of the sons of Zebedee. This explains the identification of both figures in the most puzzling Corpus Johanneum; see M. Hengel, *Johanneische Frage*, 313-25.

103. On this, see R. Bauckham, ed., *The Gospels for All Christians: Rethinking the Gospel Audiences* (Cambridge, 1998); M. Hengel, *Four Gospels*, 76ff. Concerning the success of Matthew in the second century, see W.-D. Köhler, *Matthäusevangelium*. The criticism by M. M. Mitchell, "Patristic Counter-Evidence to the Claim That 'The Gospels Were Written for All Christians,'" *NTS* 51 (2005): 36-97, uses erroneous argumentation that completely misses the point historically. The Fathers, when they set forth their hypotheses about the origins, were always of the opinion that the gospels belonged to the whole church. References to places, with respect to the origin, do not suggest that a particular gospel was written for that particular location alone. A linguistic-ethnic (not geographic) exception is the "Hebrew" collection of logia by Matthew, which then — because of the interest of the church at large — would have been translated by various translators into Greek, as suggested by Papias in Eusebius, *Hist. eccl.* 3.39.16. The opening citation of Gregory of Nazianzus, which is based on traditional information, seeks to do nothing except to emphasize the superiority of the evangelist John over against the older gospels. Point of origin and value are to be essentially separated. That Matthew had the whole church in view is demonstrated not only by Matt. 16:17-19 but also by the closing statement in 28:18-20, which is directed to all Christians. We need to put an end to speaking uncritically about *the* "community" of Q and that of Mark, Luke, Matthew, and John. In essence, the evangelists wrote for the entire church, regardless of which location was in mind when they wrote; see n. 152 below. Already Justin, who more than once speaks of the ἀπομνημονεύματα τῶν ἀποστόλων (memoirs of the apostles), and Irenaeus, who dedicates to him the entire — decisive — third volume of his work, both understood the gospels in this way.

transmission history of the gospels. At this point, it is once again surprising that this is true at least two decades before Matthew, in the oldest gospel, the one according to *Mark,* written just before A.D. 70; again in the *two-volume work by Luke,* which was written sometime between 75 and 85; and two to three decades earlier than that in the *Letters of Paul* to the Galatians and Corinthians. Along with Paul and later John, he represents the *apostolic tradition* in the New Testament.

An interesting note by *Clement of Alexandria* furnishes support for this depiction: "The teaching activity of the apostles, including the service of the apostle Paul, comes to completion at the time of Nero; those who invented heresies appeared only later, at the time of Emperor Hadrian [117-38], . . . such as Basilides, even though he claims *Glaucias, the interpreter of Peter,* as teacher, as they boast about themselves. They also pass on the story that Valentinus belonged to Theodotus; but this one was *a student of Paul.*" It is noteworthy that, roughly in the year 130, these two groups of influential Christian "Gnostics" and their students place value on a personal and direct line of "teaching succession" that is tied directly to *Peter and Paul.* That makes sense with respect to Paul, because of his letters — but why also with Peter, the onetime Galilean fisherman?

From this same time of Hadrian, we also have the earliest example of a Gentile author who was familiar with a gospel. *Phlegon of Tralles,* who was freed by Caesar, loved sensational stories. He not only describes an eclipse of the sun that took place at the time of Jesus' crucifixion but, according to Origen, produced "Pertaining to Christ's Advance Knowledge of Future Events" and, in a most remarkable way, mentions in this context also the person of *Peter.*[104]

I must directly contradict Luz when he suggests that "Peter did *not,* in the most important sense, become the authoritative figure of postapostolic

---

104. On *Clement,* see *Strom.* 7.106.4, and, on that, see W. A. Löhr, *Basilides und seine Schule,* WUNT 83 (Tübingen, 1996), 19-23, who compares this tradition about Peter with the notation from Papias in Eusebius, *Hist. eccl.* 3.39.15, and follows my suggestion to see a "conscious effort to build concurrence" (21), on the part of the presbyter John, with the older Petrine traditions in Mark. Concerning Valentinus, Theodotus, and Paul, see C. Markschies, *Valentinus Gnosticus?* WUNT 65 (Tübingen, 1992), 298-302.

Concerning *Phlegon,* see Origen, *Cels.* 2.14, and, on this, M. Hengel, "Die ersten nichtchristlichen Leser der Evangelien," in *Beim Wort nehmen — die Schrift als Zentrum für kirchliches Reden und Gestalten,* FS Friedrich Mildenberger, ed. M. Krug et al. (Stuttgart, 2004), 99-117 (110ff.). Concerning the interest of later Gentile authors, from Celsus to Julian the Apostate, see J. G. Cook, *The Interpretation of the New Testament in Greco-Roman Paganism,* STAC 3 (Tübingen, 2000), index, under Paul and Peter.

Christianity *because of his own theology.*" His effect was supposedly much rather to be attributed to the fact that he had "time and again played an intermediary role in the church as a missionary to Israel and later to the Gentiles."[105] This is an example where Peter's importance continues to be underestimated. If he had not possessed a powerful, Spirit-filled proclamation[106] during a most threatening situation right from the beginning, Peter would not have become the first leader of the original Jerusalem community, with its most amazing missionary successes,[107] and thus would not have become the Man of Rock. Not only did he have the massive number of Jesus' traditions at his disposal but, as the first witness to the resurrection and by means of Spirit-prompted enthusiasm during the early times that followed Easter, he would have participated in giving decisive shape to *the development of the pre-Pauline beginnings of Christology and soteriology.*[108] The same might also apply to the early Christian expectation of Christ's return in the near future, as one confronts this idea as a pre-Pauline tradition in 1 Thess. 4:14-17; 5:2-3 and in the Synoptic apocalypses. Luke gave shape to the sermons preached by Peter in Acts, but they are not thereby simply worthless historically because their Christology sounds antiquated when compared to what Paul articulates.[109] At the very least, they demonstrate

---

105. U. Luz, *Matthäus*, 470 [Engl: *Matthew 8-20*, 368] (italics by M.H.). According to O. Böcher, "Petrus," 269, "the actual theology of Peter is best to be considered as being in outline form." One can agree with that. But then, we have in our possession from the message and history of earliest Christianity primarily only — though generally very impressive — "fragments."

106. Cf. the Lukan formulation in Acts 4:8. It is there that the word of Jesus from Luke 12:12 = Matt. 10:20 is fulfilled for Luke. Opposition and persecution give to the witness both profile and most convincing power. In this regard, Luke emphasizes the παρρησία (boldness) of Peter and the apostles: Acts 2:29; 4:13, 29, 31.

107. Acts 2:41; 4:4: The numbers may be highly exaggerated. But one ought not to question the success of Peter's preaching in Jerusalem and Judea. Concerning the numbers, see L. Brun, "Etwa 3000 Seelen, Act 2,41," *ZNW* 14 (1913): 94-96: The 120 (1:15) are 10 × 12; the 5,000 (4:4) are connected with Luke 9:14 or else are 10 × 500 (1 Cor. 15:6); the 3,000 (2:41) are to be explained as a contrast to Exod. 32:28. In Acts 21:20 Luke even speaks of πόσαι μυριάδες (how many thousands). Peter was not without his successes as a "missionary to the Jews" — even though he was not as successful as Paul: 1 Cor. 15:10; see pp. 89ff. below.

108. O. Böcher, "Petrus," 270: "Christology presumably stood in the center of the sermon of Peter," which means "Jesus is the Messiah." One could add: including the soteriological consequences; see, e.g., 1 Cor. 15:3.

109. The tendency arose in Germany, given impetus by the commentaries of Haenchen and Conzelmann, as well as the monograph of U. Wilckens, *Die Missionsreden der Apostelgeschichte*, WMANT 5 (Neukirchen, 1961), to give a completely negative evaluation,

the overarching authority of the spokesman of the Twelve. That the other Jerusalem apostles take a back seat to him in Acts, in the gospels, and even in the Cephas-Peter traditions in the letters of Paul[110] certainly also relates to his particular *theological* competence, which one cannot deny to him, even though it did not result in a written legacy and development, as it did with Paul. Why did the onetime persecutor Saul/Paul visit *only Peter* in Jerusalem and not the other apostles after his "three years" in Nabatean Arabia and in Damascus?[111] If it had not been for the authority and theological influence of Peter, there also would not have been a Cephas party in Corinth, and Paul would not have had to speak so bitterly about the delegation of the Petrine mission in 2 Corinthians 10–12.[112]

We ought not to allow ourselves to be led astray to historical and theologically one-sided judgments because of the one-sided nature of the sources that are available to us. *The Man of Rock was certainly not merely an average "theologian who passed on the theology of others."* As is true for Paul also, in both his effect and efficacy, he was unique. Because of the uniqueness of each, in later times — despite all the points of opposition along the way — those who came after subsequently remembered both of them.[113] One also cannot reject out of hand the possibility that there was some development of a school, unless one would determine that the term "Petrine school" would be inappropriate in light of his considerable influence. In-

---

historically and theologically, to the sermons of Peter. Wilckens admittedly revised his views to some extent in the third edition of 1974, in "a new, third section" (p. 3). See the summary, p. 205: "No matter how great is the creative literary ability of Luke in these texts, still the style and the scope comes from specific Jewish preaching from Jewish Christian traditions that were available to him." Is it not likely that Peter, as the best-known Jewish missionary, would have had a decisive role in this activity?

110. See pp. 28-30 above, and pp. 77-78 below.

111. Gal. 1:18; on this, see Hengel and Schwemer, *Paul*, 136-50. James is little more than a second-tier "bystander"; see n. 303 below. Acts 9:26-28 might reflect a Jerusalem tradition, which Paul must contradict. It is likely that his visit to Peter was kept secret; the life of Paul was threatened after his conversion, since it would have made him appear as an apostate: Acts 9:29.

112. First Cor. 1:12-13; on this, see n. 73 above. This situation ought not to be minimized; see n. 215 below. One cannot avoid the question: How did it happen that, among the Christians in Corinth, in a community that was founded by Paul, there would have been a "Cephas group," and how did it come to be that these particular difficulties for Paul in Corinth took place because of Jewish Christian messengers? See pp. 66-79 below.

113. *First Clement* 5 and 6; Ign., *Rom.* 4:3; Dionysius of Corinth, in Eusebius, *Hist. eccl.* 2.25.8; Irenaeus, *Haer.* 3.1.1 and 3.3.2. Peter is always named first in these passages. In addition, one notes the numerous apocryphal works of Peter; see p. 26 above, and n. 80 above.

deed many, if not almost all, communities between Jerusalem and Rome — at the very least *also* (particularly as is demonstrated in the gospels) — in some way "went to school" under him. The fact that scholarly activity has so intensively set forth individual "images of Peter" in the various New Testament writings and their relative differentiations ought not to divert our attention from the fact that there is an inner and connected relationship from 1 Corinthians and Galatians, through Mark, and on to Matthew, in 1 Peter, and then on to the later, surprisingly frequent apocryphal works of Peter in the second century. One can capture this relationship only by using the single word *authority*. Paul himself had to engage in deep discussion — sometimes quite critically — with such authority, and he does so with the passion that corresponds to his own unique personality and to his own theological awareness of the truth. Matthew 16:17-19, the text that we examined at the beginning, gives evidence of this authority for Peter. This presupposition was created by Jesus himself when he called Simon to follow him and gave him the name *Kêphā'*. For this reason, I would still suggest the meaning "rock" as most appropriate. We ourselves need to examine critically how Protestantism has underestimated Peter theologically as a result of the difficult circumstances presented in the sources.

4. Mark, the Disciple of Peter

As I noted above, Peter is not only the "apostolic foundational figure for Matthew"; he plays the same role also for Luke and for Mark.[114] O. Böcher is correct when he emphasizes that "the Matthean view of Peter still corresponds in essence to that in Mark,"[115] whose work came into existence roughly twenty to thirty years before Matthew's, just a few years after the martyrdom of the apostle in Rome, at the very location where it took place.[116] To be sure, there is a wide-ranging critical exegesis, lacking con-

---

114. See pp. 28ff. above. On Mark, see Papias in Eusebius, *Hist. eccl.* 3.39.15.

115. O. Böcher, "Petrus," 265. For a similar view, see R. Feldmeier, "Darstellung," 269: "In Matthew — based on the view of the third generation and progressing beyond Mark — Peter becomes the man of the church. But with respect to the gospel as a whole, he does not have greater importance than he does in Mark."

116. Concerning the author and the historical situation of the Second Gospel, see M. Hengel, "Entstehungszeit und Situation des Markusevangeliums," in *Markus-Philologie. Historische, literargeschichtliche und stilistische Untersuchungen zum zweiten Evangelium*, ed. M. Cancik, WUNT 33 (Tübingen, 1984), 1-45; idem, "Probleme des Markus-evangeliums," in

vincing arguments, that rejects the idea that assertions about the authors of the gospels are credible,[117] which would rather consign the origin of the gospels to an ill-defined fog, as is also the case for the way the questions about the dates of the gospels are resolved. It is easier to read one's own ideas into texts if one falsely interposes one's own ideas about setting and time and thus avoids needing to resolve them. One might happily forget that Mark writes for an overwhelmingly Gentile population in Rome. An example of such historical criticism that leads one astray can be seen, among the many that exist, in the widely circulated *Einleitung ins Neue Testament* by Udo Schnelle. He supposes that the author of the Second Gospel is an unknown Gentile Christian who obviously must have come from Syria, since one cannot deny that the vocabulary betrays a lexical grasp of Aramaic[118] that is beyond reproof in his gospel. The only proof that he can offer for this supposition is that the anonymous author writes in the Greek language, since it is for Gentile Christians. He refuses to accept the tradition, which has the presbyter John as its source, as is reported by Papias, that Mark the evangelist is the interpreter of Peter, since "neither

---

Das Evangelium und die Evangelien. Vorträge vom Tübinger Symposium 1982, ed. P. Stuhlmacher, WUNT 28 (Tübingen, 1983), 221-65, and the article by my assistant at that time, R. Feldmeier, "Darstellung," 267-71; in addition, see M. Hengel, *Four Gospels*, 76-115.

117. M. Hengel, *Die Evangelienüberschriften*, SHAW.PH 3 (Heidelberg, 1984); see also M. Hengel, *Studies in the Gospel of Mark* (London, 1985), 64-84]; idem, *Four Gospels*, 34-56.

118. On this, see H.-P. Rüger, "Aramaismen," 73-84; idem, "Aramäisch II," *TRE* 3:602-9. Mark is the scriptural book in the New Testament — in fact, the book in the entire Greek literature — which far and away has the most lexical Aramaisms. It is to be noted that they are all removed by Luke, and mostly so by Matthew. Such "barbarisms" were, as a rule, rejected in Greek literature. The only exception is the special case in the magical literature, which as a rule is significantly later and which has no connection with Mark. The Jewish Christian source for his gospel that came into existence in Rome is apparent. Nevertheless, he writes there for a primarily Gentile Christian reader in a popular style. The alleged reasons for suggesting that the author was a Gentile Christian are completely suspect. On Mark 7:3-4, see M. Hengel, "Mc 7,3 πυγμῇ. Die Geschichte einer exegetischen Aporie und der Versuch ihrer Lösung," *ZNW* 60 (1969): 182-98; Mark 14:1, 12 assumes the Greco-Roman way of dividing the day, which, contrary to the way it was treated in Palestinian Judaism, did not commence with the onset of nighttime. For this reason, the "day of preparation," on which the Passover lamb was to be slaughtered in the afternoon and before which all the leaven had to be removed from the house, was already considered part of the *maṣṣôt* festival; see Polycrates of Ephesus concerning the Passover dates in Eusebius, *Hist. eccl.* 5.24.6; cf. 5.23.1. I have no idea what would argue for a Gentile Christian author except for the desires of some modern authors to repress, as much as possible, the importance of Jewish Christianity in the New Testament. Attempts of that variety have little to do with *historical* criticism.

... [can one] demonstrate a Petrine theology behind the Gospel of Mark, nor . . . does Peter [play] a significant role in the Gospel of Mark beyond the information provided by the tradition. No one would assume that the person of Peter can be detected to be behind the unique theology of the Gospel of Mark if there was no tradition handed on by Papias!"[119]

Just about everything about this reasoning is suspect: Where does Schnelle get to know "Petrine theology" so well that he cannot find it "behind" Mark, and its "uniqueness," in order to be able to assert that Peter does not play any "significant role" therein? Beyond the fact that we know only the theology of the genuine Pauline letters and the pre-Synoptic logia tradition from *before Mark,* one must still ask whether in fact the overarching role that Peter plays in the earliest gospel, which demonstrates a decisive initial presentation of this very tradition, points precisely to the personal connection between this gospel and its author, the Man of Rock. Is it possible that Peter might have actually played a still greater role in some aspects of the pre-Markan tradition than even that which he played in the gospel it-

---

119. U. Schnelle, *Einleitung,* 243; cf. H. Conzelmann and A. Lindemann, *Arbeitsbuch zum Neuen Testament,* UTB 52 (Tübingen, 1998[12]), 321: "About all one can say is that the author of Mark is a Gentile Christian who is not more specifically known to us." A chief argument against Mark — his apparent lack of knowledge about Palestinian geography — shows only that the critics themselves are unaware of the problem of ancient geographic knowledge (without maps), especially concerning the geography of Palestine. On this, see M. Hengel, "Der Historiker Lukas und die Geographie Palästinas in der Apostelgeschichte," *ZDPV* 99 (1983): 147ff., and G. Lang, "'Über Sidon mitten ins Gebiet der Dekapolis.' Geographie und Theologie in Markus 7,31," *ZDPV* 94 (1978), 145-60, on Mark 7:31, with reference to Josephus, *Ant.* 18.153. At that time, Damascus belonged to the Decapolis. Concerning his supposed lack of knowledge about Jewish relationships, one can say only that Mark neither studied the commentary by Billerbeck nor ever attended an introductory New Testament seminar. The critically uncritical arguments against Papias's note are repeated in the scholarly literature as if part of a catena. P. Lampe, "Petrus," 1161, does at least admit that, in Mark, "[P]eter [is] the most important disciple" but rejects the note provided by Papias without offering any reasons: "That the author of Mark belongs to . . . the followers who accompanied [Peter] cannot be maintained." To this point, I have never encountered a convincing argument against the information provided by Papias. Each scholar seems to want to appear — and there is no difference any longer between Catholic and evangelical exegetes — "critical" concerning everything in the world, and no one notices how uncritical these arguments are! Concerning the topic as a whole, see M. Hengel, "Situation," 16-21, and especially 17-18, n. 73, concerning E. Meyer's criticism of J. Wellhausen, who introduced the numerous miracle stories into the discussion as an argument against the connection between the author and Peter. E. Meyer, on the basis of his comprehensive knowledge of ancient historical sources, shows that numerous miraculous legends came into existence already during the lifetime of the heroic figures themselves.

self? Despite ongoing efforts that never seem to want to stop, when one considers Mark, it is generally not possible to clearly distinguish between tradition and redaction. What, then, should be considered the source of the numerous mentions of the disciple at decisive points in this work, which appears *just a few years after his martyrdom*? Peter's name appears 25 times in the Second Gospel, with a far higher frequency than in Luke and in Matthew, and in John as well, if one sets to the side the addendum, chapter 21.[120] In that sense, the latter two Synoptic writers are largely dependent upon the Petrine tradition as well, based on their *Markan* "starting point," which means that they are also dependent upon the authority that stands behind Mark's gospel. Matthew is thus so tied to the text of Mark that he makes use of 80 percent of it. He himself is obligated to the authority of the Man of Rock because he knows that behind the Second Gospel there is a tradition tied to Peter, whom he also esteems so highly.

As the earliest evangelist, working a short forty years after the Easter event, Mark mentions the disciple who was called first so often *because this individual is of such foundational importance for him*.[121] In a certain limited sense this still applies even to the Gospel of John, which is relatively critical of Peter and which one can assume is aware of Mark and Luke. And how can one, at the outset, eliminate the possibility of a "Petrine theology" in Mark when we know so little about the sources of the Second Gospel? The instances where Mark mentions Peter come at consciously identified scenes of importance: once at the beginning, when he is called; then in the middle, when he confesses Jesus to be the Messiah, when the coming sufferings are announced, and when the transfiguration takes place, which provides the climax;[122] and finally at the end, in Gethsemane, and when he

120. On this, see pp. 28ff. above, and especially n. 88 above.

121. On this, see M. Hengel, "Probleme," 252-57; cf. R. Feldmeier, "Darstellung," 267-71; M. Hengel, *Four Gospels*, 78-89.

122. The transfiguration underscores the importance of the confession of Peter and the predictions about the suffering to come; the voice of God in Mark 9:7 Christologically deepens the confession of Peter in 8:29 (cf. 14:61; 1:1, 11, 24, 34; 9:41; 12:6ff., 35ff.), which ought not to be understood negatively. The future events of Easter and Good Friday, along with the complete salvation-historical meaning of Jesus, are as yet not understood by Peter (9:10-13). This lack occasions his opposition against Jesus' announcement about suffering, which to him makes absolutely no sense, a response that Jesus thus must reject in such strong terms, since everything that is to take place is linked to that upcoming event (8:31-33). This is the reason for Peter's foolish utterance on the Mount of Transfiguration, in which he hopes to hold onto the three mediators of revelation (9:5-6). The voice of God from the clouds, "Listen to him!" points to the "beloved son" who has announced his passion as that of a true

denies that he knows Jesus. Peter is thus central in the three most important theological highpoints in the work.[123] Should we dismiss all this as
having nothing to do with a "Petrine theology" or with remembrances of
Peter that are theologically explained? To add to the mix, the numerous
surprising Latinisms in Mark give support to the viewpoint that is also expressed and asserted in the tradition that Mark's gospel originates in
Rome. Mark was composed there, where Peter (and Paul as well) suffered
death by martyrdom.[124] It is also noteworthy how often Mark already, as
well as Matthew, who is dependent upon him, mentions the "Sea (of Galilee),"[125] trips on boats, and the milieu of fishing activity, from whence
come Peter, Andrew, and the two sons of Zebedee;[126] the same holds true
for the localities of Bethsaida and Capernaum.[127] It would seem that the
two pairs of brothers — Peter and Andrew, along with James and John, the
sons of Zebedee — knew each other personally before they were called by

word of the revelation of God. Moses and Elijah are to give witness to him. Because of the
Son of God and his path, they have lost their own unique salvation-historical importance.
Behind this entire complex, finally, is what has been artfully composed and stylized by Mark
from what was remembered by Peter or from the theology of Peter, which places the passion
into a theological framework.

123. Mark 14:29-31, 33, 37, 54, 66-72. On this, see P. Dschulnigg, *Petrus*, 8-31. He identifies
"15 scenes" in which Peter appears in Mark. From among these, "three times three are close
to a trilogy . . . at the beginning (1:16-39), in the middle (8:27–9:8), and toward the end of
Mark (14:26-72)." The most important of the three is in the middle trilogy. Therewith "the
compositional technique is also clear, that Peter . . . stands in the middle as the transmitter
and witness of the Christological confession" (27).

124. M. Hengel, "Situation," 43ff., and idem, *Four Gospels*, 78-89. Mark 12:42 and 15:16
have Greek words that are explained in Latin, a hint that points to Rome; 7:26: Ἑλληνίς,
Συροφοινίκισσα (a Greek woman, a Syrophoenician) is best understood in the Latin West,
where one would have to differentiate between the Syrian-Phoenicians and the Libyan-
Phoenicians. See also BDR §5.4 for references to further, numerous Latinisms in Mark; see, in
addition, M. Hengel, "Mc 7,3," on Mark 7:3: πυγμῇ = *pugno, pugillo*, with the meaning "with a
handful." There is nothing in Mark that speaks for the gospel having been written in Syria, in
contrast to Matthew (4:24), though much speaks for Rome. What is going on here is simply
the old "Pan-Syrianism" of the religion-historical school, which seeks to establish a syncretis-
tic origin for Christianity. Against this view, see Hengel and Schwemer, *Paul*, 21-23, 76-80.

125. Mark 1:16: θάλασσα τῆς Γαλιλαίας. He speaks of it seventeen times. The uncommon expression θάλασσα has its roots in Num. 34:11: *yam-kinneret* (sea of Chinnereth; see
also LXX and the Targums). In contrast, Luke 5:1-2; 8:22-23, 33 reads λίμνη (Γεννησαρέτ),
"lake (of Gennesaret)."

126. Πλοῖον (/πλοιάριον), "boat(s)," appears eighteen times in Mark, more than in any
of the other evangelists: Mark 17/1, Matthew 13, Luke 7/1, John 7/4.

127. Bethsaida: Mark 6:45; 8:22; Capernaum: 1:21; 2:1; 9:33.

4. Mark, the Disciple of Peter

Jesus and were likely partners who worked together as well.[128] This more specific group of three or four among the circle of the twelve disciples were seemingly friends before they were called by Jesus. From where should these at times very personal connections have come if a "Syrian Gentile Christian" is the purported author of the Second Gospel?

It is most strange and thus needs interpretation that Simon/Peter appears both as the first-named and as the last-named disciple in the entire gospel. Directly after the comment that Jesus appeared in Galilee, Mark 1:16ff. describes the call of "Simon and Andrew, the brother of Simon"[129] as future missionaries from among those who followed Jesus. Jesus' summons: "Come here, after me! I will make you into those who fish for human beings" points to this pair of brothers as having particular prominence, as the first ones called to be part of the future "apostolic" service.[130] Mark cannot describe any activity of Jesus without disciples — more specifically, without singling out the by far most important disciple. But discipleship means concurrently being sent forth.[131] Even in individual scenes Simon is specially singled out, which is not just by chance. In Mark 1:29-31 Jesus visits "the house of Simon and Andrew" and heals Simon's mother-in-law, a unique and intimate description of healing that has its own personalized character, which shows us that Peter was married.[132] Not long after this event, those who are called first are identified in 1:36 as Σίμων καὶ οἱ μετ' αὐτοῦ (Simon and his companions).[133] In the second-to-last verse of the gospel, 16:7, the angel charges the deeply shocked women at the grave:

---

128. Mark 1:16ff.; cf. Luke 5:7: μέτοχοι (partners). Concerning the two pairs of brothers, see Mark 1:16, 19; 13:3.

129. One notes the name Simon being mentioned twice.

130. Mark 1:17: Δεῦτε ὀπίσω μου, καὶ ποιήσω ὑμᾶς γενέσθαι ἁλιεῖς ἀνθρώπων; cf. the worldwide mission in Mark 13:10; 14:9, which the evangelist already has in mind with this paradigmatic call. Galatians 2:7 still portrays Peter as primarily a missionary to the Jews. Mark writes approximately fifteen years later and already has in mind the universal mission to the Gentiles for the pair of brothers as well; see pp. 89ff. below. On Mark 1:17, see M. Hengel, *Nachfolge und Charisma. Eine exegetisch-religionsgeschichtliche Studie zu Mt 8,21-22 und Jesu Ruf in die Nachfolge,* BZNW 34 (Berlin, 1968), 85ff.

131. See Mark 3:14, the installation of the Twelve: ἵνα ὦσιν μετ' αὐτοῦ καὶ ἵνα ἀποστέλλῃ αὐτοὺς κηρύσσειν, with Simon in the first position, who has the nickname Πέτρος.

132. On this, see pp. 103-10 and 125-31 below.

133. Cf. Luke 8:45; the variant reading with the most manuscripts support: Πέτρος καὶ οἱ σὺν αὐτῷ or else μετ' αὐτοῦ (Peter and those with him); see also the shorter, secondary ending to Mark, Nestle/Aland (2001), 147: The disciples are referred to as τοῖς περὶ τὸν Πέτρον (those with Peter), and Ign., *Smyrn.* 3:2: τοὺς περὶ Πέτρον (those with Peter).

"but go and say to his disciples *and to Peter. . . .*" This καὶ τῷ Πέτρῳ (and to Peter) is not necessary in terms of content; indeed, it is intrusive. Matthew leaves it out, since Peter is the most important person among the disciples. That his name follows at the end is also strange, since (Simon) Peter is otherwise always mentioned first when the disciples are mentioned. One can best understand this unique καὶ τῷ Πέτρῳ at the end of the work, together with the twofold mention of Simon at the beginning, as an *inclusio* that Mark intentionally formulates for his gospel. It is not a veiled indicator that the first appearance of the Resurrected One was to Peter, since no reader would come to that conclusion without knowing the tradition. In my view, this completely unnecessary statement καὶ τῷ Πέτρῳ, and its connection with the first mention of the disciple in 1:16, is a signature, by means of which Mark indicates the one who for him is the most important guarantor of the tradition, an individual who at the same time was the most authoritative disciple of Jesus.[134]

It is completely misleading for Terrence V. Smith to attribute to Mark a general "anti-Peter tendency" in the gospel,[135] which he develops in a series of unlikely hypotheses about why the unknown author of the gospel, who supposedly is writing it for the Gentile Christian church, proceeds with such anti-Petrine attacks. The dance set forth by his presuppositions is, in general, lively. He follows in the tracks of F. C. Baur and others, constructing a theory that there is a Gentile Christian attack against the Jewish Christian communities in Palestine, which were under the leadership of Peter and the Twelve. But had not James taken a leadership role[136] instead of Peter in these communities in Palestine, particularly in Jerusalem, and thrust Peter out of his leadership role there? This scholar believes that the unknown author seeks to provoke opponents who were relying especially on Peter and, at the same time, wants to teach his community about what true discipleship means by using a very negative example.[137] In reality, as

---

134. A parallel, which likewise accentuates the name of Peter at the end, is 1 Cor. 9:5: ὡς καὶ οἱ λοιποὶ ἀπόστολοι καὶ οἱ ἀδελφοὶ τοῦ κυρίου καὶ Κηφᾶς (as also [do] the other apostles and the brothers of the Lord and Cephas). We find another puzzling signature with reference to the young man, Mark 14:51, whom I still consider, along with Zahn and the early church catenae, to be most likely the evangelist John Mark himself. A better explanation for this puzzling passage has not been found to date.

135. T. V. Smith, *Petrine Controversies in Early Christianity*, WUNT 2/15 (Tübingen, 1985), 162-90, 185.

136. See n. 25 above.

137. T. V. Smith, *Petrine Controversies*, 189-90. See the justified criticism of P. Achte-

the lead disciple in Mark, Peter would be the prototype of the disciple who does not understand and the disciple who denies, as is — by necessity — also the case in the later gospels as well. These "shadowy sides" are based neither on a later polemical construction, which is directed against the Jewish Christians in Jerusalem, nor on a messianic secret à la Wrede, but in the final analysis on the remembrance, specifically that of Peter and the other disciples, that they *could not understand* Jesus' actions and path before Easter and were guilty over against him. In this matter as well, Mark has a lively witness of Peter as his source, one that is theologically stylized and dramatically described. The hearts of the disciples did not understand and were hardened before Easter, and this situation could be overcome only when the Resurrected One appeared and gave them the experience of the forgiveness of their guilt.[138] This last element, in fact, belonged to the earliest kerygma of the original community. Peter proclaimed what he himself had experienced. The statement in Mark 2:17 (= Matt. 9:13) applies to the disciples too. Jesus had not called any among them who were "righteous."[139]

It is also an absurdity to suppose that such a new and revolutionary work as the oldest gospel could have been composed by an anonymous Gentile Christian, an early Christian "Mr. Nobody." Behind this work there *must be a recognized authority* who was instrumental in this brand new movement and who, because of a special importance, as would be appropriate to grant to Peter in his role as partner in dialogue with Jesus in the gospel, could be considered a greater authority yet. This is also the only way one could understand how a self-confident theological mind and brilliant storyteller such as Luke and — even more so — the unknown Christian scribe and author of the First Gospel both turn to the Gospel of Mark in such a massive way, with the latter in particular copying so much from it.[140] *They knew that they were standing thereby on a solid, recognized foundation,* by means of which Mat-

---

meier, review of Smith, *Petrine Controversies, JBL* 107 (1988): 337-39: "The weakest [material] concerns the place of Peter in the Gospel of Mark, a rather one-sided and in some cases over-interpreted view of the evidence" (339).

138. Mark 8:17ff., 33; 9:6, 10, 19; 10:32; cf. Luke 24:25-26, 31-32, 47; Acts 2:38; 5:31; 10:43; 13:38; 1 Cor. 15:3-4; on this, see U. Mittmann-Richert, *Der Sühnetod des Gottesknechts. Jesaja 53 im Lukasevangelium,* WUNT 220 (Tübingen, 2008).

139. On this, see *Barn.* 5:9 and the defense of this sentence in Origen, *Cels.* 1.63, who also makes reference to Luke 5:8 and 1 Tim. 1:15.

140. W. G. Kümmel, *Einleitung in das Neue Testament* (Heidelberg, 1980[20]), 30, n. 32a. See pp. 103-4 below.

thew adds even more strength to the Petrine cast of the writing that was before him when he adds additional, legendary material such as Peter walking on water and the pericope about the temple tax,[141] whereas Luke — here is where one can see "Pauline influence" — particularly emphasizes the missionary motif of the "justification of the sinner," which is important already in Mark. This appears with the utterance "Lord, depart from me, for I am a sinful man,"[142] and then once again after the Last Supper, when Jesus makes note of the satanic threat to Peter and the other disciples, which will be repelled by the petition of the master. At the end comes Jesus' admonition to Peter that he should "strengthen the brothers" after his "repentance," which means, after Easter.[143] The Lukan statement "and when once you have found your way back"[144] refers to Peter's remorse after his denial and his vision as the first to see the Resurrected One,[145] which means both forgiveness and a new acceptance. The original community knew: Christ died also for the sins of Peter and the disciples.[146] This means that the criticism of Peter as the protagonist of the disciples' lack of understanding, which reaches its highpoint when he denies him, rests essentially on the report of Peter himself. It is based in the self-criticism of a disciple who understands himself to be a "redeemed sinner," much like Paul, who repeatedly mentions his activity as an opponent of the church.[147]

In the second century, as Justin maintains,[148] Mark was linked to Peter,

141. Matt. 14:28-33; 17:24-27. The narrative must have taken shape during the time of the second temple. After 70 the tax, as the *fiscus Iudaicus,* was to be paid to the emperor. Concerning the importance of Peter, see also his introduction in Matt. 10:2: πρῶτος Σίμων ὁ λεγόμενος Πέτρος (first Simon, known as Peter), and see n. 86 above.

142. Luke 5:8; cf. 18:11.

143. Luke 22:31-32; cf. John 21:15-17. On this, see P. Dschulnigg, *Petrus,* 68-87, and concerning the corresponding influence of Peter in Acts: 88-115.

144. Luke 22:32: καὶ σύ ποτε ἐπιστρέψας; on the translation, see E. Klostermann, *Das Lukasevangelium,* HNT 5 (Tübingen, 1929²), 212-13. Codex D and other Western witnesses make it into an imperative: σὺ δὲ ἐπιστρέψον (and you find your way back!).

145. Luke 22:62 and 24:34. The "minor agreement" in Luke 22:62 — καὶ ἐξελθὼν ἔξω ἔκλαυσεν πικρῶς (and he went out and wept bitterly) — was taken into Matt. 26:75 from Luke, to whom it seemed that the conclusion of the Markan text, in 14:72, did not seem adequate.

146. First Cor. 15:3-5.

147. First Cor. 15:9; Gal. 1:13-14; Phil. 3:6; cf. 2 Cor. 5:16; Eph. 3:8; 1 Tim. 1:15-16.

148. Justin, *Dial.* 106.3. On this, see M. Bockmuehl, "Memories," 134ff. See also Tertullian, *Marc.* 4.5.3: "et Marcus quod edidit [evangelium] Petri affirmatur cuius interpres Marcus. Nam et Lucae digestum [Marcionitae] Paulo adscribere solent" (that [gospel] which Mark produced is stated to be Peter's, whose interpreter Mark was. Luke's narrative also they usually attribute to [the Marcionite edition of] Paul).

just as Luke was linked to Paul. We see basically the same impulse in Marcion, who identifies his abridged Gospel of Luke with the gospel that Paul himself had received from Christ.[149] This special authority of Peter that is in the background of the Gospel of Mark also had the effect that this very writing, though its content had been significantly borrowed by Luke and, even more extensively, by Matthew (in contrast to other sources for the gospels, which somehow went missing), survived as a self-contained work within the framework of the εὐαγγέλιον τετράμορφον, or fourfold gospel. This version of the gospel predates Irenaeus and the gospel of Marcion and dates back to the first decade of the second century.[150] Justin knows of it when he speaks of the "remembrances of the apostles" of Jesus, which means the later "canonical" gospels, which "were composed" by these "and by their successors." This refers, on the one hand, to Matthew and John and, on the other, to Mark and Luke, in which case the gospels of the "students of the apostles" are older than those to which the names of the apostles are attached. In the second century, works that had the characteristics of the gospels were no longer attributed to their students; the pseudepigraphic works were linked primarily to the apostles themselves.[151] The four gospels were assembled not for a particular "community" of that particular evangelist[152] but for the church at large.[153] *The leading role of Peter in all four gospels corresponds to the importance of the Man of Rock for the entire church from the very beginning.*

It is also misleading to maintain that the connection between Peter

149. Gal. 1:11-12; Rom. 2:16; 16:25; 2 Tim. 2:8. On this, see A. v. Harnack, *Marcion* (repr., Darmstadt, 1960), 39ff., and B. Aland, "Marcion," *TRE* 22:91-92.

150. The gathering of the four gospels into a collected unit took place roughly about 120 in the library of a larger community, such as in Ephesus or in Rome, and was limited at first to the larger communities. Justin already assumes its existence: *Apol.* 1.67.3; *Dial.* 103.8. On this, see M. Hengel, *Four Gospels*, 19ff. The inauthentic ending to Mark, in 16:9-20, which was composed at roughly this same time, demonstrates knowledge of Luke, Matthew, and John and is referred to already by Justin and Irenaeus; see J. A. Kelhoffer, *Miracle and Mission*, WUNT 2/112 (Tübingen, 2000), 123-56; T. K. Heckel, *Vom Evangelium des Markus zum viergestaltigen Evangelium*, WUNT 120 (Tübingen, 1999), 32-62.

151. See M. Hengel, *Evangelienüberschriften*, 18-19; idem, *Four Gospels*, 59ff.

152. The "communities" in which an evangelist taught needed at least some written gospel, which could at best depict only a shadow of the oral teaching in its fullness. From the very beginning, the evangelists had in mind a wider reading — or, more aptly, hearing — audience in many communities; see n. 103 above.

153. Admittedly, Luke makes a certain exception to this with his very uncommon dedication to Theophilus. But even he hoped for a wide dissemination of his work through the recipient.

and Mark is "spun from" the mention of the two in 1 Pet. 5:13 and that the tradition came to Papias from that source.[154] Peter and Mark, after all, both appear in the same scene in Acts 12:12, where Peter, after being released from the jail, flees immediately to the house of Mary, John Mark's mother, in order to depart from there to leave the region ruled by Herod Agrippa.[155] Another point gladly downplayed in the literature that is critical of such traditions is the information that the story about Mark as the interpreter of Peter has the *presbyter* (John) as its source,[156] whom Papias has to thank for many other traditions as well.[157] Papias writes, at the very latest, at the time of Hadrian,[158] which means that the tradition about Mark that is attributed to the "elder" John has to be at least two generations older yet. In that essential form it certainly stretches back before the time when 1 Peter was written, which came into being about 100 (in my opinion, as the result of the Letters of Paul being gathered together). The passage in 1 Pet. 5:13 — "The [community] in Babylon [i.e., Rome], which is likewise chosen, and Mark, my son, greet you" — and the notation in Papias about what the elder said both point independently to this same

154. Cf., for example, E. Haenchen, *Der Weg Jesu* (Berlin, 1966), 8; P. Vielhauer, *Geschichte der urchristlichen Literatur* (Berlin, 1975), 260-61; somewhat more circumspect is J. Gnilka, *Petrus und Rom* (Freiburg, 2002), 149: "determined on the basis of 1 Pet. 5:13"; cf. U. Schnelle, *Einleitung*, 243: "The link between Mark and Peter in the Papias tradition [could] have its point of origin in 1 Pet. 5:13." With respect to such faulty conclusions, one ought first of all to reflect upon the problems with dating Mark, 1 Peter, the presbyter John, and Papias.

155. Acts 12:17. The Mark who is in the title of the gospel, in 1 Pet. 5:13, and in the Letters of Paul (Phlm. 24; Col. 4:10: the nephew of Barnabas, cf. Acts 12:25; 15:37, 39; 2 Tim. 4:11) is not some unknown person but is known to the recipients and the readers as a well-known person of authority, identical with the John Mark from the Acts of the Apostles. See also pp. 97ff. below.

156. See, for example, L. Wehr, *Petrus und Paulus*, 199, n. 337, on 1 Pet. 5:13. It is typical that the author does not use Mark at all in his work; see the index, 414, where Matthew and Acts are cited copiously, but where Mark appears in only two unimportant passages. It is not surprising that one comes to corresponding "conclusions" when proceeding from such a selective use of sources.

157. Eusebius, *Hist. eccl.* 3.39.7, 14-15. On the "presbyter" John, see M. Hengel, *Johanneische Frage*, 96-119.

158. A.D. 117-138. For this reason, one arrived at the date of A.D. 120-130. U. H. J. Körtner, *Papias von Hierapolis*, FRLANT 133 (Göttingen, 1983), 92-100; idem, "Papias," *TRE* 25:641-44, posits a contemporary of Ignatius, approximately 110; the same is true for M. Günther, *Einleitung in die Apostolischen Väter*, ARGU 4 (Frankfurt, 1997), 92-100, and idem, "Papias," *RGG*⁴ 6:862: If both were right, one would be even more compelled to take the notation as historically accurate.

older, reliable tradition.[159] The note from Papias is additionally no defense of Mark but, rather, a mild criticism: Mark did not present the story in an orderly way, nor was he an eyewitness; his sketches were based instead on the disorganized verbal preaching of Peter. He based his writings on these, on whatever he could remember. Papias, the bishop of Hierapolis, comes from the circle of the Johannine school and expresses this criticism on the basis of what for him is the better organization (τάξις) presented in the Fourth Gospel.[160]

We have good reason to accept Papias's report about the traditions passed on from the elder, especially since we have — sometimes completely independent of him — an entire series of other references from the second century that link Peter and the Gospel of Mark. One is the information in Irenaeus,[161] which likely comes from the Roman archive and which is historically appropriate: "After the death of these two [Peter and Paul], Mark, who was a disciple of and interpreter of Peter, provided for *us* [i.e., for the Roman community], in writing, what Peter proclaimed."[162] Clement of Alexandria, who knew about what Irenaeus had written, stated in contradiction to this report that Mark had written his gospel while Peter was still alive and that this writing was given the stamp of approval by Peter himself. He thereby sought to reassert the authority of this gospel among the communities, which (according to the witness of the papyri from Egypt) in the second century no longer made much use of Mark. These witnesses go further still, into the third and fourth centuries as well.[163]

---

159. Even the reference to the Aramaic logia collection of Matthew likely comes from the presbyter (Eusebius, *Hist. eccl.* 3.39.16). On this, see M. Hengel, *Johanneische Frage*, 76-95; Papias is the first author whom we know to have reflected on the origination of the gospels. The same is done later by Justin and Irenaeus.

160. M. Hengel, *Johanneische Frage*, 86-95; T. K. Heckel, *Evangelium*, 256-60; see now also P. Trebilco, *The Early Christians in Ephesus from Paul to Ignatius*, WUNT 166 (Tübingen, 2004), 246-56.

161. Irenaeus, *Haer.* 3.1.1 = Eusebius, *Hist. eccl.* 5.8.3; on this, and concerning the Roman archive, see C.-J. Thornton, *Der Zeuge des Zeugen. Lukas als Historiker der Paulusreisen*, WUNT 56 (Tübingen, 1991), 8-69; M. Hengel, *Four Gospels*, 34-38.

162. Concerning the relationship between this reference and the note from Papias, see C.-J. Thornton, *Zeuge*, 63-67; on this, see B. Mutschler, *Irenäus als johanneischer Theologe*, STAC 21 (Tübingen, 2004), 159ff.: "Irenaeus knows more than Papias" (159), at which point one must reflect on the fact that we have only a very few fragments from Papias.

163. We have various and to some extent contradictory narratives from Clement of Alexandria, *Hypot.* 6, in Eusebius, *Hist. eccl.* 6.14.5-7; cf. 2.15.1-2 and its Latin translation, the "Adumbrationes" (GCS 17, ed. O. Stählin, 206), concerning 1 Pet. 5:13; see also the so-called

The systematic rejection of these varied historical notes about the origin of the gospels, which are dated to the second and third centuries, is the typical result of a dogmatic criticism that does not bother with history. Even apart from the types of historical evidence concerning the personal relationship between Peter and the evangelist Mark, the very fact that the person of Peter is so absolutely important in the earliest gospel deserves a historical explanation that makes sufficient sense. This involves more than just the simple remembrance about what once happened, let us say, in the short one- to two-year time frame in which Jesus was active or during the time when Peter exercised a leadership role in Jerusalem during the twelve or thirteen years that led up to the persecution under Agrippa, because of which he had to leave his motherland, if only for a time, roughly A.D. 42/43 (Acts 12:17), and the time when James, the brother of Jesus, took over leadership of the community in Jerusalem and Judea. The decisive question, which has accompanied us during the discussion from the very beginning, is much rather: *How can Peter have maintained such an overarching importance in the Synoptic Gospels — beginning with Mark and still applicable (in spite of the time difference) in John — but also in Acts and already in select Pauline letters, such as Galatians and 1 Corinthians?*

5. The Later Role of Peter and His Conflict with Paul

5.1. Peter's Activity outside of Judea

Although Luke, as he tells the story in Acts, decisively (one might say) breaks off the story about the activity of Peter with his appearance in the Jerusalem "Council," which was convened roughly A.D. 48/49, *the next 15-17 years,* which lead up to the persecution by Nero, must have played a decisive role in the high honor that Peter is accorded in the mission communities of the West. These communities were gradually becoming more and more "Gentile Christian," being located between Antioch and Rome. Such importance was noted not only by the authors of the gospels and Acts but also by Clement of Rome, by the unknown author of the First Letter of Pe-

Monarchian Prologue to the gospels in J. Regul, *Die antimarcionitischen Evangelienprologe,* AGLB 6 (Freiburg, 1969), 47ff., 1: "Marcus evangelista Dei et Petri baptismate Filius" (Mark, the evangelist of God, and, in baptism, the son of Peter); cf. Origen, *Comm. Matt.,* in Eusebius, *Hist. eccl.* 6.25.6; Jerome, *Vir. ill.* 8, among other passages. See also the citation from Tertullian, n. 148 above.

ter, and by Ignatius.[164] Such high accord, which is incomparably greater
than that of all the other disciples (even the sons of Zebedee, James and
John, play a considerably smaller role in the Synoptic Gospels and Acts
when compared with Peter),[165] can be explained only if one starts from the
fact that — in contrast to Luke, who does not let Peter get any further than
the port city Caesarea Maritima (Acts 10:1–11:18) — the Western communities knew the apostle himself or learned about him from messengers.
These messengers had been sent forth by him[166] and thus were influenced
by him either directly or indirectly, and indeed not only in Syria, Antioch,
and Rome but also in important communities located in between, in the
capital cities of provinces such as Ephesus and Corinth.[167] The five provinces of Asia Minor that are mentioned in 1 Pet. 1:1, as the homeland of the
"elect strangers" — Pontus, Galatia, Cappadocia, Asia, and Bithynia —
posit the assumption that the pseudepigraphic apostolic author carried
authority in these regions.[168] One could point to the fact that, in the later

164. *First Clem.* 5:1-4: Peter is named as the first ἀθλητής (champion, one who con-
tends), which means as a martyr "in the most recent period"; Paul follows him. Cf. Ign.,
Rom. 4:3: "I do not command you as do Peter and Paul." Both texts assume that they have
apostolic authority and that they were martyred in Rome, which Ignatius understands as being freed. This interpretation undergoes development during the second century and continues to be held during the unfolding history of the church. See n. 16 above.

165. The two sons of Zebedee appear nine times in Mark; James, in spite of his early
death (Acts 12:2), is always named before John, which points to an older tradition; once
(Mark 9:38) John is encountered alone, asking a question. We find them three times in the
group of three, with Peter at the head (Mark 5:37; 9:2; 14:33), once as a group of four, along
with Andrew (Mark 13:3), in which case one might consider that they all called Capernaum
home. Matthew names them only three other times. Luke names the brothers together five
times, John alone once (9-49), and John together with Peter (22:8). In Acts, John, beyond the
list in 1:13, appears seven times, always as accompanying Peter, and in 12:2, as the brother of
James, who was put to death with the sword.

166. H. v. Campenhausen, *Kirchliches Amt und geistliche Vollmacht in den ersten drei
Jahrhunderten*, BHT 14 (Tübingen, 1953), 21: "Later, Peter left Jerusalem altogether" (with
reference to Acts 12:17); 20: "his area of influence [extended] beyond Palestine to Syria, possibly even into Asia Minor and further still"; 142: "There were also Gentile Christian communities that honored Peter as their apostle."

167. Concerning Ephesus, cf. the ecclesiological importance of Peter in the Johannine
school in John 21:15-19; concerning Corinth, 1 Cor. 1:12; 3:22; 9:1-7, and see pp. 24-25 above
and pp. 66ff. below. If Philippians was written in Ephesus, one could point as well to the difficulties that Paul had with his own fellow believers, which might have had their roots in
Petrine influence; see Phil. 1:14-17.

168. They also should not all be seen as simply the territories of Paul's mission activity.
Pontus (the home of Aquila, Acts 18:2) and Bithynia (Acts 16:7) no longer belong to the

tradition, Andrew, the brother of Peter, was connected with the northern coast of the Black Sea (Scythia),[169] and Mark, the disciple of Peter, was linked to the establishment of the community in Alexandria.[170] Such information might be legendary, but it could also point to the many directions in which the Petrine mission spread his influence. This might have been carried out, at the very least, by those who were sent.

The important role played by Peter during the time that followed the Apostolic Council, up to the time that he resided in Rome and suffered martyrdom, was limited not only or primarily to Antioch and the territory of Syria, as is often suggested today. Peter would have played a leading role not only in Antioch after his confrontation with Paul; instead, his authority would have stretched out toward the West in a powerful way.[171] This

---

provinces that we know of as places where Paul traveled. In addition, the spread of Christianity in Bithynia and Pontus at the time of the procuratorship of Pliny (ca. A.D. 110-114) need not be rooted solely in the work of the Pauline mission.

169. Eusebius, *Hist. eccl.* 3.1.1-2, which reports that Peter preached in the five provinces of Asia Minor mentioned in 1 Pet. 1:1 and that Andrew was in Scythia. Concerning Mark in Alexandria, see Eusebius, *Hist. eccl.* 2.16.24, on which see Hengel and Schwemer, *Paul,* 259-60. The *Acts of Andrew,* dated to the end of the second century, also places the area of activity for the brother of Peter in northern Asia Minor, but also Macedonia and Achaia, which means in the territory typically connected with Paul's mission; see *Acta Andreae,* 1:68ff., 81-86, 88-89; T. Zahn, *FGNK* 6:220-21.

170. The development of Christianity in Egypt, starting with Alexandria, poses the great unsolved riddle in the history of the early church. The only report from the first century is in Acts 18:24, concerning Apollos, Ἀλεξανδρεὺς τῷ γένει (a native of Alexandria). But we know nothing about whether he came to faith there. It is only Codex D and gig that have the additional information that he was instructed in the new faith in his πατρίς (home town); on this, see Hengel and Schwemer, *Paul,* 259-60.

171. First in Origen, *Hom. Luc.* 6 (GCS 49, ed. M. Rauer, 34), is Ignatius identified as the second bishop of Antioch, "after the blessed Peter" (but see, in opposition to this statement, Eusebius, *Hist. eccl.* 3.22, where a certain Euodius comes in between). According to Jerome, Peter established the congregation in Antioch and then was sent to Rome in the second year of Claudius (A.D. 42), where he preached the gospel and was bishop for twenty-five years; see *Chron.* (GCS 47, ed. R. Helm, 179; Eusebius says something similar in *Hist. eccl.* 2.14.6). According to Jerome, *Vir. ill.* 1, after Peter established the community in Antioch and after missionary preaching among the Jewish Diaspora in Asia Minor, in the five provinces mentioned in 1 Pet. 1:1, he made it to Rome, in order to do battle there against Simon Magus. Further texts appear in K. Froelich's article "Petrus II," in *TRE* 26:275-76. Concerning the special connection between Peter and Antioch, and thereby with Matthew, who grew up in Syria, see the suppositions offered by L. Wehr, *Petrus und Paulus,* 251, 286ff., concerning the Apostolic Decree. He correspondingly wants "to consider Matthew to be the closest place in the New Testament to find the traditions from Peter," since this book supposedly is to be located

high view of his importance stands in peculiar contrast to the minimal references in the New Testament to James, the brother of the Lord, even though he had become the leading figure between, roughly, A.D. 43 and when he was stoned in Jerusalem, in about 62, being in charge of the community in the Jewish motherland, and thus would have had a claim, one might assume, on some form of a leadership role over the entire messianic community of Jesus. Theodor Zahn is not completely wrong when he calls James the "pope of the Ebionite fantasy."[172] In my opinion, James was the point of origin for the *monarchical* episcopate,[173] a pattern of leadership that migrated from the East to the West and took hold at a relatively late time in Rome.[174] In the traditions of the first century, this one-sided step

"in Syria and possibly right in Antioch," and he believes that "the theological point of view held by Peter comes clearest in Matthew" (289). That he ignores Mark completely and misses the point that the historical situation of Matthew is that of the work of a Jewish Christian scribe (Matt. 13:52; 23:34) in a mixed congregation that is directly under influence from the motherland, as well as that he does not notice the relatively late time when the work comes into existence, leads him to questionable conclusions. The earlier writings of Luke, and most especially Mark, are no less under the influence of the authority of Peter than is true of Matthew. The only new element in Matthew is the pointed theological emphasis of the salvation-historical and church-related importance of the "Man of Rock" in Matt. 16:17-19.

172. T. Zahn, "Brüder und Vettern Jesu," *FGNK* 6:280; on this, see M. Hengel, "Jakobus der Herrenbruder — der erste 'Papst'?" in *Kleine Schriften III*, 549-82; P.-A. Bernheim, *Jacques*, 251-90: chap. 8, "Jacques, le premier pape?" [Engl: *James, Brother of Jesus,* trans. J. Bowden (London, 1997), "James, the First Pope?" 191-222: "To describe James as the first pope is perhaps an exaggeration, and certainly anachronistic. However, if any figure in the primitive church merits this designation, he certainly does" (222)]. Bernheim attributes to James the leadership role in Jerusalem from the very beginning. See pp. 9ff. above.

173. James possessed a "monarchical" authority in the community, with a circle of elders around and under him. The title as first bishop in Jerusalem, who would have been installed by the apostles, is not connected with him until the time of the legends that sprang up during the second century; on this, see M. Hengel, *Kleine Schriften III,* 561-62. In the Pseudo-Clementines, *Recog.* 1.43.3, he appears as "princeps episcoporum" (prince of bishops); the installation as bishop by the apostles is reported by Clement of Alexandria, according to Eusebius, *Hist. eccl.* 2.1.3. Irenaeus, *Haer.* 3.12.15, speaks of the "circa Jacobum apostoli" (apostles who were with James); see n. 133 above, with similar formulations connected with Peter. The first known monarchical bishop, with claims of being responsible for more than one region, is Ignatius, who, according to his *Rom.* 2:2, can call himself ἐπίσκοπος Συρίας (bishop of Syria). Cf. n. 24 above.

174. The congregation at Philippi, according to Polycarp, *Philippians,* still did not have a monarchical bishop. Concerning Rome, see P. Lampe, *From Paul to Valentinus: Christians in Rome in the First Two Centuries* (Minneapolis, 2003), 397-408. The size of the city and the numerous house churches there would favor the idea of having a collegial presbytery. Clear moves toward a monarchical episcopate are to be noted only from about the time of Anice-

backward for James comes as a result of the weakening of Palestinian Jewish Christianity because of his stoning in the year 62 and because of the Jewish War that broke out four years later, from which the movement never recovered. At the same time, it also points to a growing distance that developed between the Jewish Christians who remained true to the law, particularly in the motherland, and the ever-increasing position of strength that came forth from the church of the nations after A.D. 70, which, in contrast to the authority of James, gave basic affirmation to the authority of Peter. Peter was precisely *not* the typical representative of the type of Jewish Christianity that was strongly dedicated to the law, though this is how he has been depicted again and again, ever since the time of F. C. Baur. He stood between the two wings, which are characterized by James and Paul (and by their sometimes extreme adherents). Even this mediating position, which was open to Gentile Christianity and which theologically — in spite of radical differences — finally was closer to Paul than to the wing of early Christianity that stayed true to the law, provides the basis for his great effectiveness.

I would like to point to three reasons for this development, which applies most especially to the dark period after the Apostolic Council (between ca. A.D. 48/49 and 64/66).

1. In spite of the settlement reached at the council, in the years that followed Peter *also became* a more and more committed and convincing *missionary to the Gentiles,* which resulted in a situation of rivalry that became most painful for both him and for Paul. The division of work that separated the Jewish mission and the Gentile mission, as agreed upon in Jerusalem, was just not workable in the communities outside the motherland that were, to a greater or lesser extent, mixed communities. Both apostles deeply wounded the other in the conflict at Antioch (Gal. 2:11ff.) and thus became opponents. This situation was not only still an issue in Galatians 2 but continued to have an effect in the later letters of the apostle and in his mission, which overshadowed his mission all the way to the time of his imprisonment at the Feast of Weeks in A.D. 57, about which Luke felt it necessary to pass over in silence because he wanted to present a harmonious picture about early Christianity. For this reason, he lets Peter exit from the

---

tus (ca. 155-166). See also *1 Clem.* 42:4-5, who uses the term ἐπίσκοπος (bishop), which is derived from Isa. 60:17 (which has the plural), as meaning the same thing as πρεσβύτεροι (those who are older, elders, 1:3; 21:6; 44:5; and often elsewhere), and Hermas, who also equates both terms. The Pastoral Letters, which point toward Asia Minor, ought not to be dated too early. They are probably from about the same time as Ignatius (ca. 110-114).

stage abruptly, right after his pro-Pauline speech at the Apostolic Council in Acts 15:7-11.

2. In contrast to the onetime persecutor, Paul, but also in a way that differed from James, who was more skeptical of his brother before the passion, in a sovereign way Peter stood as master over the *fullness of the Jesus tradition,* which encompassed the words and deeds of the Messiah. His unique importance in the gospels, in the final analysis, is connected to a great extent with the fact that he became a figure of authority in the Gentile Christian church, which was gradually becoming stronger and stronger, because of his ties to these traditions about Jesus, traditions that are seldom mentioned in the Letters of Paul. One might suppose that, because he was a disciple of Jesus, Peter had been shaped already by Jesus' less rigid way of dealing with the ritual commandments and by Jesus' concentration on the will of God as articulated in the double commandment to love.[175] It is worth noting that the Jewish-Messianic movement in the early church was able to go beyond the geographic borders of Eretz Israel and the religious borders of strict Judaism so quickly, in relatively few years. This chain of events is without parallel in the history of Palestinian Judaism and must have its roots, finally, in the actions of Jesus himself. The promises uttered by the prophets concerning the end times that were to come with the appearance of the Messiah included the fact that membership in the people of God would be opened to the Gentiles.

3. Theologically, Peter was not (any longer) really "legally strict," in the sense that this idea was understood by the Jewish Christians in Jerusalem. That is seen already in the story of Cornelius (Acts 10:1–11:18), which points back to a historical event that one can assume took place before the time of Agrippa I (between early A.D. 41 and early 44), in fact probably already before the mad behavior that took place earlier, during the time of Caligula (ca. A.D. 39/41).[176] One can assume that, at the end of the 30s, Pe-

---

175. Cf. Mark 2:23-28 par.; 7:18-23 par.; Luke 6:31 = Matt. 7:12; Matt. 9:13 = 12:7; 23:23; see also the Hellenists in Acts 6:14.

176. Luke depicts this transformation in the Cornelius story in dramatic fashion. In Acts 10:14 Peter, in response to the summons from the voice from heaven, refuses to eat the unclean animals that are depicted in the horrifying vision. "Indeed, Lord, I have never eaten anything unholy or impure," which means that Luke characterizes him at first to be a strict Jewish Christian. In Acts 11:2-3 he is attacked in Jerusalem because of his lax behavior over against the Torah, which is expressed in the fact that he shared in table fellowship with those who were uncircumcised. Acts 11:1 goes on to mention, in general, "the brothers in Judea." According to the judgment of Paul in Gal. 2:12, who was upset, Peter later breaks off table fel-

ter was already somewhat closer, with respect to the question about the Jewish law and its ritual commandments and the necessity of saving faith in Jesus, the Lord who was crucified and had been raised, to the position of the "Hellenists" and to that of Paul[177] than to that of James and the circle that later formed around him. This circle included the Jewish elders,[178] even though James also, as is shown by the agreement at the Apostolic Council, does not completely reject a mission to the Gentiles unless it would require circumcision.[179] He, however, over against the Jews in Eretz Israel, wanted to forestall the accusation of apostasy that was increasingly having an impact on the existence of the community and thus he sought to hold fast to the demand for a Jewish Christianity that would call the brothers in the faith in the motherland to be faithful to the law. This explains why the influence of Peter gradually waned in Jerusalem, over against that of James, at the same time as Peter's reputation was growing among the missionary communities in the Diaspora.

We find confirmation for that view in the Letters of Paul and in the

---

lowship with the Gentiles only out of fear ($\phi o \beta o \acute{\upsilon} \mu \varepsilon v o \varsigma$) of the emissaries sent by James, not because of his own convictions. Concerning the threat to the temple by Caligula, which brought Judea to the brink of a war with Rome, see Hengel and Schwemer, *Paul*, 182-86.

177. This is true even though Peter does not agree with the specific way that Paul understands the law, which is typified in the Letters to the Galatians and to the Romans, but also in texts such as 1 Cor. 15:56, 2 Cor. 3:6-11, and Phil. 3:2-11. As a Galilean Jew, he had been too influenced by the Jesus tradition. It is no wonder that Matthew attributes to him such a unique importance as a teaching authority. Concerning the Hellenists, see M. Hengel, *Kleine Schriften III*, 1-67.

178. It is surprising that the Letter to James has such a completely reduced Christology and soteriology, which does not correspond to Petrine or to Pauline theology. On this, see M. Hengel, *Kleine Schriften III*, 511-82. It is not by chance that 1 Peter stands closer to the Letters of Paul than it does to the Letter of James, even if, with J. Herzer, *Petrus oder Paulus? Studien über das Verhältnis des ersten Petrusbriefes zur paulinischen Tradition*, WUNT 103 (Tübingen, 1998), we would correctly attribute to him a theologically unique position over against the Corpus Paulinum. I would admittedly not speak of a specific "Syrian-Antiochene tradition" for the letter, but more likely of a Roman one. For Antioch at about A.D. 100, Ignatius is typical. The community or communities in Rome have close ties to Jerusalem from their founding, roughly at the time of Caligula (A.D. 37-41), or maybe early in Claudius's rule (as is true for the synagogue communities that were there earlier). This is observed even in the Letter to the Romans. Even Matthew is not shaped by an "Antiochene theology" — which we really do not know — but by being close to the Jewish motherland and to the developments taking place there. We should not narrow the "Petrine mission territory" too much geographically (Herzer, ibid., 264), or else the unique meaning of Peter for the developing churches would be hard to explain.

179. Gal. 2:9; Acts 15:13-21; 21:21-25.

Acts of the Apostles. The compromise that was worked out, according to the characterization of Paul at the Apostolic Council, between the three "pillars" James, Cephas, and John, on the one side, with him and Barnabas, on the other side — that "we [will go] to the Gentiles, but the others to the Jews [αὐτοὶ δὲ εἰς τὴν περιτομήν]" (Gal. 2:9) — is based on the insight that, already at that time, Paul and Barnabas had proclaimed the gospel to the "uncircumcised" but that Peter had oriented his preaching toward the "circumcised," and in fact that he had also been working outside the motherland.[180] The arrangement demonstrates that Peter had already achieved the status of the most successful proclaimer of the new message, over against those who were part of the same brotherhood, a portrayal that squares with Acts 2–5 and 9:32-43 in the motherland, but also in Mark and Matthew with the metaphor of "a fisher of human beings."[181] In a unique way he claimed the role of ἀποστολὴ τῆς περιτομῆς (Gal. 2:8). It is quite likely that, after he fled from Jerusalem in A.D. 42/43, he enjoyed success as a missionary among the Jews outside of Palestine as well. The first scene would be in the region of Syria, which had significant numbers of the Diaspora, but one cannot exclude the possibility that he traveled to other regions as well, in fact that he even got to Rome already at that time.[182] But the distinction that was agreed upon at the Apostolic Council in Jerusalem between the mission to the Jews and the mission to the Gentiles turned out later to be unrealistic, since it could not be main-

180. Gal. 2:7-9. It is striking that 2:7-8 first speaks about the fact that "the gospel . . . for the circumcised" was entrusted to Peter, or, stated another way, that Christ had worked with him in the mission to the circumcised, whereas in v. 9, by contrast, all three pillars function as missionaries to the Jews (αὐτοὶ δὲ εἰς τὴν περιτομήν). In any case, Peter appears here as the leading missionary to the Jews, and in fact beyond the territory of Judea.

181. Mark 1:17 = Matt. 4:19; cf. Luke 5:10; on this, see M. Hengel, *Nachfolge*, 85ff.

182. Concerning the Syrian Diaspora and concerning the establishment and early history of the community in Rome, see n. 92 above; Hengel and Schwemer, *Paul*, on Syria: 51-54, 55ff., 80ff.; on Rome: 257-60. According to Eusebius, *Hist. eccl.* 2.14.6, and Jerome, *Vir. ill.* 1, Peter came to Rome at the beginning of the reign of Claudius, roughly A.D. 42. Such dating references are admittedly questionable. Peter is once again in Jerusalem in 48/49 and presumably in Antioch in 51/52, where there was such a serious confrontation with Paul (see pp. 57ff. below). Paul perhaps avoids naming Peter among those in Rome because of the conflict described in Gal. 2:11-12. He mentions none of the earlier apostles, and Jerusalem appears in Rom. 15:30-32 more as a repulsive place, indeed as an inimical place. He reckons with the possibility that his collection will be refused there and that his life will be threatened. The opponents who slander him are referred to only as τινές (some people, Rom. 3:8). See nn. 228 and 240 below. An exception is the puzzling married couple Andronicus and Junia in 16:7 and their particular relationship with the apostles; see part II, n. 83.

tained consistently in practice outside the motherland, especially since the "Gentiles" were originally closely tied to the synagogue as "God-fearers" and were more or less congruent with Judaism. For this reason Paul also started at each new site at the synagogue, since he could speak to the Godfearers there, who were considered legally still to be uncircumcised Gentiles.[183]

It is astounding how much Paul starts out on the basis of the presuppositions of Jewish tradition and exegesis in his letters. If it had not been for the Old Testament–Jewish instruction of the majority of his hearers, such as would have taken place in sermons in the synagogue, neither his missionary proclamation nor his letters to the communities would have been understandable. By contrast, outside Eretz Israel and against his original impulses, Peter increasingly *also* became a "missionary to the Gentiles," since the communities there were mixed and the worship service was celebrated in common, so that there was no practical way to keep a strict division of persons between the Jewish and Gentile Christians, as it had been conceived by the Apostolic Council. Luke knew that such was the case in actual fact and laid the groundwork for the mission to the Gentiles relatively early by presenting Peter's preaching before the God-fearing centurion Cornelius in Caesarea, but he excludes Peter from the description of the mission to the Gentiles after this time. By contrast, Luke goes against the autobiographical portrayal by Paul and against what is in all likelihood historically accurate;[184] he commences the mission to the Gentiles on the part of the "Hellenists" and of Paul in Antioch only after Peter had given

183. Paul's preaching before the Godfearers began already in the synagogues in Damascus (on this, see Josephus, *B.J.* 2.560-61): Acts 9:19-22 and, on this, Hengel and Schwemer, *Paul*, 50-54; on the "Godfearers," see 76-80 (also see the excursus in the German edition, *Paulus zwischen Damaskus and Antiochen. Die unbekannten Jahre des Apostels*, WUNT 108 [Tübingen, 1998], 101-39). Paul was also always a missionary to those who were of his own nationality; see Rom. 1:16; 11:14; 1 Cor. 9:20ff. The Jewish Christian part of his communities was not all that small. For this reason Peter and his emissaries had the possibility, in light of the decision of the Apostolic Council, to visit "Pauline" communities as well.

184. Paul's report in Gal. 1:15ff. about the turning point in his life (ἵνα εὐαγγελίζωμαι αὐτὸν ἐν τοῖς ἔθνεσιν, that I might proclaim him [the Son of God] among the Gentiles) and the narrative about the vision that Luke himself reports, in Acts 22:17-21; 26:16-18, both contradict the Lukan mission pattern. Based on his own testimony, Paul was called, from the very beginning, as an "apostle to the Gentiles." As "Apostle to the Gentiles" (Rom. 11:13; cf. 1:14), after the turning point in his life, he went to Arabia and not up to Jerusalem, to those who were "apostles" before him (Gal. 1:17). See Hengel and Schwemer, *Paul*, 42-43, 47-50, 82ff., and often elsewhere.

the green light with the Cornelius episode.[185] It is possible that those who were associated with Peter later considered him to be the actual "founder" of the mission to the Gentiles on the basis of the narrative about Cornelius.[186]

5.2. The Conflict with Paul in Antioch

The communities that were established outside of Judea became increasingly mixed communities, in which the Gentile Christians gradually became the majority, even though the "leading powers" as a rule remained the Jewish Christians for a longer period of time.[187] The *disagreement in Antioch between Peter (and Barnabas), on the one side, and Paul, on the other,* which is most often downplayed in terms of the depth of the effects that were caused by it (Gal. 2:11-21), demonstrates the impossibility of keeping the agreement detailed in Gal. 2:7-9, which proposed separating the areas of mission activity in the communities outside of Jewish Palestine; too many problems, such as table fellowship with the Gentiles and the danger that came therewith, that of enjoying meat that had been offered first to idols, libation wine, and other "unclean foods," were issues that remained unresolved at the Apostolic Council. At the very least, for the Jewish Christians in Eretz Israel who remained strictly faithful to the law, the agreement that was reached in Jerusalem remained most difficult to accept without further clarifications.

The *protracted split* between the two leading missionaries, which came about as a result of the conflict at Antioch, can probably be dated to a few years after the Apostolic Council, between the "second" and "third missionary journeys," roughly in the year A.D. 52/53, which Luke purposely

185. Acts 11:20, where Ἕλληνας (Greeks) is to be read; see also Paul and Barnabas on the "first" missionary journey: 13:7ff., 43-48. On this, see Hengel and Schwemer, *Paul*, 178-204.

186. On this, see A. Strobel, "Das Aposteldekret als Folge des antiochenischen Streites," in *Kontinuität und Einheit,* FS Franz Mußner, ed. P.-G. Müller and W. Stenger (Freiburg, 1981), 81-104.

187. Most of the New Testament authors are still Jewish Christians, as is true of the three evangelists Mark, Matthew, and John. Luke was likely a Godfearer. The unique importance of Gentile Christianity in the early period has long been overemphasized. The leaders in the community in Antioch, in Acts 13:1ff., were all still Jews. See Hengel and Schwemer, *Paul*, 198-99.

discusses in Acts 18:22-23, with enigmatic brevity just before the "third" journey, as he discusses an apparently uneventful stay of Paul in Antioch. Corresponding to the overall thrust of his work, he remains silent about the disagreement itself. At least with respect to the second part of his early Christian mission history, he knows considerably more than he reports and skips over anything that might displease the most excellent Theophilus. That this dispute between Peter and Paul could have a negative effect on the ancient reader can be detected in the way that the most important critic of Christianity makes sport of the confrontation, as he reacts with mockery to Paul as depicted in Gal. 2:11ff. Porphyry speaks of the "childish squabble," about how Paul "burned with envy over against Peter's successes . . . and wrote boastfully." The Gentile philosophy of Macarius Magnes and Julian the Apostate took the other side, criticizing Peter on the basis of this conflict and because of his questionable morality.[188]

The very fact that Barnabas split with Paul (Acts 15:39) shows that there was a certain tension between these two, who had been partners in mission, and it could, among other things, explain why this man also joined with Peter and the other Jewish Christians in Antioch, according to Gal. 2:13. And that Paul, on his so-called third missionary journey, no lon-

---

188. Luke reports in Acts 15:37-39, however, about the break between Paul and Barnabas before the second journey. This is to some extent a prelude to the later conflict and shows the intensity of the disagreement, with the harsh formulation: ἐγένετο δὲ παροξυσμὸς ὥστε ἀποχωρισθῆναι αὐτοὺς ἀπ᾽ ἀλλήλων (and such a sharp disagreement arose that they separated from one another; cf. 1 Cor. 13:5: [ἡ ἀγάπη] οὐ παροξύνεται, [love] is not provoked, and Acts 17:16). There is no other passage in which Luke more sharply characterizes a disagreement among the brotherhood; cf., as well, Acts 6:1; 11:1-3; 15:7. Even the collection for Jerusalem goes unmentioned by Luke in Acts 21:18ff., though he does speak of it in Acts 24:17, within Paul's speech by which he defends himself, as "alms for my people." It is likely that it was not accepted by James; instead, Paul was to redeem the Jewish Christian Nazirites with that sum, in Acts 21:23ff., in order to demonstrate that he was no apostate. Luke says nothing further about the contact of the prisoner with the Jerusalem community after his imprisonment. It is likely that the procedure against Paul was a heavy burden for them. Cf., however, the support given by the ἴδιοι (his own [people, friends]) in 24:23, though it remains unclear who is meant thereby, and by the "friends" in Gentile Sidon, 27:3.

Concerning *Porphyry,* see A. v. Harnack, *Porphyrius "Gegen die Christen,"* APAW (Berlin, 1916), no. 1, frg. 21B, p. 54. Idem, *Kritik des Neuen Testaments von einem griechischen Philosophen des 3. Jahrhunderts,* TU 37/4 (Leipzig, 1911), 56f., lines 25ff. (III, 22): "It concerns a πολλὴ . . . καὶ μεγάλη κατάγνωσις [great and large condemnation]."

Concerning *Julian* and his mockery of Peter, because Peter had been judged by Paul as a "hypocrite," see *Juliani Imperatoris librorum contra Christianos quae supersunt,* ed. K. J. Neumann (Leipzig, 1880), 222, 17ff., and, on that, J. G. Cook, *Interpretation,* 158-59, 315-16.

ger had anyone from Jerusalem who joined with him as a missionary coworker, and that Luke and the Letters of Paul never describe any further contacts with Antioch, make it likely that this conflict came rather late.

The problem with the depiction of the conflict in Gal. 2:11ff. is that only the Pauline side of the story — one might indeed say: one-sided and overstated — is reported and that precisely at this point Protestant exegesis breaks the rod too easily over Peter, not only with respect to theology but morally as well, so that he who would also certainly have had reasons for his actions can no longer defend himself. One ought not to suggest that this behavior is simply "cowardice," even if the verb ὑπέστελλεν (Gal. 2:12), "he recanted," can be interpreted polemically in the sense of "turn away in a cowardly manner."[189] That Paul reacted in such a curt manner and described Peter's behavior as "worthy of condemnation" (2:11: κατεγνωσμένος ἦν) is easily understandable. According to Paul's way of thinking, by means of his behavior, Peter had "condemned" himself. One must now fear that the Gentile Christians, who were not yet well-grounded, could become confused by the separation that was called for by the messengers from James when it came to the Eucharistic celebration, which was celebrated as a real meal.[190] And, consistent with this separation, these Gentile Christians could also be asked to observe the Jewish legal prescriptions such as circumcision, purity laws, and food laws as also being "necessary for salvation" or at the very least "recommended with respect to salvation." In this manner, "justification by faith in Christ *alone*"[191] would be brought into question.

Paul's harsh accusation of hypocrisy against Peter and the Jewish Christians of Antioch,[192] including Barnabas,[193] that they had given in to the demands of the messengers from Jerusalem, is based for him in the fact that they did this out of fear of those who came,[194] that it involved

189. See BDAG, 1041; cf., in the middle of the discussion, Hab. 2:4 (LXX) = Heb. 10:38.

190. It is likely that, externally, this preserved the old form of the daily "breaking of bread," as in the original community.

191. Gal. 2:16: ἐκ πίστεως Χριστοῦ καὶ οὐκ ἐξ ἔργων νόμου (by faith in Christ, and not by doing the works of the law). Cf. also Rom. 3:28 and the contrasting position of those who were Paul's opponents: καὶ οὐκ ἐκ πίστεως μόνον (and not by faith alone, Jam. 2:24); on that, see M. Hengel, *Kleine Schriften III*, 523-28.

192. According to Acts 13:1 they still had a leadership group made up of "prophets and teachers."

193. Gal. 2:13: συνυπεκρίθησαν . . . ὥστε καὶ Βαρναβᾶς συναπήχθη αὐτῶν τῇ ὑποκρίσει (they joined [him] in this hypocrisy, so that even Barnabas was led astray by their hypocrisy).

194. Gal. 2:12: φοβούμενος τοὺς ἐκ περιτομῆς (for fear of the circumcision faction).

going against their own faith convictions, and that the Gentile Christians, who were by and large those counted at an earlier time among the Godfearers, could be led astray so that they would attribute to the "works of the law" some sense of *meaning for salvation*. In his view, it suggested "coercion," which means, at the same time, the confusion of the consciences of the Gentile Christians of Antioch. For this reason Paul, in his anger at Peter, charges him with suddenly changing the way he was practicing table fellowship, thereby "forcing" the Gentile Christians to "live in a Jewish way."[195] In essence, Peter was effectively hiding himself as he all of a sudden started reerecting the walls that Paul had torn down, which Paul said would make Peter a transgressor (Gal. 2:18: παραβάτην) of the law, whereas Christ would be mistaken thereby as one who was a "promoter of sin" (2:17: ἁμαρτίας διάκονος). But the reality was that the atoning death of Christ meant that the law once and for all lost its meaning as a way of salvation: "For I through the law died to the law, so that I live for God. I have been crucified with Christ." For this reason one ought not in any way soften Paul's attack against Peter and the other Jewish Christians and merely speak of a "reprimand," as does O. Cullmann.[196] According to Gal. 2:3-5, with respect to the contested point of conflict concerning the meaning for salvation at the Apostolic Council in Jerusalem, Paul did not give in for a moment and thus prohibited the circumcision of Titus. The two times that "anathema" is used in the first verses in the Letter to the Galatians (1:8-9) show already that he was not willing to give an inch in this matter in the future or to soften his position.

But was it the intention of Peter, Barnabas, and the other Jewish Christians really to reinstitute circumcision and the observation of the entire ritual law for the Gentile Christians in any way, shape, or form? For the Jewish Christians, participating in community with Peter as the head pointed to the situation from a quite different perspective. From their vantage point, they must also have had good reasons for their behavior. For them it dealt with the introduction of separate times for meals — even at the Apostolic Council the "missionary realms" for the "Jews" and "Gentiles" were clearly demarcated — one might suppose because of a

---

195. Gal. 2:14: πῶς τὰ ἔθνη ἀναγκάζεις ἰουδαΐζειν; (how can you compel the Gentiles to live in a Jewish way?).

196. Gal. 2:19. The basic Pauline statements are to be understood in light of texts such as Gal. 3:13-14; 4:4-5; 2 Cor. 5:14-15, 20; Rom. 3:20-31; 8:3ff. Concerning "reprimand," see O. Cullmann, *Petrus*, 35, 58-59.

measure of respect for the ritual understanding of purity for the guests from Jerusalem, and thus also, at the same time, because of the situation faced by the Jewish Christians in Jerusalem and throughout Judea, which was increasingly more difficult and oppressive; they would have understood their actions in a basic sense as an act of brotherly love with respect to the early community and its pressing circumstances, which Paul himself had articulated with great clarity not all that long before, in the first letter that we have from him, in 1 Thess. 2:14-15.[197] One might say, paradoxically, that observing separate meals served as an advantage for the preservation of the communal relationship of the church between Jerusalem and Antioch, which was being threatened by the persecution in Jerusalem, which means at the same time between the Palestinian Jewish Christians and the Gentile Christians of Antioch. They did not want to force the Jewish Christian guests from the Holy City to deny their Jewish identity in Gentile Antioch. Paul himself could say of himself just a few years later, because of the requirements of missionary service: "To the Jews I became as a Jew, in order to win the Jews. To those under the law I became as one under the law (though I myself am not under the law) so that I might win those under the law. . . . I have become all things to all people, so that I might by all means save some."[198] At the beginning of the so-called second journey, right after the Apostolic Council but still before the conflict in Antioch, he himself also circumcised Timothy, who was born in a mixed marriage to a Jewish mother and a Gentile father in Lystra, in order to keep open the possibility for him to preach in synagogues.[199]

In contrast, because of this incident Peter and Barnabas did not once again become "preachers to the circumcision" (cf. Gal. 5:11). We do not

197. On this, see A. M. Schwemer, "Verfolger," 170ff. Cf. Gal. 4:29 as well.

198. First Cor. 9:20-21, 22b; cf. 19-23. In 1 Corinthians, where Paul is dealing with an entirely different situation, circumcision plays a secondary role at best; it has practically become an adiaphoron, or matter of indifference: 7:18ff.; by contrast, cf. the other judgments in Gal. 5:6 and 6:12-15.

199. Acts 16:1-3. The historicity of this incident has been wrongly cast in doubt. One ought not to turn Luke into a pious storyteller. According to the law, Timothy was Jewish and Paul, who was sent to the Diaspora synagogues, would have precluded entry for himself as an apostate if he had not circumcised him. In 1 Cor. 7:18ff. he handles the issue in the sense of a pastoral word of advice and not in the foundational sense with which he treats it in the Letter to the Galatians, which he would have written not all that long afterward. The open question remained whether Jewish Christian married couples were to circumcise their children in Pauline missionary communities in order not to renounce their external membership in the Old Testament people of God.

know, in connection with this conflict, whether even a single Gentile Christian in Antioch allowed himself to be circumcised. Paul speaks in 2:11ff. only about the hesitation with respect to συνεσθίειν (eating together) and in general about the necessity of ἰουδαΐζειν (living like a Jew). He mentions nothing here about circumcision. Those who were causing trouble in the province of Galatia certainly had very little in common with Peter and Barnabas. It is possible that this involved a group of radical Jewish Christians. After Paul, because of the conflict on the "third trip," had set out toward the north and had traveled across the Taurus Mountains (Acts 18:23), this group perhaps came after him and, as citizens of Jerusalem, impressed and confused the communities in southern Galatia.[200]

From the vantage point of Peter, Barnabas, and the people of Antioch, the matter unfolded quite differently: Because of the resolution to the conflict that happened afterward, at the instigation of James through the means of the Apostolic Decree, the word "circumcision" no longer appears at all,[201] to say nothing of fulfilling demands that the commandments of

200. Concerning the legal and ritualistically shaped piety of the population in Inner Anatolia, where Judaism had expanded since the third/second century B.C., see C. E. Arnold, "'I am astonished that you are so quickly turning away!' (Gal 1.6): Paul and Anatolian Folk Belief," NTS 51 (2005): 429-49. The summons to accept legal obligations could have fallen here on particularly fruitful ground for the Gentile Christians as well.

201. Acts 15:23-29; cf. 19–21; 16:4; 21:25. Concerning the complicated transmission of the text, see B. M. Metzger, *Textual Commentary* (London, 1971), 429-35. According to Luke, the decree is based on a suggestion by James. He repeats it when Paul visits in Jerusalem. Concerning the understanding of this difficult text, see C. K. Barrett, *The Acts of the Apostles*, vol. 2 (Edinburgh, 1998), 730-36. The question of the laws given later to Noah, Str-B 3:37-38, ought not to be directly tied to the decree; by contrast, the requirements of Leviticus 17 and 18 concerning non-Israelites in the land of Israel, which were applied later to proselytes, may have played a certain, though not decisive, role. The Hebrew *gēr*, which originally had the meaning "protected citizen, foreigner," is translated by the LXX as προσήλυτος (proselyte). Codex D and a few other Western witnesses left out καὶ τοῦ πνικτοῦ (and from what is strangled), which later became disruptive, and replaced it at times with the Golden Rule in its negative form (positive: Luke 6:31 = Matt. 7:12). Here the primarily ritual requirements are turned into ethical statements. It also remains unclear whether Luke actually transmitted the entire decree in its original form. Pseudo-Clementines, *Hom.* 7.8.1 (GCS 42, ed. B. Rehm, 120), provides an expanded statement that is connected with 1 Cor. 10:21 as well; cf. 8.19.1 (129). W. G. Kümmel, "Die älteste Form des Aposteldekrets," in *Heilsgeschehen und Geschichte. Gesammelte Aufsätze, 1933-1964*, ed. E. Grässer (Marburg, 1965), 278-88, sees that "as making possible the fewest number of requirements . . . , so that the legally demanding Jewish Christians could have contact with the Gentile Christians in the same community" (287); H. Lietzmann, *Kleine Schriften II*, TU 68 (Berlin, 1958), 297, suggests that it is an "authoritative Jerusalem answer" that Paul knew

the Torah be observed, but only the call to stay away from being defiled by the meat of animals offered to idols, serious sexual offenses (πορνεία), drinking blood,[202] and, what is just about the same thing, eating what had been "stabbed," which means meat that had not been properly butchered. These strictures certainly deal with matters of respecting Jewish identity when Jewish and Gentile Christians engaged in table fellowship, which is the stone of stumbling that brought about the division in Antioch. It seems that it was reestablished once again by means of the decree.[203] Paul himself makes no mention of it, which makes sense, since it was not binding on him. But his disgust about such a horrid example of πορνεία (immorality) and his instructions in the matter of eating flesh offered to idols in Corinth[204] do show that such problems were not unknown there. One might suppose that Cephas/Peter, or else his messengers, might have informed the Corinthians about what had happened. It certainly is surprising that Paul categorically forbids, in two letters to the Corinthians, one following close after the other, any sharing in fellowship with repulsive sinners, which includes the Eucharistic συνεσθίειν.[205]

The deep divide that was signified by the dramatic, public, drawn-out dispute between Peter and Paul is something we cannot portray deeply enough. Paul accused Peter and those who followed him, in front of the entire community, of cowardly hypocrisy and of a betrayal of the "truth of

---

and that he uses in 1 Corinthians 8–10, with "masterful skill" (298). The decree would have been brought by Peter to Corinth and would have occasioned the letter that included the inquiry of the Corinthians mentioned in 1 Cor. 8:1.

202. Acts 15:19, 28; 21:25; cf., by contrast, Gal. 5:3-4. See now, as well, R. Deines, "Das Aposteldekret — Halacha für Heidenchristen oder christliche Rücksichtname auf jüdische Tabus?" in *Jewish Identity in the Greco-Roman World*, ed. J. Frey, D. R. Schwartz, and S. Gripentrog, AGJU (Leiden, 2007), 323-95. Deines does not see any remnant from halakic demands from the Torah of Moses; instead, in essence, these are the basic orders of the Creator, which are valid for all human beings. It admittedly remains an open question about how Paul understood them. Partaking of blood was forbidden, since the blood was the carrier of life (Lev. 17:11-12; cf. Gen. 9:5).

203. Acts 15:20, 29: ἀπέχεσθαι . . . αἵματος (abstain from blood) does not mean pouring blood out at this point but is to be understood in the context as a food prohibition.

204. First Cor. 5:1-5, 8-10. On this, see now the comprehensive study by V. Gäckle, *Die Starken und die Schwachen in Corinth und Rom*, WUNT 2/200 (Tübingen, 2005), who admittedly underestimates the importance of the conflict in Antioch and of the Apostolic Decree for the situation in Corinth.

205. First Cor. 5:9-13. Already in a previous letter, which is no longer available, he had forbidden contact (συναναμίγνυσθαι) with the "immoral" in the community (5:9). The practice of συνεσθίειν (eating with) was also a matter of contention in Antioch (Gal. 2:12).

the gospel."[206] In the eyes of the Jewish Christian contingent of the community, however, Paul thereby isolated himself by being aggressive and a legalistic destroyer of peace. The Gentile Christian contingent was not yet strong enough to play an independent role. Paul says nothing to suggest that the Gentile Christians allied themselves with him and defended him. We also do not know whether and how Peter and Barnabas (the recognized Jerusalem authority *and* the successful missionary to the Gentiles) plausibly stated their case in response. But above all else, Paul says not a single word that the two, along with the Jewish Christians from Antioch, in any way acknowledged their mistake and were swayed to change. In purely harsh, obvious words, he does nothing but describe the scandal, which must mean that the wound stayed open. The results were apparent in Antioch itself, in Galatia, in another form in the Apostolic Decree, and finally even in Corinth.

The break between Paul and the community in Antioch that came as a result, with whom he had been in partnership for over a decade, even though he did not stay there during that whole time, can be seen in that — with the exception of 1 Thessalonians[207] — he mentions Antioch only one single time after that conflict, which is in the description of the dispute when he describes it in Gal. 2:11, but in no other passage ever again,[208] whereas in his authentic letters Jerusalem/Hierosolyma is mentioned ten times.[209] The bridges to Antioch were apparently broken, but by contrast he was not able to, nor did he want to, abandon the connection with Jerusalem.[210] That was the city of the prophetic promises of the events of salvation, which were coming true at that time; that is where Jesus was crucified and resurrected from the dead. It was there that his return was anticipated, and it was from there that the gospel went out into all the world (Rom. 15:19). Furthermore, the apostle had to gather the col-

---

206. Gal. 2:14: ὅτι οὐκ ὀρθοποδοῦσιν πρὸς τὴν ἀλήθειαν τοῦ εὐαγγελίου (that they were not acting consistently with the truth of the gospel), the truth that Paul, according to 2:5, had successfully defended in Jerusalem.

207. First Thessalonians was written in Corinth about A.D. 50, during the so-called second journey. The Jerusalemite Silvanus/Silas is still Paul's travel companion, 1 Thess. 1:1; 2 Cor. 1:19; 1 Pet. 5:12; cf. Acts 15:22, 27, 40, etc. He is no longer present in this capacity on the third journey.

208. Even in Gal. 2:1 he does not mention that he went up to Jerusalem from Antioch with Barnabas; we learn of that only from Luke, in Acts 15:1ff.

209. Jerusalem: 1 Cor. 16:3; Gal. 4:25-26; Rom. 15:19, 25-26, 31; Hierosolyma: Gal. 1:17-18; 2:1.

210. Gal. 2:2b; Rom. 15:19, 25-26.

lection for them.[211] The connection with the Jewish Christian "earliest community" in the holy city stood externally as a guarantee, at least until the Jewish War in A.D. 66, for the unity of the church.

As I have said already, it is likely that the reason Peter pulled back when the messengers of James came was very possibly because of a compromise to maintain the unity between the missionary communities outside of Eretz Israel and Jerusalem itself, which was under threat. He had to take into account the sharpening of the Zealots' nationalistic tendencies in Palestinian Judaism from the 40s on,[212] a situation that was becoming more threatening all the time, which included increasing persecution of Jewish Christians in Jerusalem, a situation that became severe enough ten years later so as to reach a highpoint with the stoning of James and other leading Jewish Christians as "lawbreakers" (ὡς παρανομησάντων).[213] By avoiding table fellowship with the uncircumcised, the Jewish Christians in Antioch guarded themselves from appearing to be notoriously "unclean" opponents of the Torah or, even worse, "apostates" in the eyes of the residents of Jerusalem. For this reason, the Gentile Christians were thus obligated to abide by the few "necessary" basic rules in the end, to practice table fellowship as described in the Apostolic Decree.[214]

---

211. Gal. 2:10; cf. 1 Cor. 16:1ff.; 2 Corinthians 8–9; Rom. 15:25ff., 31; Acts 24:17.

212. M. Hengel, *Zeloten*, 349-61. Hengel and Schwemer, *Paul*, 180-86: The leaders of the Zealots were given strong impetus most especially when Caesar Caligula (A.D. 37-41) took control of the temple, which had brought the Jews to the brink of war with Rome; in addition, there was the politically unhappy return of Judea to the status of a Roman province after the early death of Agrippa I at the beginning of 44 and the dispatch of inept procurators. Their "zeal for the law" influenced the Jewish Christians (Acts 21:28ff.) over a long time period as well. James had the difficult task of trying to find some middle ground. The original community existed under pressure from several directions. Since the time of Jesus' crucifixion, their chief opponents were those in the leadership level from among the high priestly family and from among the Sadducees; in this regard, especially the Annas clan was their chief opponent. Annas II (son of the Annas who is in the passion history) had James and other Jewish Christians stoned in 62. The leadership group of the Sadducees, which was so threatened by the fanatic national, religiously fervent element, ended up distancing themselves, at least to some extent, from the Roman leadership during the two decades before the Jewish War and came closer to the Zealots, who maintained a position of hatred against foreigners. For the original community, which was under pressure from so many different directions, the only option, when the Jewish War broke out in 66, was to flee to the Gentile polis of Pella in the Jordan valley; see Eusebius, *Hist. eccl.* 3.5.3. These tensions can also be seen in the fears expressed by Paul in Rom. 15:30-31 and in the way his arrest is depicted in Acts 21:27ff.

213. Josephus, *Ant.* 20.200ff.

214. Acts 15:28: μηδὲν πλέον ἐπιτίθεσθαι ὑμῖν βάρος πλὴν τούτων τῶν ἐπάναγκες (to

5.3. Peter in Corinth

Most especially in the two *Letters to the Corinthians,* from the years A.D. 55/56, the ramifications of the Petrine (rival-)mission, which now included both Jews and Gentiles without distinction, can be clearly detected. A "Cephas party" developed in Corinth, which resulted in the "splits" and "disputes" that are noted in 1 Cor. 1:11-12.[215] This community

---

impose on you no further burden than these essentials). Over against the demand in 15:5, the commands in 15:20, 29 provide, in any case, "a decisive moderation" (H. Lietzmann, *Kleine Schriften II,* 296). On the other side, for Paul, who "was no man who went half-way with a measured response," the "demand about kosher meat . . . was 'law,' and it had been done away with, through Christ" (297). He says that clearly in 1 Cor. 10:25-26, when he uses the citation from Ps. 24:1. He resolved the issue in 1 Corinthians 8–10 and in Romans 14, concentrating on the "meat offered to idols" in a completely different way. On this, see V. Gäckle, *Die Starken.*

215. W. Schrage, *Der erste Brief an die Korinther,* EKKNT 7/1 (Zurich, 1991), 144-45, using the argumentation of M. Karrer, "Petrus im paulinischen Gemeindekreis," *ZNW* 80 (1989): 210-31 (211ff.), underestimates the role of the "Cephas Group" and thus also the importance of Peter and the negative resultant events from the conflict at Antioch. If the σχίσματα (divisions) and ἔριδες (quarrels; cf. 1 Cor. 11:19: αἱρέσεις, factions) were simply an easily eliminated *quantité négligeable,* as Karrer assumes, then why does Paul mention them as his first point of irritation at the beginning of the letter and link them, in a way that is similar to that in Galatians, with the basic question about the meaning of the cross of Christ for salvation (1 Cor. 1:13)? And with respect to 1 Cor. 9:1-5, who would have been influential enough to question his apostolate, if not the Cephas group? The exegete ought not to fall into the same mistake that Luke is accused of, namely, that of minimizing and harmonizing early Christian conflict. Between 1 Cor. 15:5, which refers to Peter as being the first resurrection witness, information Paul had shared years earlier when he established the community in Corinth, and 15:11, with its reference to the foundational unity of the kerygma shared by all who proclaim it, there is the surprisingly ambivalent self-praise that the apostle offers in 15:9-10. Why did Paul think it necessary to state this to the Corinthians? I consider it extremely unlikely that these were merely "some nondescript people, who were possibly driven into Corinth, who identified with Peter, without him being involved directly" (Schrage, *Brief an die Korinther,* 145). Schrage forgets the harsh confrontation in Antioch just a few years earlier and its impact on the Pauline mission. Because of the unique importance of Peter, Paul cannot polemicize against him or Jerusalem publicly. He could not and did not wish to break completely with Jerusalem, since the gospel went forth from there. Because of his position as an outsider, he "evades," whenever possible, a "direct polemic against the people and the regulations of the original community." "The story of his criticism against Peter in Gal. 2:11-14 has to be told only because of the most pressing need of battle for the Galatian soul, and it is very carefully constructed," according to the apt judgment of H. Lietzmann, *Kleine Schriften II,* 297. Galatians, which was likely written between 1 Corinthians and 2 Corinthians, gives evidence that the wound is still open.

had specific knowledge about the other missionary methods that were practiced by the Jerusalem apostles and Jesus' brothers, according to 1 Cor. 9:4ff., where Cephas is mentioned specifically by name once again, together with the numerous accusations against Paul, especially with respect to the dispute about his apostleship (1 Cor. 9:1-7). These facts make it quite likely that the Man of Rock[216] — who is mentioned after Apollos,[217] a man who got along better with Paul during the time that Paul was in Ephesus[218] for a period of three years — had visited the capital city of Achaia,[219] an event that caused significant problems for the apostle to the Gentiles, which can be seen even more clearly in the second letter. The surprising emphasis on Paul's worthiness to be an apostle[220]

216. Also 1 Cor. 3:10ff. and Rom. 15:20: ἵνα μὴ ἐπ᾽ ἀλλότριον θεμέλιον οἰκοδομῶ (so that I do not build on someone else's foundation) indirectly plays on this. Paul was naturally aware of the particular importance of the name Πέτρος. On this, see A. M. Schwemer, "Verfolger," 185-86, and P. Vielhauer, "Paulus und die Kephaspartei in Korinth," *NTS* 21 (1975): 348-49 (= Vielhauer, *Oikodome*, 177-78). On 1 Cor. 3:11, see n. 73 above.

217. On the visit of Apollos, see Acts 18:24. The sequence of names in 1 Cor. 1:12 and 3:22 might hint at the order of the visits. Apollos came to Corinth before Paul arrived in Ephesus. He stood closer to the apostle to the Gentiles than he did to Cephas. It is to be noted that the name Cephas does not appear in 3:4-9 but resurfaces again only in 3:22; cf. also 16:12: Paul hopes that a new visit from Apollos will have a positive effect on the communities in Corinth, but there is no further mention of Cephas. Paul apparently values him much less, in spite of (or perhaps precisely because of) his unequally greater importance. The problems in Corinth are hardly coming as a result of what Apollos was doing but more likely from radical "antinomian Pauline figures," on the one side, and from the Cephas group, on the other side. In contrast, James, who is also not a complete stranger to the Corinthians (15:7; cf. 9:5), plays no role there any longer, in contrast to Galatia, where he is a leading figure.

218. Acts 20:31 (and 20:18 in D) has Paul speaking of a three-year stay in Ephesus, according to Luke, and 19:10 reports this visit to have included two years of teaching activity in the hall of Tyrannus, which Paul had rented. Before this, he would have spent roughly three months in discussions in the synagogue (19:8). On the basis of 2 Corinthians 1 and Acts 19:23ff., one must assume that his activity in Ephesus broke off violently, and it is possible that there was also a short imprisonment during which — possibly — Philippians was written. See 19:21-22 as well.

219. A stay by Peter in Corinth was thought possible by E. Meyer, *Ursprung und Anfänge des Christentums*, vol. 3 (1923; repr., Darmstadt, 1962), 441, n. 1; H. Lietzmann, *Kleine Schriften II*, 289; C. K. Barrett, "Cephas and Corinth," in *Abraham unser Vater*, FS O. Michel, ed. O. Betz et al., AGSU 5 (Leiden, 1963), 1-12, and P. Vielhauer, "Kephaspartei," 341-52 (= Vielhauer, *Oikodome*, 169-82). Vielhauer emphasizes correctly that "the Cephas party played a key role in the conflict among the parties in Corinth" (341-42/170). See Bishop Dionysius of Corinth in Eusebius, *Hist. eccl.* 2.25.8: Peter and Paul (just like in Rome) both also "began the planting in our city of Corinth."

220. First Cor. 9:1ff.; cf. 2 Cor. 10:1-6; 11:5; 12:11-12; Gal. 1:1.

and the assertion[221] that, because he had once been a persecutor of the church, he was "not worthy to be called an apostle," but that by the grace of God he "had done more than all of them," is directed against the minimizing of his apostolic claims, as articulated by the Jerusalem apostles "before me" (Gal. 1:17), whose most important missionary had always been Peter. Those who offered allegiance to Cephas would have "boasted" about him because of his particular importance and authority.[222]

An important issue in that connection is that Paul as a rule took care of his own living expenses and did not allow himself to be supported by the mission communities, a practice that was used against him to suggest that he did not possess full apostolic authority.[223] The tentmaker or leatherworker could support himself as a missionary by his own skills, which would not have been possible for someone who had once been a Galilean fisherman or a farmer, particularly since they permitted themselves to be accompanied by their wives.[224] The sharp tension that developed, clearly in evidence here, because of the catastrophe in Antioch and the personal wounds on both sides that followed is softened somewhat by the decisive closing sentence in 1 Cor. 15:11: "Whether it is I or they,[225] so we [one could add: all] preach, and so you have believed." This means: the one gospel about Jesus' atoning death and resurrection, by means of which Paul established the community in Corinth, unites *all* of us, in spite of serious differences, and it remains the objective basis for the common faith.[226] Paul places all the tension, without prejudice, simply on the unity of the church that is established by Christ. For him, that is necessary for salvation; without it, he would have "run in vain" (Gal. 2:2).

---

221. First Cor. 15:9-10; cf. Rom. 15:17-21.

222. First Cor. 3:21-22; cf. 1:31; 2 Cor. 10:17 = Jer. 9:23-24.

223. First Cor. 9:3-18; 2 Cor. 11:7ff.; 12:13.

224. First Cor. 9:5, 14; concerning the duty to take care of those staying there, see also Luke 10:7 = Matt. 10:10. On the other side, see Phil. 4:12-18 concerning Paul as a prisoner. On Paul's trade, see Acts 18:3 and Hengel and Schwemer, *Paul*, 113. Concerning Peter's marriage, see pp. 104ff., 125ff. below.

225. At the highest point of these ἐκεῖνοι (they, those) stands Cephas, as the first witness to the resurrection, but the Twelve and the Lord's brother James are included as well. The "truth" of the "gospel" that is constitutive of the community mentioned in 1 Cor. 15:1ff. establishes the unity of the church, in spite of all schisms and difficulties.

226. Cf. also Phil. 1:14-17 and 1 Cor. 3:21b-23: "For everything is yours, whether Paul, Apollos, Cephas, world, life, death, present, or future. Everything is yours. But you belong to Christ, and Christ to God." The last sentence is decisive. The considerable tensions between Paul and Cephas do not affect that affirmation in any way.

I believe that these conflicts, which are front and center in the accusations that call into question whether the Pauline apostolate is on a par with the others, continue to unfold in the *Second Letter to the Corinthians* — this time with representatives from the Petrine mission or else from the community in Antioch, with whom Paul had broken and who were at that time closely allied with Peter. The situation in Corinth was significantly different from that in the province of Galatia, to which radical Jewish Christians had come from Jerusalem, who had already caused the trouble in Antioch and who, after a certain period of time, had traveled further yet[227] and had demanded circumcision and obedience to the law in such a way that it openly went against the resolution offered at the Apostolic Council (Gal. 2:1-10). Peter himself could have hardly been in agreement with such people, even if he had gone too far — according to what Paul thought — when he acted as he did with them in Antioch in the interest of unity in the church because of Jewish Christians who were under threat in the motherland. By this means, the main point of contention was more clearly visible in Galatians than in 1 and 2 Corinthians. It is to be noted, for the latter situation, that in the very section of 2 Corinthians in which Paul most openly defends himself in a most wounded (one might even say self-doubting) way, in *chapters 10 and 11,* at that point the profile of the opponents of Paul and their message remains most ill-defined. That section does not describe some "heretics" whose errant teaching comes forth clearly; it is not the "legalists" of Galatians, who demand the circumcision of the Gentile Christians, since the terms περιτομή (circumcision) and περιτέμνειν (circumcise) are never employed in the second letter.[228] Nor is

227. Cf. Gal. 2:12. Paul is still speaking in 1 Cor. 16:1 about the collection in (South) Galatia; that is no longer the case in the Letter to the Galatians and in 2 Corinthians 8 and 9. It is possible that messengers from Jerusalem took the money along with them.

228. With respect to 1 Corinthians, we find περιτέμνειν (circumcise) twice in 7:18 and περιτομή (circumcision) in 7:19, admittedly not within the setting of an acute conflict situation, but rather in a pastoral context; see n. 198 above. In Romans περιτομή is used fourteen times, eight times in Galatians, and περιτέμνειν is used six times. The term νόμος (law) does not appear in 2 Corinthians; in its place there appears only γράμμα (letter), in 3:6-7, contrasted with πνεῦμα (Spirit). Not paying attention to this distinction occasioned the error in the depiction of Peter by F. C. Baur, who was followed by H. Lietzmann, *Kleine Schriften II,* 287-91, when he suggests that Peter appeared "after initial hesitation as a sharp Judaist" (287) and supposedly sought with James, by using "Judaistic emissaries, to Judaize" the mission communities of Paul. James was supposedly "the leader who directed sending this propaganda, and Peter was on point in the mission field" (288). The complicated relationships in early Christianity are simplified way too much here. By contrast, the observation is correct

it the "Gnostics" or "Docetists" (since they did not even exist at the time), and not the Hellenistic θεῖοι ἄνδρες (divine men) or even libertines.

Rather, these opponents are Jewish Christians from Palestine or Syria who are — as Paul himself — "servants of Christ,"[229] which means missionaries whose demeanor is admittedly distorted[230] in the worst possible way by the apostle, so that he speaks at one point of such individuals as ψευδαπόστολοι (false apostles) and twice as ὑπερλίαν ἀπόστολοι (super-apostles), without stating specifically *whom* he has in mind.[231] According to

---

that the conflict in Antioch resulted in "a harsh break between the two leaders of the Christian mission" (288). The only point is that the issue later was no longer the question about the Jewish law. On one level it dealt with the deep personal wounds. More important, it involved the question about who had decisive authority in the missionary communities. In my opinion, this included the authoritative significance of the ethical Jesus tradition, contrasted with the Pauline theology of the cross. If the dispute had been about the ongoing validity of the Jewish law as a way of salvation, the Letters to the Corinthians would have had a whole different look. According to Rom. 3:8 (see also n. 239 below), in a passage that came into existence in Corinth shortly after 2 Corinthians, someone had accused Paul of advocating libertinism. The ethical grievances in Corinth, which are likely connected with a false understanding of what Paul meant by freedom from the law (1 Cor. 6:12ff.; 7:19; 10:23; cf. 3:21-23), could have given rise to such accusations. It is likely that these also had to do with a false interpretation of Paul's teaching about the law; on this, see the corrective statements in 1 Cor. 6:9-13; 7:19 and Gal. 5:6, 13ff., 25. Experiences of the Corinthians may be behind this as well. We find a clear foundation for the newly formulated ethic definitively in Romans 6 and 12:1ff. Lietzmann actually considers the possibility that Peter traveled farther, from Corinth to Rome, and was living in Rome at the time of the Letter to the Romans: "Peter arrived there ahead of him and brought his great authority to bear" (*Kleine Schriften II*, 290). This question can remain open.

229. Second Cor. 11:22-23. On the term Ἐβραῖοι (Hebrews), see M. Hengel, *Kleine Schriften III*, 19-22. Concerning the close connection between Judea and Syria, see M. Hengel, "Ἰουδαία."

230. Second Cor. 11:12-15. On 11:14, cf. Mark 8:33 and Matt. 16:23!

231. Second Cor. 11:13; 11:5; 12:11; see n. 240 below. Pointing in the right direction is M. E. Thrall, *The Second Epistle to the Corinthians*, vol. 2, ICC (Edinburgh, 2000), 667-76, 926-45: The messengers "are part of the Petrine mission to the Jews (cf. 1 Cor. 9:5)." On 11:16, she notes: "The Petrine mission, if it was to progress successfully westwards beyond Palestine, must surely have been served by some reasonably fluent Greek-speakers" (941). Thrall could have pointed as well to Antioch as an intermediate station and to the break that came about for Paul with that community, which sided with Peter. See also her study "Super-Apostles, Servants of Christ, and Servants of Satan," *JSNT* 6 (1980): 42-57. She is followed by T. V. Smith, *Petrine Controversies*, 193-95. See E. Meyer, *Ursprung*, 432-59: "The Second Letter to the Corinthians is a lively example of the conflict between the original conception of Christianity, as it was shaped by Peter and the Twelve, and its forced alteration by Paul. The picture of a peaceful and harmonizing development, which Luke is forced to describe after the

2 Cor. 3:1-3 they apparently bring "letters of recommendation" addressed to the Corinthians, which must come from authorities that are known to the Corinthians, since they would otherwise be worthless. Paul cannot produce any letters to match these.[232] These emissaries are missionaries who praise their particular charismatic abilities and visionary experiences and who point to their powers of persuasion and physical power and health, which are lacking in Paul, even though he is superior to them with respect to the literary rhetoric of his letters.[233] He avoids mentioning names and provides no specific details about those who had sent forth these missionaries, who in his eyes are leading others astray. The Corinthians know only too well about what is going on. Only their geographic point of origin is clear. They are Jewish Christians who are Ἑβραῖοι (Hebrews) — as is Paul himself (Phil. 3:5) — and who still have ties to the motherland.

The chief point made by Paul is that the Corinthians allow themselves to "hear preaching about a different Jesus," that they "take on a different spirit" — in fact, that they have "let themselves fall prey to another gospel."[234] The nature of this "other message" remains unclear (in contrast to

---

horrible catastrophe of Nero's persecution because of the religious necessities that developed after that time, does not correspond to reality in any way. Instead, both sides fought with impassioned bitterness. . . . The personal conflict could not be bridged; a reconciliation between Paul and Peter was completely out of the question" (459). Only the last sentence seems to me to be worded too strongly; see pp. 97ff. below. But it would have taken years for the wounds to heal. M. Karrer, "Petrus im paulinischen Gemeindekreis," *ZNW* 80 (1989): 210-31, who completely denies that there was any conflict (211, n. 6), overlooks the fact that there are highly significant situations of conflict in which the names of the opponents are purposely not mentioned or are reduced to being referred to as τινές (some; 2 Cor. 3:1; 10:2, 12; Gal. 1:7; 2:12; Rom. 3:8; cf. Phil. 1:15). Such silence about the names of opponents applies to Paul in Galatians and Philippians, to 1 and 2 John, *1 Clement*, the Ignatian correspondence, and the Essenes in Qumran. It is part of ancient polemic. The worst opponents go unmentioned: this is very clear in Ign., *Smyrn.* 5:3: such names are not written; in fact, one ought not to think about them until they repent; cf. 7:2. On this, cf. M. Hengel, *Johanneische Frage*, 141-42. Who could have appeared with such authority, after the Jesus movement had existed for roughly five years in Corinth, to bring Paul thereby into such difficulties, if these were not emissaries from the Petrine mission?

232. Such letters of recommendation could come from Peter, who had visited the community.

233. Second Cor. 10:7-11.

234. Second Cor. 11:4. It is possible that the messengers from Peter connected the communication of the Spirit in a special way with ecstatic phenomena, as they are detailed in Acts 2; 4:31; 10:44; 11:15; cf. Joel 2:28-32 and Acts 2:17-21, which the Corinthians valued most highly.

Gal. 1:6).[235] One could ask the question about whether this newer teaching took on a more markedly "Synoptic" form that put Jesus' teachings and miracles more into the foreground. In 2 Corinthians 10–13 one finds neither the Pauline articulation about justification nor, apart from 13:4, any reference to the cross of Christ. The only thing that is clear is that the opponents accuse him of being sorely lacking with respect to charismatic gifts and credibility. This is similar to what is mentioned already in 1 Cor. 9:1ff., where his worthiness to be considered an apostle is questioned and other severe personal accusations are raised against him.[236] This certainly makes sense, because it came into play because of his passionate character, which ended up at certain times drawing him into sharp polemic and which we ought not to deny.[237] In response to the accusations, the only thing that he can do — with grim irony — is to point to his "apostolic" suffering in service to Christ and thus show that the power of the Kyrios is demonstrated for him precisely in his agonizing struggle and in his weakness.[238] When we consider these strong differences of opinion, which shook the young Pauline congregation to the core, we have the vantage point of one side only, with the deeply upset and, at the same time, stirring and impressive voice of that one side, with its theological reflection; the other side cannot answer, and thus much remains puzzling for us.

235. On this, see M. E. Thrall, *Second Corinthians,* 667-71. In this section she notes, "The rival missionaries represent a branch of the Christian mission whose policy has some affinity with the outlook of the final mission charge in Matthew's Gospel: Mt 28:16-20." To that belong (1) the worldwide mission charge, which is limited no longer to the Jewish mission; (2) Jesus as "a being of power and glory"; (3) obedience with respect to Jesus' messengers, who are grounded in the Torah; (4) special experiences of the Spirit; and (5) demonstrable deeds of righteousness. "The main problem in Corinth was the self-exaltation of the opponents, and the favourable impression they have made thereby." The result was "a detrimental effect on Paul's own authority" (669-70). Against E. Grässer, *Der zweite Brief an die Korinther,* vol. 2, *Kapitel 8,1–13,13,* ÖTK 8/2 (Gütersloh, 2005), 128, who reaches back once again to the questionable Gnostic hypothesis, the exact nature of the "errant teaching" that Paul rejects is not actually clear in 2 Corinthians 10 and 11. The angry and, to some extent, bitterly ironic polemic, with unsurpassed sharpness, in the form of a "speech of a fool," does not permit us to clearly detect the contours of the opponents' teaching.

236. Second Cor. 10:2: acting "according to the flesh" or else "fleshly strategies"; cf. 1:17; 5:16; unbounded praise of self: 10:13, etc.

237. Second Cor. 11:2: ζηλῶ γὰρ ὑμᾶς θεοῦ ζήλῳ (for I feel a divine jealousy for you); 29b: τίς σκανδαλίζεται καὶ οὐκ ἐγὼ πυροῦμαι; (who is made to stumble and I am not indignant?), cf. Gal. 5:11; Phil. 3:2; 1 Cor. 16:22; 1 Thess. 2:15, and still others.

238. On this, see U. Heckel, *Kraft in Schwachheit. Untersuchungen zu 2 Kor 10–13,* WUNT 2/56 (Tübingen, 1993).

5. The Later Role of Peter and His Conflict with Paul

A later reminiscence of this disagreement is included for us in the theological testament of Paul, which was composed just a short time later in Corinth as the *Letter to the Romans*, which was written in the winter of A.D. 56/57, in which the apostle hints at accusations made against him in 3:8, suggesting that certain individuals (τινές) maintain that Paul teaches "let us do evil, that good may come."[239] Their condemnation (by God) in the final judgment will be justified.[240] The judgment in 2 Cor. 11:15 concerning the "diabolical servants of righteousness" would apply to them as well: "their end will correspond to their deeds." At the same time, it becomes clear in Romans that Paul finds no fault, in this very same part of the letter, with Peter, the other apostles, or even some who accompanied him for a time as a missionary partner, such as Barnabas. For him at this point, it is as though they did not even exist.[241] He makes reference only to his own apostolate and the success of his own mission, which at this point, in a most remarkable way, goes forth from Jerusalem,[242] even though the letters written not all that long before this time to the Corinthians were very explicit about the activity of other missionaries. He also makes no observations about the founding of the Roman community. He simply reiter-

239. See particularly Rom. 3:5-8 and cf. 6:1; 7:7; 11:1. His message about freedom from the law, which was understood by some radical "Paulinists" in a manner that was inimical to ethics, caused some to accuse him of encouraging libertinism. Cf. also n. 228 above.

240. Rom. 3:8: ὧν τὸ κρίμα ἔνδικόν ἐστιν (whose condemnation is deserved); 2 Cor. 11:15: ὧν τὸ τέλος ἔσται κατὰ τὰ ἔργα αὐτῶν (their end will match their deeds). Cf. 1 Cor. 3:12-15, as well, for the judgment about those who build, with various levels of quality, on the foundation that Paul laid, and whose work does not stand the test of fire: εἴ τινος τὸ ἔργον κατακαήσεται, ζημιωθήσεται (if the work is burned up, the builder will suffer loss, v. 15).

241. We can leave Rom. 16:1-23 to the side. If these verses are directed toward Rome (and not, as is less likely, toward Ephesus), they apply especially to the house community of Prisca and Aquila (v. 3) and, in verse 7, to Andronicus and Junia (a married couple?); the formula "my relatives and fellow prisoners, who are famous among the apostles," remains historically an unsolvable puzzle. It is the only time that ἀπόστολοι (apostles [plural]) is used in the entire letter; the word appears elsewhere in the letter only in 1:1 and 11:13, with reference to Paul himself. The warning conclusion in Rom. 16:17-20 mentions people who bring διχοστασίας and σκάνδαλα (dissensions and offenses), with reference to the teaching, and who at the same time lead astray their naive hearers "by means of pretty speechifying and honoring praise." Here, as well, Paul points to tensions that he expects to find in Rome, possibly in the other house communities. Are these the reason why Luke never reports in Acts 28 about the other communities that were located there, with the exception of v. 15? Except for Acts 21:18-26, Luke reports that the situation is similar for Paul in Jerusalem. A different situation is assumed for Acts 21:10-16 and the brief mention in Caesarea, in 24:23 (see n. 188 above).

242. Rom. 15:19; on this, cf. Acts 22:17-21 and, against it, Gal. 1:15-23.

ates that he had often wanted to visit them in the past but had been hindered, thus hinting that the community there is relatively long-standing.[243] At the same time, the unity of the church lies close to his heart, as is shown by the risky trip he planned to Jerusalem to deliver the collection; he knows that his life is threatened there and that he must remain unsure about whether the congregation located there will even accept the service of love that he will bring. In spite of the tense situation over against the "holy ones" in the Jewish metropolitan region, he does not want to break his promise, which is typically Pauline.[244] Far too little attention has been paid to the growing schism in the later missionary activity of Paul that is evident here. If one sets aside what is said in Galatians 2, where he writes because he is forced to do so and offers an answer to the personal biographical activities of the Galatians and has to set them straight, Paul cannot openly go into his own personal struggles in the communities by naming the names of those who instigated the trouble. Luke also chooses not to go into these conflicts.

It thus remains a rather well-supported suspicion that Peter was the direct missionary opponent of Paul in these tension-filled years that affected both of them after their clash in Antioch. As we have mentioned already, the so-called Apostolic Decree,[245] which Luke presents as the decision at the end of the Apostolic Council in Jerusalem, would thus be the reminiscence of a decision actually made some years later between the people of Antioch and Peter in their dealings with James and Jerusalem. That reports a decision about elementary demands for purity that are necessary in order to reestablish table fellowship, with respect to the Eucharist, between the Jewish and Gentile Christians in Antioch (and in other mixed communities in Syria and parts of Asia Minor), which had been disturbed by the objections of the Jewish Christians from Jerusalem. In Gal. 2:10 Paul mentions only the request of the Jerusalem authorities for support for the "poor" who live there; according to 2:6 he had received from them no spe-

243. Rom. 1:13; 15:22.
244. Cf. Gal. 2:10; 1 Cor. 16:1, 15; 2 Cor. 8:4; 9:1, 12; Rom. 15:25-31.
245. Acts 15:19-20, 28-29; cf. 16:4; 21:25; see pp. 62ff. above. The fact that, instead of Barnabas, Silas/Silvanus accompanied Paul after the council in Jerusalem makes it very unlikely that the split with Antioch came before the second missionary trip (cf. 15:40-41). It happened first after this trip; see Acts 18:22-23, a puzzlingly short text, which refers to a very brief visit to Jerusalem and to a somewhat longer stay in Antioch. Luke writes here in surprisingly laconic brevity. He knew only too well what had happened there. See pp. 78ff. below, and n. 261 below.

cial legal requirements. The decree thus seems to have been issued a considerable time after the council, approximately A.D. 52/53, as a result of the conflict in Antioch, without the direct involvement of Paul. By contrast, he proposes for Corinth, and later for Rome, a very different solution to the problem that is not tied to a strict prohibition of all eating. In spite of their freedom with respect to the legal strictures, the "strong," who were closely allied with Paul, were to act on account of love because of the "legal" scruples of the "weak" who were struggling, and because of their "consciences." In order to prevent the dangers that might come to the weak, the strong were encouraged to stay completely clear of partaking of meat and wine.[246] The statement in Rom. 14:17 — "The kingdom of God does not consist of eating and drinking, but rather in righteousness and peace and joy in the Holy Spirit" — sounds, then, like the final conclusion to the battle about the συνεσθίειν (eating together) in Antioch approximately four years earlier, about which the Roman Christians would not have remained uninformed.

If Paul presents himself as the successful "Apostle to the Gentiles," who offered himself up to the nations when he was sent forth, Peter could appear as the authoritative disciple of Jesus and the first leader of the original community in Jerusalem, who was head and shoulders above Paul with respect to the *fullness of his traditions about Jesus.* As a missionary, he also would have seen, as quite important, that he would deliver the "words and deeds" of Jesus, the Messiah and the Son of God, which he himself had experienced, to his Jewish and his Gentile hearers. It is possible that the hesitancy of the apostle to the Gentiles to explicitly use the traditions about Jesus has to do with this deficiency of the former persecutor. As a former enemy of Jesus,[247] Paul knew him "only in a fleshly manner" (or, better said, "mistakenly" knew him); he had no personal experiences with him before Easter, though Peter by contrast had known him in manifold ways. When talking about the foundation of the community, Paul also made reference to the "foundational elements" of the Jesus tradition; he had to report about *who this crucified Jesus was and is,* as is shown by texts such as 1 Cor. 15:3ff.; the words of institution in 11:23ff., with a reference to "the night in which the Lord Jesus was betrayed"; or also Gal. 3:1; 4:4; 1 Cor. 2:2;

---

246. First Cor. 8:1-13; cf. Rom. 14:15-23. In 1 Corinthians he speaks of συνείδησις (conscience): 1 Cor. 8:7, 10, 12; 10:25-29; in Rom. 14:1, 22-23 he speaks of πίστις (faith). On this, see V. Gäckle, *Die Starken.*

247. Acts 9:4; 22:7; 26:14; cf. 2 Cor. 5:16-17. The reference to "fleshly knowledge" of Christ might go back to a (hypothetical) charge by the opponents.

2 Cor. 8:9; Rom. 1:3-4; 9:5; and 15:8.[248] Even though, as for example in his parenesis in Romans 12 and 13, he frequently refers indirectly to traditions about Jesus, with only a very few exceptions he does not cite the words of the Lord *expressis verbis*.[249]

With respect to the community in Rome, which likely would have been just a bit more recent than the one in Antioch and, one would suppose, was also established by those who came from Jerusalem,[250] he apparently did not want to "bring owls to Athens." At this point, in comparison to Peter and "the apostles who preceded him" in Jerusalem (Gal. 1:17), Paul would have felt himself to be in an inferior position, even though he naturally cannot state that publicly. By contrast, it was at this point that there was a unique strength in the Man of Rock, who was accompanied by the visible charisma of apostolic "deeds of power," as Luke describes them in Acts and as they are described elsewhere in the gospels only when speaking about Jesus.[251] It would seem that they exercised decisive influence among the opponents of Paul in 2 Corinthians.

Stated the other way, it is not by chance that, at the very place where Paul enters into a "rivalry" with the mission of Peter, or else with those whom he had sent forth, as is emphasized in Rom. 15:19 and in 2 Cor. 12:11ff., he performed "the signs of an apostle with signs, wonders, and powerful deeds," so that he — though being "a nothing" — "did not need to take a back seat to the super-apostles," just as little as the Corinthians needed to assume such a position with respect to the "other communities."[252] That

---

248. See M. Hengel, "Das Mahl in der Nacht, 'in der Jesus ausgeliefert wurde' (1 Cor. 11,23)," in *Le Repas de Dieu/Das Mahl Gottes,* ed. C. Grappe, WUNT 169 (Tübingen, 2004), 115-60 (118ff.). Second Corinthians 5:16 ought no longer to be cited against this situation.

249. It is not by chance that this happens in 1 Corinthians, where he must do battle for the moral order in the community: 7:10, cf. v. 25; 9:14; cf. also 1 Thess. 4:15 and 5:2. Concerning the Jesus tradition in Pauline parenesis, see the extensive discussion by D. Wenham, *Paul: Follower of Jesus or Founder of Christianity?* (Grand Rapids, 1995).

250. See Hengel and Schwemer, *Paul,* 257-60. Close ties existed for Judaism between Jerusalem and Rome ever since the capture of the Jerusalem temple by Pompey in 63 B.C., which brought many Jews to Rome as captives of war. The community in Antioch was established about A.D. 36/37, that in Rome at the time of Caligula (37-41). See, as well, n. 176 above.

251. Cf. the miracle stories that Luke recounts in Acts 5:15-16; 9:32-43; on this, see Mark 6:7, 12-13 par.

252. Concerning the "apostolic signs," see now E. Grässer, *Der zweite Brief an die Korinther,* 220ff.: Paul presents himself as a "pneumatic figure par excellence" (222). Would he have said this in opposition to a "Gnostic opposition group" that cannot be otherwise re-

would have held true with respect to all the rest of the communities, and not just those that had been founded by Paul. Could it be that the puzzling phrase ὑπερλίαν ἀπόστολοι (super-apostles),[253] after the disastrous conflict in Antioch, primarily refers to Peter, his friends in Antioch and Jerusalem, and his messengers? It is certainly possible that other disciples from the circle of the Twelve might have been included among the messengers sent by Peter, possibly his brother Andrew. The era of the apostles in Jerusalem comes to an end for Luke with the Apostolic Council.[254] It is not by chance that Luke's account in Acts, which, with one exception,[255] denies the title of apostle to Paul, in deference to Peter and the circle of the Twelve, and merely refers to him as the "thirteenth witness,"[256] makes these two opponents the greatest post-Easter miracle workers.

This ongoing tendency of Luke, *auctor ad Theophilum,* to harmonize and to reconcile also clarifies one of the most intractable problems in Acts, namely, the sudden narrative division between the activities of Peter and those of Paul. Luke assumes a rigorous separation. He takes leave of Peter when Peter makes his decisive pro-Pauline speech in Acts 15:7-11 and never mentions him again, not even once. But Luke leaves the decisive suggestion, which resolves the conflict that is portrayed so dramatically,[257] to be uttered by James.[258] This is the one who has the last word; correspond-

---

constructed? Such a group did not exist at that time yet (see M. Hengel, *Kleine Schriften III,* 473-510). Were not acts of power and signs more common in the original community and performed by those apostles who had been sent forth by Jesus?

253. Cf. 2 Cor. 11:5: λογίζομαι γὰρ μηδὲν ὑστερηκέναι τῶν ὑπερλίαν ἀποστόλων (I think that I am not in the least inferior to these super-apostles) and 11:23: διάκονοι Χριστοῦ εἰσιν; παραφρονῶν λαλῶ, ὑπὲρ ἐγώ (Are they ministers of Christ? I am talking like a madman — I am a better one). The expression that refers to the "super-apostles" reminds one of Gal. 2:6: his judgment demonstrates that he clearly distances himself from those ἀπὸ δὲ τῶν δοκούντων εἶναί τι, — ὁποῖοί ποτε ἦσαν οὐδέν μοι διαφέρει (and from those who were supposed to be acknowledged leaders — what they actually were makes no difference to me), and 2:9: οἱ δοκοῦντες στῦλοι εἶναι (those who were acknowledged pillars).

254. Concerning Andrew, see John 12:22 and nn. 60, 169 above. According to a story that was widespread in the second century, the apostle is said to have left Jerusalem twelve years after the resurrection of Jesus. That might point to the time of the persecution by Agrippa (Acts 12:1ff.); see Hengel and Schwemer, *Paul,* 256-57; cf. R. Riesner, *Die Frühzeit des Apostels Paulus,* WUNT 71 (Tübingen, 1994), 106, in agreement with A. v. Harnack.

255. Acts 14:4, 14. In my opinion, Luke makes this exception very consciously.

256. On Paul as μάρτυς (witness), see Acts 22:15; 26:16 and the fine study by C. Burchard, *Der dreizehnte Zeuge,* FRLANT 103 (Göttingen, 1970).

257. Cf. Acts 15:1, 5, 7.

258. Acts 15:13-21.

ingly, it is he who stands also by Paul in Gal. 2:9 as the most important of the three pillars. Apparently, by A.D. 48/49 James had become the most important personage in Jerusalem. As so often elsewhere, Luke is closer to the truth here than many are willing to credit him. The circle of the Apostles disappears with Peter as well, which means the group for which he serves as leader, according to Luke. In chapter 15 they are mentioned five more times, always linked to the "elders," and it is with that group that they send the letter concerning the Apostolic Decree to "the brothers in Antioch, Syria, and Cilicia."[259] By contrast to the mention of the apostles, the "elders" show up once again as the circle that works with James during Paul's visit to Jerusalem during the Feast of Weeks in A.D. 57.[260] The thirteen chapters that follow the council, Acts 16–28, are dedicated solely to the mission to the Gentiles. Peter and the apostles disappear completely.

With some awareness of what he is doing, Luke presents Paul as the successor to Peter, even though the "Cephas party" in Corinth and the further expansion of Petrine authority both show that his role outside of Eretz Israel increased, not decreased. This means that Luke — unfairly in terms of history — allows Peter to be pushed aside by Paul. At the very least, the situation in Antioch was just the reverse — and one might assume not only there. Paul finds Christians in Rome already, though Luke does not say anything about how they came there.[261] According to Luke, Peter was able to establish the mission to the Gentiles on the border of the Gentile region in Caesarea,[262] in the house of Cornelius, but Luke is completely silent about any (missionary) trips and visits to communities out-

259. Acts 15:22-23; cf. 16:4. This is the last time that Luke uses the collective for "apostle." This construction by Luke has its reasons.

260. Acts 21:18.

261. Acts 28:14-16. Even Paul makes no mention in the Letter to the Romans about what group established the community and who the founders were. He assumes that there was a long history of that community already (Rom. 1:1-15; 15:22) but praises only his own missionary activity from Jerusalem as far as Illyricum, and he emphasizes that he does not want to intrude in foreign missionary territories, "so that he does not build on a foreign foundation": ἵνα μὴ ἐπ' ἀλλότριον θεμέλιον οἰκοδομῶ (Rom. 15:19-20; cf. 1 Cor. 3:11; see nn. 73-74 above). Even here there is a play on the Petrine mission, with the rivalry occasioned thereby; cf. Phil. 1:15-16, and other passages as well. See n. 167 above.

262. The port city was considered a Hellenistic polis since the time it was reestablished by Herod, when it replaced the ancient Phoenician Tower of Strato, a place where Jewish and Gentile interests came to be at odds. The city provided the gateway to the West; see E. Schürer et al., *History,* 2:115-18. The conflict between Jews and Syrians in the city occasioned the outbreak of the Jewish War in A.D. 66.

side of Palestine.[263] Luke knows much more about what happened here than he writes. In this way he arrives at a *clear geographic and temporal break* between the activity of Peter and that of Paul. Luke can avoid mentioning to Theophilus the difficult disagreement in Antioch and the tensions that persisted for years afterward, which accompanied the Pauline mission from that time on and which can be detected in his letters, in 1 Corinthians, Galatians, and 2 Corinthians, and even within individual observations in Romans and Philippians. These comments are significantly brought about by the way the Man of Rock forced his way into the Gentile Christian mission territory of Paul. This sharp break and Luke's subsequent silence that is connected to it, which irritate us, serve to make a comparison between the two most important missionaries and thus serves to characterize peace in the church during the most difficult years after A.D. 70, that is, a time when the church began to expand successfully once again[264] but when it was, at the same time, sorely tempted and in many ways threatened.[265]

6. The Unknown Years for Peter and His Theological and Missionary Importance

6.1. Concerning Peter's Theology

In spite of Luke's tendency to harmonize everything, which irritates modern historians, he performed a great service for the church of his time with his two-volume work, and his influence extends into the present, in that he attempted to depict the continuity between the proclamation of Jesus and the Pauline mission.[266] At this point Peter holds the position — in its basic nature a historically significant one — of serving a unique *bridging func-*

263. Acts 12:17: ἐξελθὼν ἐπορεύθη εἰς ἕτερον τόπον (he left and went to another place) is consciously expressed by him in an undefined way. Luke would have certainly been well informed about the basic elements of the journeys undertaken by Peter. Cf. Acts 8:14-25 and 9:32–11:18, concerning Peter's travels in Jewish Palestine.

264. See the final sentence in Acts 28:31 and the promise in 1:8.

265. Cf. Acts 5:41; 14:19; 20:29-30; cf. Luke 21:12-19. I would assign dates to the gospel and Acts roughly between A.D. 75 and 85. See M. Hengel, "Der Lukasprolog und seine Augenzeugen. Die Apostel, Petrus und die Frauen," in *Memory in the Bible and Antiquity,* ed. S. C. Barton, L. T. Stuckenbruck, and B. G. Wold, WUNT 212 (Tübingen, 2007), 195-242.

266. In contrast to the portrayal by Luke, they were admittedly not free of conflict.

tion between the activity of Jesus and Paul's mission to the nations. If Peter's student Mark serves as the most important of the πολλοί (many, see Luke 1:1) in Luke's first volume, meaning the first of the many who set forth the story about Jesus as mentioned in Luke's prologue, then Peter is the leading figure for the *auctor ad Theophilum* — in fact, one might even say that he is purely and simply the paradigmatic figure in this regard among the "eyewitnesses and ministers of the word" on behalf of those who came later. Luke counts himself among those who follow; they were most thankful to that earlier group for the traditions about Jesus that established the basis for their faith.[267] Luke appropriately allows Peter and John to confess before the leading authorities of the people: "It is impossible that we could keep silent *about that which we have seen and heard*,"[268] and Peter can give support to his story about Jesus in the presence of Cornelius with the postscript: "*We are witnesses* of all that he did in the land of Judea and in Jerusalem."[269]

We ought not to forget at this point that Luke as an evangelist was himself an expert in setting forth the tradition about Jesus, and we owe him thanks as the one who provides the richest and most variegated collection of this type. It is likely that, as a follower of Paul, he also went to Jerusalem in A.D. 57 and thus became personally acquainted with these traditions in a way that also altered his theology as it took shape during the time he accompanied Paul on his journeys.[270] The example of the "beloved

267. Luke 1:2: καθὼς παρέδοσαν ἡμῖν οἱ ἀπ᾽ ἀρχῆς αὐτόπται καὶ ὑπηρέται γενόμενοι τοῦ λόγου (just as they were handed on to us by those who from the beginning were eyewitnesses and servants of the word); cf. also Heb. 2:3. On this, see S. Byrskog, *Story as History — History as Story*, WUNT 123 (Tübingen, 2000), and M. Hengel, "Lukasprolog."

268. Acts 4:20; cf. 2:32; 3:15; 5:32 for references to (eye-)witness testimony.

269. Acts 10:38-39; cf. 13:31, where Luke has Paul being directed to the apostles who were eyewitnesses.

270. Both the gospel and Acts forbid us from dating this double work to too late a period. We are confronted here by a New Testament author who, as is demonstrated in his entire development of the work into the gospel and the Acts of the Apostles, shows that the eyewitnesses stood in relatively close proximity. Matthew, John, 1 Peter, Hebrews, *1 Clement*, Ephesians, and most especially the Pastoral Letters came into being considerably later. The sources that were available to Luke are more varied than is normally assumed. They are not limited merely to Mark, Q (which is not a unity), and other special materials. Luke, as the first Christian historian, did more than the other evangelists as he engaged in basic research, and the oral tradition that was gathered together by him ought not to be underestimated. Matthew is founded not only on Mark but also on Luke to some extent. In the way he worked with the logia tradition, Luke as a rule stayed with the more original, which means at the same time the more trustworthy, version.

physician" (Col. 4:14), who goes from being one who accompanied Paul to becoming the author of the gospel that is filled with the most detail of any, could clarify why Peter, or else his messengers, also had success in the Pauline communities on their own later missionary journeys, such as in Corinth, which the apostle to the Gentiles, who had no personal contact with the earthly Jesus, would have seen as threatening. In a way that differs from the rabbinic traditions[271] or the biographical tradition about Muhammad, Luke mentions just as little about the names of the disciples who served as guarantors of his sources as did Mark before him and Matthew after him. In the same way, with respect to specific eyewitnesses, except for the closest circle of disciples with Peter at the forefront and with only the rarest of exceptions, the Synoptic authors mention none of the others, and then primarily in the Passion Narrative.

This lack of mention might have its reason, on the one hand, in the pattern of the sacred historical narrative of the Old Testament, in which guarantors of the tradition are mentioned seldom or do not appear at all.[272] But primarily it is because the traditions in the gospels concentrate *solely* on *just one person*, Jesus himself. The disciples do not have their own unique function in such traditions but are presented solely in their relationship with this *One*. This holds true for Peter as well; what he says and does is always in relation to Jesus. Even he plays no *independent* role. For this reason, the names of the disciples are completely lacking in the *logia tradition*. (I choose this open-ended term instead of Q, a concept that refers to the overloaded standard designation referring to a unified "gospel" framed around the hypothesis of a "Logienquelle," which does not stand up to scrutiny.)[273] The only decisive element therein is that Jesus speaks as

271. Also in the early rabbinic tradition, the halakot, about which consensus exists, were transmitted anonymously: They are "(oral) Torah from Sinai."

272. On this, see M. Hengel, "Lukasprolog."

273. The textual evidence that *The Critical Edition of Q*, ed. J. M. Robinson, P. Hoffmann, and J. S. Kloppenborg (Minneapolis, 2000), gives in the concordance for μαθητής (disciple) in Q, with respect to the persons who are disciples of Jesus, is basically all unclear: The only examples where Luke and Matthew agree refer to the disciples of John (Luke 7:18) or else to a word from Jesus that describes the relationship between "disciple" and "teacher" (6:40). For 6:20 there is no parallel passage in Matthew; for 10:2 there is no Lukan parallel; for 14:26 there is once again no parallel in Matthew. A more exact examination shows how much the Q hypotheses, in their usual form, derive from the comfort level of the exegetes, but in reality they are built to a great extent on sand. Most of all, one ought no longer to speak of one or more "communities" of Q or about various "redactions." These simply cannot be demonstrated. By contrast, the role of Luke as a transmitter of traditions

the Son of God and Messiah.[274] Even the word μαθηταί (disciples) appears in this collection only marginally. Everything is concentrated there on the words of Jesus himself.[275] The names of the disciples appear in the Synoptics (and here, by a wide margin, that of Simon Peter, more than any other) only in the stories that are recounted or in individual sayings; in each case, the disciples either are questioned by Jesus or pose questions to him.

On the other hand, since Jesus is normally surrounded by a large crowd of disciples, the primary role attributed to Peter as a leader in the Synoptics, that of being a direct partner in discussions, is particular surprising. Said another way: For the evangelists he serves as *the authoritative disciple;* one could even say that he stands in, as the "Rock," on behalf of the large crowd of disciples. By this means he becomes *the decisive "apostolic witness,"* who almost takes on the character of one who functions as a mediator. One could thus describe him as the one who holds the keys to the kingdom of God, or, with a grain of salt, as *mediator ad Mediatorem,* mediator to the Mediator.[276] Mark in essence describes him in a similar way in his gospel,

---

cannot be valued highly enough. In the *Gospel of Thomas,* which hardly came into existence before 150, Peter appears twice: logion 13, where Thomas is brought before him, and logion 114, where Jesus corrects him because he has sent Mary (Magdalene) away. Both logia are secondary.

274. Cf. on this, for example, *Pss. Sol.* 17:43 concerning the unique words of the Messiah. They are to be preserved.

275. For this reason I doubt, in the strictest sense, that any longer narrative stories were preserved in the logia tradition/in Q. Matthew could have been influenced throughout concerning such material, and also by Luke.

276. The same phenomenon surfaces in the tradition about James. In the legendary *Martyrdom of James,* Hegesippus has the "scribes and Pharisees" ask the brother of the Lord: "Just One, whom we are all obligated to obey, . . . proclaim to us: 'Who is the door to Jesus [τίς ἡ θύρα τοῦ ᾿Ιησοῦ]?'" He answered by uttering a confession to the enthroned and coming Son of Man, whereupon many who were convinced by the confession expressed agreement, but James was thrown down from the pinnacle of the temple by the leaders of the people: Eusebius, *Hist. eccl.* 2.23.8-18. The door to Jesus is James the Just himself, according to his witness, right to the point of martyrdom. See above, as well, pp. 8-9, for a discussion of *Gos. Thom.* 12. In a certain sense one could naturally also say this about Paul and about the ideal Beloved Disciple in John. Paul had received the gospel, which gives σωτηρία (salvation) to every believer (Rom. 1:16) by means of a very personal revelation from Jesus Christ (Gal. 1:11-12). And the Beloved Disciple is not only the closest one to Jesus and can provide access to him (John 13:23ff.) but also the decisive witness at the cross (19:26-27, 35ff.), the first one to come to faith in the Resurrected One (20:8) and the first one to recognize him (21:7). The central, paradigmatic role that the three "pillars" (Gal. 2:9) play in the most varied texts of the New Testament is unique. At their side, Paul comes as the "thirteenth witness"; see n. 256 above.

and most especially Luke does the same in the first half of Acts. We can only assume that he would have functioned in similar fashion during the period that remains dark to us — between A.D. 43 or else 48/49 up to his martyrdom ca. 64/65 — directly *in persona* or else indirectly through his messengers in the congregations of the West, from Antioch through Corinth and as far as Rome. The significant tensions between him and Paul that stem from this time period, which we know about from Paul's own references, are only too clear when viewed from this perspective.

Forgive me for attempting a psychological evaluation: Both major characters were very much alike — in fact, too much so.[277] This might hold true also for *aspects of their theology*, about which we admittedly have too little information with respect to Peter because of the nature of the sources. We admittedly know only the "first theologian" Paul, who confronts us in his letters, in the earliest Christian literary evidence, as a powerful missionary and thinker who is oriented on the basis of the truth of the gospel, which he had received from Christ himself.[278] That Paul, by the providence of God, wrote such unique letters and that these have been preserved for us is a historical wonder. If one expected the world to come to an end in the very near future (Rom. 13:11-12) and if "the time is short" (1 Cor. 7:29), it would have made intensive literary activity more unlikely than likely. Peter, who was not a literary figure, remains almost completely unknown for us as a writer. But one does note that the Cephas party in 1 Corinthians did not advocate circumcision and observance of the ritual laws; otherwise, Paul would have reacted in a very different manner. And that he can use the first person plural in Gal. 2:16, and can thus attribute to Peter as well the knowledge "that a person is not justified by works of the law but only through faith in Jesus Christ," supports the same conclusion.[279] That suggests there was a basic consensus.

Stated from the opposite vantage point, Luke describes the situation for Peter in Acts 15:7-11, in his last speech before the council, by using the formula that sounds Pauline: God's election works "so that out of my mouth the Gentiles hear the word of the gospel[280] and come to faith." He

277. Paul himself emphasizes his emotional nature, with which he can wound as well; according to the judgment of the evangelist, it could hardly have been different with Peter either; see Mark 8:32-33 par.; 14:31 par.; 14:71 par.; Acts 5:3ff.; 8:20ff., etc. See also n. 237 above.

278. Gal. 1:11-12; 2:5, 14; cf. 2 Cor. 11:10; 13:8.

279. Thus, at the very least, according to the wording of his speech, which he cites for the Galatians as that which he had spoken to Peter in Antioch; Gal. 2:14b-21.

280. Εὐαγγέλιον (gospel) appears in Luke only in Acts 15:7, in the mouth of Peter, and

gave them "the Holy Spirit just as to us" and "purified their hearts through faith."[281] For this reason one ought not to lay upon them the yoke of the law, "but rather we believe that we are saved through the grace of the Lord Jesus, just as they are."[282] Corresponding to this, at first Peter obviously lived in Antioch with those who were not Jews by sharing in Eucharistic table fellowship and thus, according to the evaluation of Paul, "lived as a Gentile and not as a Jew" (Gal. 2:12, 14). This means that, for him also, the purity laws had become adiaphora. It was only when messengers from Jerusalem came that he broke away, for the sake of peace and for the unity of the church, and because he did not want to make any problems for the Jewish brothers among their extended family in Jerusalem, who lived under pressure of the Zealots.[283] Peter thus stepped back from the table fellowship and brought about the angry — and theologically well-founded — protest of Paul that personally hurt him so deeply.[284]

---

in 20:24, in that of Paul; on this, cf. Gal. 2:7-8 and, as the single example outside the Letters of Paul, in 1 Pet. 4:17 (Rev. 14:6 uses the term, but not yet with a specific, Christological meaning). On its Jewish Christian background, see now W. Horbury, "'Gospel' in Herodian Judaea," in *The Written Gospel*, ed. M. Bockmuehl and D. A. Hagner (Cambridge, 2005), 7-30. Afterward, as previously, still consult the extensive work of P. Stuhlmacher, *Das paulinische Evangelium*, vol. 1, *Vorgeschichte*, FRLANT 95 (Göttingen, 1968). Peter also seems to have used the term and thereby — as does his student Mark — included with it the story about Jesus. Mark himself uses it seven times with reference to the message of salvation; in 14:9 it is identical with the "story about Jesus"; see M. Hengel, *Four Gospels*, 78-89.

281. Acts 15:7-9. This refers to the wonderful conversion of the Gentile centurion Cornelius in Acts 10:1–11:18 and to the contested question about purity in 10:14ff. = 11:8ff.

282. Acts 15:11. Cf., as well, the speech of Paul in Pisidian Antioch, 13:38.

283. His conduct there could be interpreted as apostasy; see Acts 21:21, 28 and p. 65 above, and n. 212 above.

284. In an article about the theologian Joseph Ratzinger, presently Pope Benedict XVI, in the *FAZ* of May 17, 2005, no. 112, 8, Eberhard Jüngel maintains that, according to Gal. 2:11-14, the "apostle Paul . . . [opposed] the apostle Peter to his face, when this one was not conducting himself according to the truth of the gospel," which was "the birth hour of responsible theology." But does this birth hour not lie earlier, at the first open proclamation by Saul in the synagogues of Damascus, after the turning point in his life, and in the preaching of Peter on that first Feast of Weeks festival after Easter, in Jerusalem, which announced that the crucified Jesus of Nazareth was the Lord and Messiah, who had been raised by God (Acts 2:22-36)? Does real missionary preaching ever exist without responsible theological reflection? But in Gal. 2:11ff. we are confronted with the *first theological conflict in early Christianity, about which we have an eyewitness account*, which did not end with a resolution (cf. Acts 6:1ff.; 15:1ff.; Gal. 2:1ff.) but rather with a breach that lasted for a longer period of time. The reaction by Paul caused wounds and achieved quite the opposite result at first, on the part of the opponent, whose arguments we do not know. And yet its consequences were, as a whole,

6. The Unknown Years for Peter

But we are not completely uninformed concerning the theology of Peter, and one ought not to underestimate this theology from the outset and thus treat it as unimportant. Because of the leading role played by this authoritative disciple of Jesus, who was also the first witness among the Twelve to the resurrection in the original community, one must assume that he was also a participant in giving shape to the beginnings of the "teaching of the apostles" (Acts 2:42). The speeches of Peter in Acts 1–5, which sound so "antiquated" in their unpretentious Christology and soteriology, are possibly not quite as completely worthless as is generally suggested. To be sure, they were formulated in a substantive way by Luke and thus can also serve as a witness to Luke's own theology — but what is the source of this theology? Would he who was so zealous in assembling the significant traditions about Jesus not have asked about what Peter himself taught and even asked the apostle and adapted from that teaching certain "archaic" emphases, which are so typical of him? Might this state of affairs, which is such an irritant to many, that Luke is no pure-as-the-driven-snow follower of Paul (if such a person ever existed),[285] but that he had his own peculiar way of stating his theological observations, possibly be connected with the fact that he had a closer acquaintance with the traditions about Jesus and the early church?[286] It is for this reason that he was faced with the task, during

---

positive. The Antiochene party and those who were not part of the radical wing of the Jerusalemite party found a solution in the Apostolic Decree. With respect to Paul we find, in this unhappy disagreement, the stimulus to write the Letter to the Galatians and, indirectly, essential points that are important in his extensive letters to the Corinthians and his Letter to the Romans. To that extent the observation of Jüngel finds its broad justification.

285. On this, see A. v. Harnack, *Lukas der Artz. Der Verfasser des dritten Evangeliums und der Apostelgeschichte* (Leipzig, 1906), 101: "*He is no Paulinist,* but he demonstrates very clearly that he knows Paulinism and harvests much from it." At the same time, he poses the question: "Where, then, did Paulinism remain except for Marcion and what Marcion made of him?" I remember the famous dictum of Karl Barth: "I am no Barthian."

286. This would be more understandable if the radical Paulinism would have developed further in an anti-Jewish and antinomistic sense after the judgment upon Jerusalem in A.D. 70; see Acts 20:29ff. One ought not to speak yet in such circumstances about "Gnosis." But there was a "pre-Marcionism," which spread at the beginning of the second century through the *Letter of Barnabas* and through Cerdo to Marcion. Its beginnings might be related to the destruction of Jerusalem, which would have been interpreted as God's judgment. See M. Hengel, *Kleine Schriften III*, 507ff. Cerdo, who according to Irenaeus, *Haer.* 1.27.1, was influenced by the students of Simon Magus (Eusebius, *Hist. eccl.* 4.11.2), and who supposedly came to Rome under Hyginus (ca. 136-140), already distinguished between the God of the Old Testament and the Father of Jesus Christ. Marcion supposedly adopted his teaching a short time later. According to Irenaeus, *Haer.* 3.4.3 (= Eusebius, *Hist. eccl.* 4.11.1),

a time of crisis between the churches of Paul and the earliest community, to effect a reconciliation by means of a narrative.

Something similar might hold true for Mark. Since he was the pupil and possibly also the interpreter of Peter, that neither proves the historical veracity of his narrative in the modern sense nor calls for giving up on the attempt to describe Mark's own theological profile, which he no doubt possessed. But there are emphases in his work that might be linked to Luke and possibly also to 1 Peter, which could be "pre-Pauline" and which might point back to the early period of the early community,[287] during which Peter was the leading authority figure.

This is not the proper place to attempt to unfold a "Petrine theology," since this would go beyond the parameters of this investigation, and it is additionally possible only in a purely hypothetical sense, but I would like to make reference to a few points. Baptism "for the forgiveness of sins,"[288] as performed by John the Baptist, now takes place "in the name of Jesus." This happens when one looks upward in faith toward the Glorified and Coming One and is linked to the gift of the Spirit. The concluding summary statement to Peter's Pentecost sermon is the summons to let oneself be baptized "in the name of Jesus,"[289] an invitation from this same individual who serves as an example of a sinner in all four gospels, who is sorry for his sins, and who is restored to his position once again by the crucified and risen Lord. The act of turning toward the sinner and the promise of "the forgiveness of sins" characterize not merely Jesus' activities, according to Mark,[290] as well as Luke[291] and Matthew,[292] which are to some extent dependent upon Mark, but also the preaching of Peter and

---

Cerdo at first belonged to the Roman community but gradually distanced himself from it; on this, see P. Lampe, *Paul*, 394.

287. Concerning the "pre-Pauline" development during the first two to three years of earliest Christianity, see M. Hengel, "Christologie und neutestamentliche Chronologie," in *Neues Testament und Geschichte. Oscar Cullmann zum 70. Geburtstag*, ed. H. Baltensweiler and B. Reicke (Zurich, 1972), 42-67; Hengel and Schwemer, *Paul*, 24-35; L. Hurtado, *Lord Jesus Christ* (Grand Rapids, 2003), 155-58.

288. Mark 1:4; Luke 3:3; differently, Matt. 26:28.

289. Acts 2:38.

290. Mark 2:5ff. par.; 2:17 par.; 10:45 par.; 14:24 par.

291. For him — in my opinion under the influence of Peter and Paul — Jesus' turning to sinners is particularly emphasized: Luke 1:77; 5:8; 7:48-49; 15; 18:9-14; 19:1-10; 22:31-32; 23:43; 24:47. For Luke the sentence from Luther's *Small Catechism* is really true: "Where there is forgiveness of sins, there is also life and salvation."

292. Matt. 1:21; 6:12, 14-15; 18:21-35; 26:28.

the apostles, as recorded in Acts[293]; it is confirmed by the self-offering of Jesus as the "servant of God" according to Isaiah 53,[294] which plays a role several times in the speeches in Acts 3 and 4.[295] Also 1 Pet. 2:22-25 cites portions of this text. And behind the ancient Jerusalem confession of faith in 1 Cor. 15:3 — ". . . that Christ died for our sins according to the Scriptures" — is most clearly a reflection of the fourth Servant Song from Isaiah. In this connection one should ask whether the Markan version of the description of the Last Supper in Mark 14:22-25, which is reproduced faithfully in Matt. 26:26-29, goes back to a Petrine tradition, whereas Luke 22:19-20 seeks to harmonize and to link the Pauline and Petrine traditions together.

One could point additionally to the spiritual enthusiasm of the earliest church, which is motivated by the coming of the end of time, in which the promises of the prophets are fulfilled and in which, according to Paul, the Aramaic word *abba* is used to articulate one's being a child of God.[296] That term, along with *Maranatha,* which preserves the wording of the oldest known prayer to Jesus,[297] is an expression of the continuity between Jesus himself, the original community, and the Gentile Christian missionary churches, since Jesus himself had already used it as a form of address in prayer and had taught the disciples to pray in this way as well.[298] That Jesus could have already been addressed as "our Lord" in Jerusalem is related, on the one hand, to looking back upon him as the "Lord" of the community of disciples, but, on the other, it can also be linked very closely with the interpretation of the resurrection of Jesus as the elevation to be enthroned at the right hand of God on the basis of Ps. 110:1, which, next to Isaiah 53, is the most important Christological text in the Old Testament: "The Lord said to *my Lord,* 'Sit yourself down at my right.'" Mark, Matthew, and Luke all place this in the mouth of Jesus, and in his Pentecost sermon, Peter articulates the confession that "God has

---

293. Acts 2:38; 3:19; 5:31; 10:43; 13:38.

294. Mark 10:45; 14:24; Luke 22:19-20, 27, 32, 37; on this, see U. Mittmann-Richert, *Gottesknecht.*

295. Acts 3:13, 26; 4:27, 30; cf. also 8:32-33 = Isa. 53:7-8.

296. Gal. 4:5-6; Rom. 8:15-16; cf. Mark 14:36.

297. Cf. Rev. 22:20 and, on that, the twofold prayer of the dying Stephen in Acts 7:59-60.

298. First Cor. 16:22; cf. Rev. 22:20; *Did.* 10:6; on this, see M. Hengel, "Abba, Maranatha, Hosanna und die Anfänge der Christologie," in *Denkwürdiges Geheimnis. Festschrift für Eberhard Jüngel zum 70. Geburtstag,* ed. I. U. Dalferth et al. (Tübingen, 2004), 145-83; M. Philonenko, *Das Vaterunser,* UTB 2312 (Tübingen, 2002), 33-43.

made [Jesus] both *Lord and Messiah.*"[299] Furthermore, 1 Pet. 3:22 makes a connection with Ps. 8:6.[300] The Christological interpretation of the Psalms must have begun very early on.[301]

It is obvious that not all of these ancient Christological confessional statements of the original community are to be attributed to Peter alone, but one still ought to pose the question in the reverse: Is it possible that the decisive foundational insights for their faith within the earliest (i.e., pre-Pauline) community, which means during the first two or three years of existence for this new movement, could have taken place without the significant participation of the first witness to the resurrection and the leader of the earliest community in Jerusalem? He would have played a decisive, if not *the decisive,* role in the development of the earliest kerygma. Even the term εὐαγγέλιον (gospel) — which goes back to the Aramaic *bᵉśôrā᾿ ṭôbā᾿* (bring good news) and the verb *biśśar* (proclaim), which occur in prophetic and Psalm texts and which are translated in the LXX by using εὐαγγελίζεσθαι (preach the good news) — would have been used, in my opinion,[302] already by Peter and his circle. It is certainly not just by chance that Paul, a few years after his conversion, visited with Peter alone in Jerusalem and that he stayed with him for fifteen days — that is, not an extremely short period of time.[303] During this two-week period, they would each have learned from the other, but at that time Paul would have certainly learned more from Peter than vice versa.

In addition, the wealth of traditions about Jesus is there because of the witness of Peter in the Synoptic Gospels, more than because of the other apostles.[304] This, at the same time, provides the foundational material for the Christian ethos, as we encounter it in parenetic sections in Paul. Form-critical scholarly activity, most especially in Germany, has long suppressed

---

299. Mark 12:36 = Matt. 22:44 = Luke 20:42-43; Mark 14:62 = Matt. 26:64; cf. Luke 22:69; Acts 2:34-35.

300. On Ps. 110:1 see M. Hengel, "Setze dich zu meiner Rechten!" in *Le Trône de Dieu,* ed. M. Philonenko, WUNT 69 (Tübingen, 1993), 108-94. Concerning the relationship between Ps. 110:1 and Ps. 8:6, see, in addition, 1 Cor. 15:25ff., Eph. 1:20-22, and, with regard to Christ as the intercessor at the right hand of God, the pre-Pauline, confession-like formula in Rom. 8:34.

301. See M. Hengel, *Studies in Early Christology* (Edinburgh, 1995), 227-91.

302. On this, see n. 280 above. It is absurd to continue to suggest, as happens again and again, that one should derive these forms of speech from the cult of the Caesar.

303. Gal. 1:18; on this, see Hengel and Schwemer, *Paul,* 133-50. One might guess that this visit was secret, since the life of Paul, as an "apostate," was under threat in Jerusalem.

304. See pp. 82-83 above.

the idea that the Synoptic tradition was not singularly the work of creative anonymous collectives within the community, but also that authoritative personalities were connected as the bearers of the tradition.[305] This would not exclude important secondary traditions, let us say from women or from other special eyewitnesses.[306] But the form-historical "dogmas" about the complete anonymity and collective nature of the traditions about Jesus have been believed for too long and too intensively. Because of his unique authority as confessor, missionary, and teacher — and in this role importantly also because he was the transmitter of the traditions about Jesus — as well as in his position as leader within the community and at the end as a martyr, Peter is placed into the role of "rock," upon which the Resurrected Lord, according to Matthew, would build his church, and for this reason he carries — seen as well within a historical framework — "Peter" as a name of honor, with justification. For this reason also he did not establish some narrow school, for that would have been too little. Instead, significant numbers of people in the early church, first in Jerusalem and Judea, but then later in the missionary congregations in the West, from Antioch to Rome, would have been schooled by him. Concerning Mark, but then also concerning Luke and Matthew, in fact in some partial sense concerning Paul and John, one could even say, *concerning the apostolic witness,* that he is — without having left us with a single sentence that he himself wrote — the teacher of us all.

6.2. *The Organizer and Mission Strategist*

Another point is significant as well, which in my mind has been too lightly appreciated. Peter was not merely a Spirit-empowered preacher and theologically creative caregiver but also — in a way that matched Paul himself — a *successful organizer and "mission strategist,"* an aspect about him that played an important role in the conflict between the two opponents. It was he who suggested in Acts that an election be held to maintain the basic number of the Twelve. It is he who takes the initiative to speak at Pentecost, who speaks the judgment against Ananias and Sapphira, who serves as speaker for the new messianic community in its confrontation with the Je-

305. On this, see M. Hengel, "Eye-witness Memory and the Writing of the Gospels," in *The Written Gospel*, ed. M. Bockmuehl and D. A. Hagner (Cambridge, 2005), 70-96.
306. M. Hengel, "Lukasprolog."

rusalem hierarchy, who joins John in visiting the newly won Christians brought to faith in Samaria by Philip, who restrains Simon Magus, and who brings many to faith through the miracles that he performs in Jerusalem, Lydda, the Sharon Plain, and Joppa. The highpoint of the legends about Peter, which are assembled and artfully described by Luke, is the conversion of the God-fearing centurion Cornelius. Is it going too far to say, if one proceeds on the basis of these narratives being paradigmatic for Luke and makes the assumption that Peter is depicted therein in a leadership role, that he certainly played, not only a role, but actually *the* most significant role in consolidating the as-yet unorganized movement of the followers of Jesus (and the Baptist?) in the motherland after Easter? It is my opinion that this self-confident messianic community, active in a missionary sense and successful in its own right among the Greek-speaking Jews in Jerusalem, among the so-called Hellenists, is not the least of his accomplishments as well. Because of this man's authoritative position, Paul visits only him in Jerusalem and is his guest for two weeks. Herod Agrippa I has Peter taken into custody as the leading figure of this new movement and wants him to be executed. He also plays the leading role in the conflict in Antioch. Paul — in a theologically appropriate way — can contradict him, but he cannot find fault with any of Peter's organizational activity and has to back off, since in the eyes of the Jewish Christians, who were still in the majority at that time, the missionary to the Gentiles was in the wrong.

Based on this mass of vastly different indicators, one can assume, not only that Peter's heart was concerned to make sure that the missionary proclamation went forward, but that his concern extended to matters of the development, structure, and unified activity of the admittedly very different communities, initially in Jewish Palestine, but after the conversion of Cornelius and after the expulsion at the time of Agrippa, also beyond its borders into Syria and finally all the way to Rome. And thus, just as Paul developed a "network" of communities that were beholden to him, there would also have been such a network of communities that would have been aligned with Peter. With respect to Antioch, one could speak of a "displacement" of Paul by Peter, and for a time one could fear that the same situation could unfold in Corinth. There would have been Pauline and Petrine house communities next to each another in Rome. The occasion for conflict in various places would have always been close to the surface.

Frequent exhortations for unity through the entire New Testament show that this threat was always real and that such unity was not always the mind-set of everyone. Even the two-volume work of Luke, which came into existence in the time between A.D. 75 and 85, had — among other goals — that of overcoming the tensions in the church. When finally, in such a unique way in Matt. 16:18, roughly ten to twenty years later, such a close link is established between Christ himself and the Man of Rock with respect to the development of the church, this is supported by the fact that Matthew is convinced that Peter had been involved, in a special way, with holding together the Jesus communities that were to some extent so very different. One could even say that Peter's concern was for the unity of the church. It is in fact remarkable that, in spite of the variety of conflicts and tensions, the earliest church did not fall apart into various splinter groups, which at times fought with each other already in the first century. It may be that the influential actions of Peter, who through his own trips and through those of messengers to the Pauline mission communities, such as in Corinth, might in his mind have been connected with such desires for unity — according to his way of conceptualizing it. An impatient, overconfident pressure for "unity" can admittedly bring about deeper conflicts yet.

It is surprising that — in contrast to Paul — Peter does not reportedly establish any of his own communities according to Acts but that he visits those already established; one might almost say that he "inspects" them, as in Samaria and Lydda, or that he goes there because of some special need, such as in Joppa.[307] According to Luke, the conversion of Cornelius in Caesarea is a special case that takes place by the wondrous intervention of God, in which one ought not to overlook the fact that Luke reports Philip's ongoing activity in that region.[308] The rank held by the Roman centurion clearly calls for the leading apostle to be the one who proclaims the message to convert him and his household to Jesus. Finally, in Antioch, Peter visits the most important community in Syria.

The *opponents of Paul in Corinth,* who were very confident of what they were doing, who traveled with letters of commendation,[309] and who denied to him the status as an apostle, come making a claim that he — which is naturally stated in bitter irony from his side — "dare not place himself on the same level" with them "or compare himself with them [τισίν]." At the same time, he accuses them that they, in contrast to himself,

---

307. Acts 8:14ff.; 9:32ff., 36ff.

308. Acts 8:40; cf. 21:8ff. The conversion of the Ethiopian finance minister, in which it remains unclear whether he is a full proselyte or just a Godfearer, points to a first, cautious step into the mission to the Gentiles.

309. Second Cor. 3:1ff. The term συνιστάνειν (recommend) is used surprisingly frequently in 2 Corinthians: cf. 4:2; 5:12; 6:4; 7:11; 10:12, 18 (twice); 12:11.

"break into foreign [missionary] areas of work and extravagantly praise themselves with respect to what has already been accomplished [by others]."[310] Concerning these influential missionaries, behind whom stands one who can claim a greater authority — I refer back to what has been stated already[311] — it is most likely that these are representatives who have been sent by the Petrine mission. They in essence call the validity of his apostolic activity in Corinth into question; Paul, however, who had established the community there on the basis of the gospel,[312] did not agree. He did not think that he had "overstepped" the boundary of his mission charge, in contrast to the opponents;[313] in fact, Paul is confident that, when things have settled down in Corinth, he will also go into regions beyond Achaia, which means as far as Spain, which was the end of the settled world at that time (Rom. 15:24, 28). There he would proclaim the gospel, without in the process poking into an area of mission activity that had been started by others, as the opponents were doing.

The appearance of the Jewish Christian missionaries from Jewish Palestine or from Syria, who in my opinion have ties to the Petrine mission and who contest Paul's apostolic mission, attack him personally and denigrate the value of his missionary activity, which is so painful and indeed threatening to Paul because the communities that he had established are the very ones who are openly to offer him "honor" in the parousia: they are his "hope, joy, his crown of boasting [στέφανος καυχήσεως] and his glory [δόξα]" (1 Thess. 2:19-20), or in a word: his καύχημα (boasting) "on the day of Christ" (Phil. 2:16; cf. 2 Cor. 1:14). This honoring also involves his renun-

---

310. Second Cor. 10:12-18: εἰς τὰ ἄμετρα καυχώμενοι ἐν ἀλλοτρίοις κόποις (we do not boast beyond limits, that is, in the labors of others, v. 15), οὐκ ἐν ἀλλοτρίῳ κανόνι εἰς τὰ ἕτοιμα καυχήσασθαι (without boasting of work already done in someone else's sphere of action, v. 16). On this difficult text, see M. E. Thrall, *Second Corinthians*, 100-109. On the term κανών (10:13, 15), it has a "geographic" meaning here, in the basic sense of the missionary territory that is "appropriated" to Paul by God's leadership; see BDAG, 507-8, and the passages cited by W. Beyer, *TWNT* 3:603, lines 24ff. [Engl: *TDNT* 3:509, lines 11ff.]. Cf. H. Windisch, *Der zweite Korintherbrief* (Göttingen, 1924⁹), repr., ed. G. Strecker (Göttingen, 1970), 312: "They have inserted themselves into his field of labor, and they boast about accomplishments that are not even their own."

311. See pp. 69-72 above.

312. See 1 Cor. 3:10ff.; 15:1ff.

313. Second Cor. 10:14: οὐ . . . ὑπερεκτείνομεν (we were not overstepping our limits); on this, see BDAG, 1033. In Jam. 4:13ff. there is, in my opinion, an indirect polemic against the mission plans of Paul that extend beyond land and sea; 2:20-26 is not the only criticism of Paul in this letter; see M. Hengel, *Kleine Schriften III* (511-48), 529-33.

ciation of remuneration from the community, which is held up against him as a deficit with respect to his full apostolic authority (1 Cor. 9:15ff.; cf. 2 Cor. 11:9-10). Even though he knows that praise of one's self is foolishness, he has to do so anyway because of his opponents, whom he allows to remain in anonymity, striking them with their own weapons, himself making use of this "foolishness" in his gripping "speech of a fool" (2 Cor. 11:16-33), which reaches its highpoint as he paradoxically gives honor to his "weakness." One is moved to compare this disagreement with that of the Twelve (Mark 9:33-37 par.) about "who is the greatest," and with Jesus' answer: "Whoever wants to be the first among you must be the last and servant of all."

Paul writes the *Letter to the Romans* in the winter of A.D. 56/57 from Corinth, not all that long after 2 Corinthians, which he had written in Macedonia in preparation for his arrival in Corinth.[314] He deals with such issues most particularly in Romans 15, which also played a role in his disagreement with his Petrine opponents in Corinth and which shows that this did involve, not just a marginal group when he was dealing with them, but an influential, well-informed "opposing" mission movement. In a way that is similar to 2 Cor. 13:3, he emphasizes the evidence of his (apostolic) full authority "in the power of signs and wonders" in Rom. 15:18-19.[315] This is followed by a geographic indication of the areas of his missionary activity to this point. "Thus I could begin in Jerusalem and draw a circle around the region where I could bring [the proclamation] of the gospel about Je-

---

314. Cf. Acts 20:1-3; 2 Cor. 2:13; 7:5; 8:1. I am skeptical of the various proposals about how to divide up the letter. The last portion of the letter, in 2 Corinthians 10–13, might stem from correspondence that was written separately; it is unlikely, however, that it is identical with the letter of tears mentioned in 2:3. I follow, now as before, the considerations offered by H. Lietzmann and W. G. Kümmel, *An die Korinther,* 2 vols., HNT 9 (Tübingen, 1949⁴), 139-40, as worthy of reflection: The letter certainly did not come into existence in one day, and as regards the break between chapters 9 and 10, it may be that "the acceptance that there was a sleepless night in which he stayed awake [would be sufficient]." Furthermore, "Paul is no letter writer, to be measured according to the usual norms, and for this reason the problem for the exegesis of his letters is less that of a literary-critical nature (as had been considered previously), but a psychological one. We find temperamentally inserted later additions even in 1 [Cor.] 16:22 [and] Gal 6:11-17; Rom. 16:17-20 even includes an attack on opponents about whom nothing else is said in the entire letter, which thus provides a good parallel for our chapters." W. G. Kümmel, in his addendum to Lietzmann's commentary, points out that A. Schlatter is "correct in emphasizing that Paul first speaks in detail about his plans for the future in Corinth in 10–13."

315. See pp. 76-77 above.

sus to completion, as far as Illyricum."[316] Paul adds abruptly: "In this I lay my honor, not to proclaim the gospel in those places where Christ has [already] been named, so that I do not build on a strange foundation,"[317] and he provides support for this with a citation from the Septuagint, from the Servant Song in Isa. 52:15. This reference, which is materially unnecessary, can best be understood if Paul is thereby distancing himself from another competitive mission movement that, according to his view, finds pleasure in building on "a strange foundation" (ἐπ᾽ ἀλλότριον θεμέλιον), which is almost surely the Petrine mission. For this reason he does not announce himself in Rome as a missionary (see Rom. 15:23ff.), but only as a visitor passing through on the way to Spain who hopes for a joyful chance to meet the brothers in the faith in the Roman metropolis and hopes for support for his further travels.[318]

Concerning the founders of the community in Rome, Paul mentions not a word, which is exactly how Luke handles it in Acts. As Rom. 1:10-13 and 15:22 show, the community has existed for a long time already. Because of the numerous contacts between Jerusalem and Rome, having been established by those who came from the Holy City, this community could have been almost as old as the community in Antioch. From the outset this would also make it likely that there was a connection between Peter and the unknown Jewish Christian founders of the community, a connection that would also explain why Peter later made a trip to Rome. Unfortunately, we do not know when (and how often) he came there. The Letter to the Romans, by means of which Paul sets forth the gospel that he proclaims as an apostle, has an apologetic character as well. He deals with questions there that are posed to him by the Roman Christians, from which one must assume that they are close with the Jerusalem, Petrine tradition — otherwise, Peter would not have had such a central role in the later gospel tradition stretching from Mark to John, but also in Acts and in *1 Clement*. It is possible that he had been in Rome even before Paul got there. When the apostle to the Gentiles states so bluntly that he had long

---

316. Rom. 15:19b; on κυκλῷ (around), see BDAG, 574; on πεπληρωκέναι (fully proclaimed, brought to completion), see ibid., 828, under 3. Concerning the apparent contradiction to Gal. 1:15-24, see Hengel and Schwemer, *Paul*, 86-87, 99, 142, 144.

317. Rom. 15:20: ἵνα μὴ ἐπ᾽ ἀλλότριον θεμέλιον οἰκοδομῶ (so that I do not build on someone else's foundation). The closeness to the way this is expressed to 1 Cor. 3:10 is remarkable; see pp. 16ff. above.

318. Rom. 15:22-24; cf. 2 Cor. 10:16. In Rom. 1:13-14 he speaks differently; apparently he changed the nature of his argumentation during the time the letter was taking shape.

wanted to see the Roman Christians,[319] why would the same not have been the case for the Man of Rock after he was forced to leave Jerusalem, ca. A.D. 42/43?[320] As the leading man up to that point in the earliest community, and then also in Syria and beyond, he would certainly have exercised leadership over a large number of primarily Jewish Christian mission helpers, who would have had no trouble mastering the Greek language accurately. At this point, he was certainly in a better position than was the outsider Paul, who had no fellow travelers from Jerusalem by the time he went on his third journey.

The stature and influence of Peter in the many missionary communities of the Diaspora outside of Palestine that were still led by Jewish Christians must have been considerable — which is demonstrated for us in the conflict in Antioch — and the same would have applied to Rome. It is possible that the scattered house communities in the large city of Rome were at the same time "communities that each had a particular character." That would at least be an accurate reading of the "house community" of Prisc(ill)a and Aquila (Rom. 16:3-5a), which alone is designated as an *ekklēsia,* which would have had a Pauline character; the rest would have been influenced by Peter or — with still stronger Jewish Christian influence — would have followed the leadership of James. The Jewish Christian element controlled the spiritual leadership before A.D. 70, which is shown by the traditions that were processed there a generation later in the Letter of Clement.[321] The "Petrine mission" would have played an important role in the capital city, which can hardly have been less important, and was likely more important than, that of Paul. This would support our thesis that Peter was not merely a predominant authority but also a competent organizer and "mission strategist." The task of a "worldwide mission," which confronts us already in clear form in Mark,[322] the earliest gospel,

---

319. Rom. 1:11-15; cf. 15:22.

320. This applies at least to the time the Jews (Jewish Christians) were banished from Rome at the time of Claudius, roughly in the year A.D. 49 (Acts 18:2), and then once again after his death in 54 and at the beginning of Nero's reign. On this, see R. Riesner, *Frühzeit,* 139-80; Hengel and Schwemer, *Paul,* 257-60.

321. The closing prayer still has a markedly Jewish character; on this, see H. Löhr, *Studien zum frühchristlichen und frühjüdischen Gebet. Untersuchungen zu 1 Clem 59 bis 61 in seinem literarischen, historischen und theologischen Kontext,* WUNT 160 (Tübingen, 2003). Even the worship service at Rome, as it is described by Justin, *Apol.* 1.67, is completely dependent in its first part on the synagogue worship service. Paul rejects any accusation of animosity toward Judaism in Romans 9–11 and warns against such thinking in 11:17-24.

322. Mark 13:10 par.; 14:9 par.; cf. 1:17.

and which is patently obvious in both Luke and Matthew as well, was supported — certainly in Peter's later period of activity — by him as well, which for him also included proclamation among the Gentiles. That was no Pauline monopoly. But the onetime fisherman from the Sea of Gennesaret did not compose letters for us, as is the case with the onetime Pharisaic scribal scholar from Tarsus. It is for this reason that his theology cannot be so convincingly demonstrated for the later church.

Peter's final roughly sixteen years, from the time of the Apostolic Council, in A.D. 48/49, to his martyrdom, sadly remain in almost total darkness. We must — at least at the outset — assume that the deep and consequential, also very personal, conflict with Paul, in A.D. 52/53, was a decisive experience for his later activities. At the same time, precisely these sixteen years were decisive for Peter's growing influence in the church in the West, which was becoming increasingly "Gentile Christian."[323] Based on everything that has been said to this point, the Galilean fisherman ought not to be underestimated or brushed to the side with respect to his activities in both the church and theological-historical matters, even during this period between ca. A.D. 48/49 and 64/66, over against the Pharisaic scribal scholar from Tarsus, who can be characterized for us as the first early Christian theologian because of his majestic writings. The word about the rock in Matt. 16:17-19, the reference to the faith of Peter, which will not waver because of Jesus' prayer on his behalf and through which he is to strengthen his brothers (Luke 22:32), as well as the threefold charge

323. P. Vielhauer, *Kephaspartei*, 351-52 (= Vielhauer, *Oikodome*, 180), insinuates that the Cephas party in Corinth "elevated for their . . . teacher a claim for exclusivity and absoluteness" and emphasizes, in conclusion: "But the Cephas ideology lived on. It was not limited to Corinth; it had been introduced there from elsewhere and existed elsewhere as well." To counteract that claim, he suggests that "opposition to the Petrine claim of primacy developed within the Johannine circle." In the end it led to "very circuitous ways" of dealing with "Matt. 16:17-19 to arrive at the Roman doctrine of primacy," whereas "deep darkness . . . surrounds the origins, the 'setting in life,' and the 'historical center' of the Cephas ideology" (352/181-82). Here, in spite of historically apt observations, an ideological construct is spun at the end. The striking importance of the "Man of Rock" in the early church — as also for Paul and for the Lord's brother James — lies in the special *authority* of his personhood as a disciple of Jesus, theological teacher, missionary, and leader of communities that were located in many regions, which survived through the decades up to his death, and one can add: after his death as a martyr. Concerning the "primacy" of Peter — if one must use this weighted terminology — there is, in my opinion, no demonstrable historical and theological way to arrive at what later became papal "primacy." The unique apostolic nature of the disciple of Jesus, as well as the relatively late appearance of the claim for primacy, speaks against any direct link.

from the Resurrected One to feed his flock (John 21:15-17), are not to be minimized by applying them only to the earliest period; *they apply to the entire activity of Peter right to the point of his martyrdom.* Such texts about Peter in the gospels would not have come into existence and would not have been transmitted to us without him having been intensively active in these years that remain dim to us.

6.3. Reconciliation with Paul?

At the end, did it come to the point that the parties moved closer together or even reconciled? We do not know for sure, but we can consider it possible. For both of them, for the former denier and for the former persecutor, the unity of the church, which is centered Christologically in its essence, was on their heart: For them, Christ was not "divided" (1 Cor. 1:13). They both also knew from personal experience that their faith lived on the basis of the forgiveness of sins, and both of them well knew of Jesus' commandment to personally forgive others, which superseded all human and theological differences. It was not simply to fill space that Jesus took this commandment up into the fourth petition of the Lord's Prayer.[324] It is certainly possible that they were in personal contact between the time Paul came to Rome and the time of the persecution by Nero, that is, between A.D. 60 and 64/65.

A small indicator for closing the gap could be the mention of *Mark* in Col. 4:10 (identified there as the nephew of Barnabas), 2 Tim. 4:11, and Philemon 24, among the fellow workers with Paul, always mentioned at the same time as Luke.[325] Admittedly, only the Letter to Philemon comes with certainty from Paul's own hand, and we do not even know where this smallest of the Prison Letters was written, though we could suppose Ephesus or, later, from Caesarea or Rome.[326] The Letter to the Colossians was certainly written by a student, and 2 Timothy, as is true of the Pastoral Letters in general, was written very late, roughly at the same time as the Ignatian correspondence, and it assumes clear knowledge of Acts.[327] In a

---

324. Luke 11:4; in Matt. 6:12 it is the fifth petition.

325. Col. 4:14: ὁ ἰατρὸς ὁ ἀγαπητός (the beloved physician); Phlm. 24; 2 Tim. 4:11. Cf. Acts 12:12, 25; 15:37: John Mark; 15:39: only Mark; 13:13: only John.

326. The question remains unresolved.

327. On this, see 2 Tim. 3:11 for the geographic sequence Antioch (in Pisidia), Iconium, Lystra, which does not stem from oral tradition but points to literary dependence, and also see Acts 13:14, 51; 14:1, 6, 8, 19; see also the very personal details about Timothy in 2 Tim. 1:3ff.;

certain sense as a continuation of Acts, the letter manifests the character of a testament before the death of the apostle by martyrdom.[328] Thus 2 Timothy 4:11 — "Bring Mark with you, for he is useful for service" — seems almost like a reconciling gesture, which would put an end to the break described in Acts 15:37-39. At that time, Paul was involved in a harsh disagreement with Barnabas,[329] since he considered John Mark to be unfit as a helper for the mission. "Deutero-Paul" wants to heal the wound.

In a like manner, the First Letter of Peter[330] has, among other elements, the character of a testament and a primer for suffering for those who would follow in the footsteps of Jesus and of the apostle, who in 1 Pet. 5:1 is called "a witness of the sufferings of Christ." First Peter 5:13 would have a deutero-Petrine correspondence to the role of Mark in the later Pauline traditions; the addition "my son" points in fact to a close teacher-student relationship.[331] First Peter and the later book 2 Timothy both point to Rome.

Although we know very few of the details concerning the deaths of Peter and Paul as martyrs in Rome, during or soon after the persecution of Nero, which links them together once again, no one any longer ought to question these events.[332] The traditions passed on by the church in connec-

---

3:15; Acts 16:1 and, beyond that, the place-names provided in 2 Tim. 4:12, 20 and the echoes of the departure speech at Miletus: 4:3 = Acts 20:29 and 4:7 = Acts 20:24; 4:16 and Acts 22:1; the verbal connections with the Lukan work are striking, but on the other side, there are also great differences. Luke knows of no monarchical office of bishop and no high Christology. One could almost conclude that the author of the Pastoral Letters was a student of Luke. It seems, beginning with Luke and extending through the Pastoral Letters and to Polycarp, that there was something like a "school of Paul" that carried forth conservative ideas.

328. Second Tim. 4:6-8, 16-18.

329. Acts 15:37-38 and 13:13; see pp. 58-59 above, and n. 188 above.

330. The same is true of the second letter, which comes into existence twenty to thirty years later.

331. On this, see later interpretations, pp. 131ff. below. The mention of the "faithful brother" Silvanus, who had been Paul's companion on the second trip, after the Apostolic Council, and who was the present letter carrier to Asia Minor, moves in this same direction. Apparently 1 Peter also seeks to build a bridge. Second Peter 3:15-16 goes further yet, speaking of "our beloved brother Paul," who has no control over the fact that heretics misused his letters.

332. The disagreement in this matter can be seen from the time of the Waldensians in the Middle Ages and was bitterly waged with some justification since the Enlightenment. A short overview of those who opposed it and those who favored it, until 1961, is provided by W. Bauer in *NTApocr*[3] 2:22 [Engl: 2:49]. Above all others, K. Heussi, in numerous publications about Peter, has advocated the view that there is no historical truth to his stay in Rome,

tion with these two great teachers of the early church place their death at roughly the same time and in the same city, as those who gave their witness to the point of death. This is reported already in *First Clement,* which means toward the end of the 90s; it is based on a Roman tradition that was already solid and that Ignatius also knew.[333] Even though serious differences at times existed between them, and in spite of all theological differences, with respect to their unique activity, they were *appropriately* considered together by the church of Jesus Christ and have been united as lasting witnesses for the "truth of the gospel." Possibly one ought to make June 29, the festival of Peter and Paul, for which evidence exists already in the middle of the fourth century, in some special way into an ecumenical festival day.[334]

The corpus connected with both Peter and Paul, and with them a third individual in the community, by the name of John, provides for us *the weight-bearing pillars of the new message,* which is for all human beings. More than any others, to them we owe thanks for the *apostolic witness* that is the foundation for our common faith and the starting point for all ecumenical reflection. Just as their witness, upon which the church bases its faith, is not carried forth arbitrarily and expanded at will, thus also their apostolic witness is in itself unique and their authority cannot be replaced or expanded. There is thus also no "office of Peter," which keeps expanding during the history of the church and which can set forth ever new, developing authoritative claims. The very fact that a variety of Petrine texts exist, such as Matt. 16:18-19, Luke 22:31-32, or John 21:15-18, which impresses anyone who visits St. Peter's Basilica in Rome, *points back to the reality of the special, unique "apostolic service" that the Man of Rock performed for the growing church.*

---

nor to his martyrdom. How extensively a significant scholar can err methodologically is demonstrated in his last study on the theme: *Die römische Petrustradition in kritischer Sicht* (Tübingen, 1955). See also pp. 5-7 above and pp. 125-26 below.

333. Ign., *Rom.* 4:3. Ign., *Smyrn.* 3:2 mentions Peter as the leader of the disciples and as a witness to the resurrection; Ign., *Eph.* 12:2 mentions Paul as founder of the community in Ephesus, as a letter writer, and as a martyr.

334. Most especially W. Bauer, *Rechtgläubigkeit und Ketzerei im ältesten Christentum,* BHT 10 (Tübingen, 1934; 1964²), 115-33, saw in the linking of Peter and Paul since *1 Clement* 5 a "way to seek support and to do battle" against heresy, a view that is certainly incorrect. For all their differences, the two were in reality the leading figures in early Christianity, and that they died in the capital city of the empire is connected with the fact that they both took great pains to be there. The "antiheretical" role of Rome in the second century is highly overrated by Bauer. The Roman community was surprisingly kindhearted toward the "theological diversity" of the second century.

7. Summation: Ten Points

The result of our reflections can be drawn together in ten points.

1. With his discourse about the rock, the Matthean Christ identifies the first disciple as the authoritative, unique person in the circle of the Twelve and distinguishes him thereby also as a later teacher, missionary, and leader of the community over against the other disciples.
2. Peter's nickname *Kêphā'* goes back to Jesus himself, which means that the meaning "rock" or "rock fragments" is more likely from early on, instead of the currently favored connotation "stone."
3. The play on words in Greek πέτρος/πέτρα is thus not something that Matthew discovered but is put into use early after Easter, possibly by the Hellenists in Jerusalem.
4. Looking back, we see that the key word "rock," upon which Christ builds his church, is not related solely to certain functions Peter performed, such as speaker for the disciples, recipient of the first vision of the Resurrected One, or leader of the original community in Jerusalem. Rather, it is descriptive of the entire thirty-five years of his activity, from his call to his martyrdom in Rome.
5. On the one hand, Peter plays a decisive role in Jerusalem in the opening of the new messianic movement for the "peoples," since Jesus' work of salvation broke down the national Jewish barriers and fulfilled the prophetic promises for all peoples. From the time of the persecution under Agrippa and afterward (ca. A.D. 43), he was increasingly the leading missionary for the Jews outside of Eretz Israel and thus addressed the Godfearers in the synagogues as well, who were actual Gentiles.
6. On the other hand, Peter wanted to pay careful attention to the Jewish Christian community in Jerusalem. It was being increasingly oppressed and, from about A.D. 43, when Peter had to flee, was under the leadership of the Lord's brother James. Peter sought to avoid any activity that would provoke an accusation of apostasy by Judaism, as was raised against Paul. For this reason, at the Apostolic Council in Jerusalem, Peter specifically called for the Gentile mission to be released from any requirement for circumcision. But then, only a few years later in Antioch, he came into severe conflict with Paul, who sharply disagreed with Peter that the Jewish Christian and Gentile Christian celebrations of the Eucharist were to be practiced separately because

of issues of purity, out of respect for the oppressed Jewish Christians in Jerusalem.

7. The later ramifications of this conflict can be detected in a variety of Paul's letters (Galatians, 1 and 2 Corinthians, and parts of Philippians and Romans). In these letters it is hinted that Peter himself had increasingly become a missionary to the Jews *and* to the Gentiles. In this regard, as the onetime disciple of Jesus and as the authoritative representative of the Jesus tradition, including in communities that were primarily Gentile Christian, he stood in high regard. The "Cephas party" in Corinth gives one indication of this development. The importance of Peter in the later "postapostolic" writings, including the gospels, is framed from the end of the 40s within this expanded missionary activity. A problem is that Luke has Peter establish the mission to the Gentiles with respect to Cornelius but then says nothing about Peter's later activity after the Apostolic Council, no doubt in order to avoid discussing the conflict between Peter and Paul.

8. As the empowered guarantor of the traditions about Jesus, Peter appears clearly in the gospel of his student Mark, in which he plays a leading role that is patently underestimated at present, which is expressed in greater detail in the later gospels of Luke and especially Matthew. Even John cannot avoid discussing him. Traditions reported by Peter lie behind the Second Gospel and they motivate Luke and Matthew to base their work extensively on his gospel. In the second century there was still recognition of this, and for this reason Mark was included in the "Canon of the Four Gospels."

9. Though he neither had training in being a scribe, as Paul had received, nor was conversant in the rhetorical and literary skills of the Greek language, Peter was still a theologically powerful thinker, an impressive proclaimer, and a competent organizer; otherwise, he would not have played such a unique role within the circle of Jesus' disciples, in Jerusalem, and later as missionary to both Jews and Gentiles, and he would not have been able to achieve a unique position and be held in such high regard. The Christological-soteriological bases of the Christian kerygma, which developed astoundingly quickly right after Easter, as well as the early Christian ethos, could not have come into existence without Peter's considerable influence. In later years one must assume that there was an independent mission relationship between Jerusalem and Rome that started with him. The traditions about Jesus played a considerable role in this mission, and Peter was in that respect

superior to Paul, the more successful missionary to the Gentiles. At the same time, Peter was distinguished from Paul theologically by a divide that was not insurmountable. The points of agreement in the basic elements of the new message would have carried the day, in spite of the conflict that broke out in the meantime in Antioch between the two of them and in spite of the bitter disagreement with the missionary messengers sent by Peter, as revealed in 2 Corinthians 10–12.

10. Both Peter and Paul were premier — in fact, unique — early Christian teachers; *we thank both of them for the decisive content of their apostolic witness,* which Paul conveys by means of his letters and which Peter provides for us through the Synoptic Gospels, especially Mark and Matthew. Luke, by contrast, in his two-volume work, seeks of necessity to convey the story by seeking common ground with both of them. John (or, better said, the Corpus Johanneum) is the unique, individual third witness, which from his side assumes knowledge of both of the other bodies of witness.

This *common "apostolic witness,"* in spite of the apparent tensions that are preserved therein, is *unique* for the church and — in the full sense of the word — *foundational.* Appropriate explication of it is the central task for all Christian confessions. Ecumenical discussion can go forward in a meaningful way only on the basis of this foundation, which is held in common by all. This original witness does not continue to develop ad infinitum in terms of content, but it seeks rather *to call back to itself* each generation anew. Through such turning back and returning, Christ, according to Matthew, builds his community upon the "rock," Peter.

II. The Family of Peter and Other Apostolic Families

1. Mark and the Other Evangelists

According to Papias, the bishop of Hierapolis in Phrygia about 130, according to Irenaeus of Lyon about 180, and according to Clement of Alexandria about 200, the evangelist Mark was the interpreter and student of Peter. Clement adds the information that Mark's gospel came into existence in Rome. This means that the Gospel of Mark rests upon solid Petrine tradition. Papias refers to the testimony of the "Elder John," which means that this information must have been a generation or two older and that it is rooted back in the first century.[1] To be sure, "progressive" evangelical and Catholic exegetes today confidently assert that these references are to be decisively contested, even though not only 1 Pet. 5:13 — "the elect [community] in Babylon [i.e., Rome] and Mark, my son, greet you"[2] — but also Justin Martyr write about this same relationship in the middle of the second century.[3] The unique emphasis on Simon Peter in the Second Gospel itself speaks in favor of the testimony. Simon and Peter are the first and last names of a disciple in the gospel; he thus provides an intended *inclusio* and is at the same time, by a significant margin, most often named as a disciple.[4]

---

1. According to Eusebius, *Hist. eccl.* 2.15 and 3.39.15; cf. Irenaeus, *Haer.* 3.1.1. See pp. 36-48 above.

2. The letter was written by one of Peter's students and does not come from the apostle himself. See pp. 12-13 above. On 1 Pet. 5:13, see also pp. 131ff. below.

3. Justin, *Dial.* 106.3 cites Mark 3:16-17 as the gospel of Peter. Because the authority of Peter stands behind it, the Gospel of Mark survived, even though more than 80 percent of it was copied by Matthew, whose gospel is much more extensive. See n. 140 above.

4. Cf. Mark 1:16 and 16:7; on this, cf. R. Feldmeier, "Die Darstellung des Petrus in den

We receive from Mark, this student of Peter, a very personal and trustworthy remark about this first and clearly most important disciple in the gospel, which Luke and Matthew take hold of as well:[5] Simon, to whom Jesus gave the name *Kêphā'*, which is rendered *Petros* in Greek, was married. Mark admittedly says this only indirectly in his narrative about the healing of this disciple's mother-in-law, but at the same time, that clearly says enough. The ancient church kept this tradition alive, at least to some extent. Just before Mark tells this story, he relates the narrative about a possessed man being freed in the synagogue in Capernaum, as evidence for the special power of Jesus. Thereafter follows the description of a miracle that appears out of place:

> And as they had left the synagogue, they went right away into the house of Simon and Andrew, together with James and John. The *mother-in-law* [πενθερά] *of Peter lay sick with fever,* and someone told him about her right away. And he went there, helped her get up, as he took [her] hand, and the fever left her, and she served them [at table].[6]

The Synoptic parallels in Luke and Matthew are completely dependent at this point on the "Gospel according to Mark," which for them was authoritative and stood in the Petrine tradition.[7] As often elsewhere, Matthew shortens it and attempts to smooth the somewhat awkward report of the Jerusalemite Mark,[8] who does not write in rhetorically informed Greek

---

synoptischen Evangelien," in *Das Evangelium und die Evangelien. Vorträge vom Tübinger Symposium 1982,* ed. P. Stuhlmacher, WUNT 28 (Tübingen, 1983), 267-71; M. Hengel, "Probleme des Markusevangeliums," in ibid., (221-65) 244-57; idem, "Entstehungszeit und Situation des Markusevangeliums," in *Markus-Philologie. Historische, literargeschichtliche und stilistische Untersuchungen zum zweiten Evangelium,* ed. H. Cancik, WUNT 33 (Tübingen, 1984), 1-45. Cf. also idem, *Studies in the Gospel of Mark* (London, 1985). More extensively on the topic, see pp. 36ff. and 41ff. above.

5. But compare the other, possibly more original, sequence of those called in John 1:35-42 and, on this, the list of disciples by Papias in Eusebius, *Hist. eccl.* 3.39.4 and M. Hengel, *Die johanneische Frage. Ein Lösungsversuch,* WUNT 67 (Tübingen, 1993), 8off.

6. Mark 1:29-31 = Luke 4:38-39 = Matt. 8:14-15.

7. In my opinion, the form of the title of the gospels goes back to Mark, as the earliest of the gospels; cf. M. Hengel, *Die Evangelienüberschriften,* SHAW.PH 3 (Heidelberg, 1984); idem, *The Four Gospels and the One Gospel of Jesus Christ* (London, 2000), 118ff.; cf. Mark 1:1, 14; 10:29; 13:10; 14:9.

8. In my opinion, Mark is identical to the John Mark of the Acts of the Apostles, the nephew of Barnabas (Col. 4:10): The earliest gospel, written just a few years after the death of the leading men Peter, Paul, and James, the brother of the Lord, circulated shortly before

style. Luke, "the beloved physician,"[9] uses medical terminology and speaks of a "high fever,"[10] and he also describes the healing by using the format of an exorcism: Jesus positions himself by the head and restrains (ἐπετίμησεν) the fever as if it were a demon,[11] so that this must leave the sick person immediately.

It is unique that the mother-in-law is lying down in "the house of Simon and Andrew" and gets up, after being made well, to take over the duties of the mother of the house. With the uncommon imperfect "and she served them" (καὶ διηκόνει), the effect of the healing is clearly to be demonstrated, but just standing up right away would have been sufficient to show that.[12] The imperfect has a durative meaning here for all three evangelists; Matthew and Luke, by contrast, remove the intruding reference to Andrew. We thus know that the mother-in-law lives in the house of her son-in-law.[13] By contrast, nothing is said about Peter's wife. It is a hard-and-fast rule concerning the narratives in the gospels that all "secondary figures," about whom we have such interest, are rigorously left out of the picture. Mark might have chosen to depict the scene in the house of a large family in Capernaum, in which case the historical question is admittedly made more difficult by the fact that John 1:44 states that the home town of "Andrew and Peter" is the nearby town of Bethsaida, at the mouth of the Jordan, where it flows into the Sea of Gennesaret. John also knows the name of Simon's father, John.[14] The narrative would be much easier to understand if Mark and those who retold his story had simply spoken of Peter's mother.

---

the destruction of the temple, would not have been composed by an anonymous authority but rather by one who was recognized.

9. Col. 4:14; on this, see a work that is still unequaled: A. v. Harnack, *Lukas der Artz. Der Verfasser des dritten Evangeliums und der Apostelgeschichte* (Leipzig, 1906), 122, 127; M. Hengel and A. M. Schwemer, *Paul between Damascus and Antioch: The Unknown Years* (Louisville, Ky., 1997), 6-11.

10. Luke 4:38: πυρετὸς μέγας (a high fever); on this, cf. BDAG, 899, with references to medical literature.

11. Luke 4:39; cf. Mark 1:25; 3:12; 9:25; Luke 4:35; 9:42.

12. Cf. the Matthean and Lukan parallels Mark 2:9-12 = Matt. 9:5-7 = Luke 5:23-25. On the διακονεῖν (providing, service) of women, see Mark 15:41; Luke 8:3; 10:40; John 12:2.

13. Matt. 8:14: οἰκίαν Πέτρου (Peter's house); Luke 4:38: οἰκίαν Σίμωνος (Simon's house).

14. John 1:42; the *Bar Yona*, "Son of John," in Matt. 16:17, is perhaps actually a shortened Aramaic form, even though we have no examples of it; cf. M. Hengel, *Johanneische Frage*, 278, n. 13, and see part I, n. 58.

The fact that the evangelist instead leaves it to read "mother-in-law" is in my opinion a sign for its *historical* veracity, even down to this detail, which we might think interrupts the narrative flow. Though he is often accused of it, Mark does not simply sacrifice the historical veracity for the larger main purpose of his narrative or because of the "needs of his community." Rather, he assumes, without going into any more detail about it, *that the fisherman Simon was married,* which means that he had a family[15] and lived either in the house of his mother-in-law (or parents-in-law) in Capernaum or else that she (or they) lived with him. In Capernaum we in fact have archaeological evidence of a church from the fourth century that is constructed on top of a private house that was built in the first century. This house complex seems to have served Jewish Christians of the third and possibly already the second century as a "house church," in which graffiti refers to the name Peter.[16] According to an early rabbinic reference and in contrast to the situation in the rest of Galilee, from the time of the turn from the first to the second century Capernaum was to some extent a Jewish Christian village. It seems that there were a significant number of large Jewish Christian families there.[17] Should the house "of Simon and Andrew" in Mark 1:29, together with the unique description of the healing of Peter's mother-in-law, be taken as a reference to an actual house, at which those who associated with Jesus also met after Easter, which then developed into a "house church" and in the final analysis goes back to Peter and his family?[18]

That Peter was married and that a family stood behind him points, in

---

15. O. Cullmann, *Petrus: Jünger — Apostel — Märtyrer; das historische und das theologische Petrusproblem* (Zurich, 1960²), notes with brevity: "Based on the witness of the Synoptic Gospels (Mark 1:29ff. par.), as well as that of Paul (1 Cor. 9:5), Peter is married. The later notes about his children and the martyrdom of his wife, which he was there to witness, are legendary." On this, see pp. 125ff. below.

16. E. Testa, *I graffiti della casa di S. Pietro,* vol. 4 of *Cafarnao* (Jerusalem, 1972); J. F. Strange and H. Shanks, "Das Haus des Petrus," in *Das Petrusbild in der neueren Forschung,* ed. C. P. Thiede (Wuppertal, 1987), 145-62 [Engl: "Has the House Where Jesus Stayed in Capernaum Been Found?" *BAR* 8, 6 (Nov./Dec., 1982): 26-37].

17. Str-B 1:159-60 (*Midr. Qoh.* 1:8): The Jewish Christian "heretics" from C[apernaum]. brought the nephew of R. Jehoshua to the point that he allowed himself to be baptized (?) and rode around on the Sabbath on a donkey. His uncle "healed" him of his error by anointing him with oil and sent him to Babylon, where he became a respected teacher of the law. In a similar way, misguided family members were sent to America during the nineteenth century.

18. On this, cf. R. Riesner, *Jesus als Lehrer. Eine Untersuchung zum Ursprung der Evangelien-Überlieferung,* WUNT 2/7 (Tübingen, 1988³), 437-39.

another passage in the Gospel of Mark, to the possibility of a conflict. After the pericope about the rich man who declines the call to follow Jesus because of his possessions and Jesus' warning about riches,[19] Mark gives Peter the opportunity to confess: "Behold, we have left everything and have followed you." Jesus answers, "Amen, I say to you, everyone who has left behind house or brothers or sisters or father or mother or children or fields for my name's sake and for the sake of the gospel will receive again one hundredfold." It is unique that in this sequence there is no mention of the wife;[20] only in Luke is "wife" inserted after "house," in the place of "father or mother."[21] And in the sharpened form in the parallel in Luke 14:26, which stems from the logia tradition,[22] in contrast to the related text from Matt. 10:37, the wife is mentioned in addition to parents and children. It may be that, even though he places great emphasis in Acts on the importance of the house communities, Luke consciously sharpens the requirements for following Jesus at this point. It is clear that Mark also notes that becoming a disciple means relinquishing ties to family and possessions already in the call of the first four disciples: Simon and Andrew leave their nets and follow the summons of Jesus to make them into "fishers for human beings," and James and John leave their father, Zebedee, in the boat with his day workers.[23] Origen sees the problem and thus interprets Peter's

19. Mark 10:17-27 = Matt. 19:16-26 (Matthew makes the young man rich) = Luke 18:18-27.

20. On this, see R. Pesch, *Simon-Petrus. Geschichte und geschichtliche Bedeutung des ersten Jüngers Jesu Christi*, PuP 15 (Stuttgart, 1980), 22, who poses the question: "Was Simon the oldest of the disciples of Jesus, and is there any possibility that he was the only one who was married?" Since Jews in Palestine often married at a very young age, this is most unlikely. Against this view, one can also cite evidence from 1 Cor. 9:5; on this, see pp. 111ff. below.

21. Luke 18:29b: οἰκίαν ἢ γυναῖκα ἢ ἀδελφοὺς ἢ γονεῖς (house or wife or brothers or parents), which means that parents first appear in the fourth position of those to be set aside. Matthew makes it simpler, on stylistic grounds, but follows Mark, who is authoritative for him; the only difference is that he places the father before the mother (19:29).

22. I use "logia tradition" instead of *Logienquelle* (or "Q"), since, in the form that the term is overwhelmingly used today, it sets forth a hypothesis that cannot be verified. This extraction of the traditions that are common to Luke and Matthew, after abstracting the material in Mark, is not a "gospel" that has a unity that can actually be proven convincingly. In many cases Matthew can also be dependent on the older Luke. With this solution, the unexplained minor agreements between Luke and Matthew against Mark fall to the side. On this, see M. Hengel, *Four Gospels*, 169-207.

23. Mark 1:16-20 = Matt. 4:18-22; cf., as well, Luke 5:11; on the entire problem, see M. Hengel, *Nachfolge und Charisma. Eine exegetisch-religionsgeschichtliche Studie zu Mt 8,21-22 und Jesu Ruf in die Nachfolge*, BZNW 34 (Berlin, 1968).

question in Matt. 19:27 ("Behold, we have left all and followed you, so what will we get as a result?") in the following way: "In the full context it is right to think that he abandoned not only the nets but also family [οἶκον] and *wife* [γυναῖκα], whose mother was freed of her fever when Jesus came to her," even though in the list of those left behind in 19:29, as in Mark so also in Matthew, the wife is not mentioned. The learned ascetic points further to Matt. 8:21 and adds the observation that those who had been called had "to some extent forgotten family members at home [τῶν οἶκοι]" and followed him, for which actions Peter "would be a judge in Israel" (19:28).[24]

The anecdotes that describe following Jesus that are in the logia tradition in Luke 9:57-62 and Matt. 8:19-22 point in the same direction and are likewise cited by Origen. But the question still remains whether Mark and Matthew, who reflect on every word placed in their gospels, did not purposely leave out the wife from this long listing that takes many circumstances into account, since they knew that the disciples of Jesus, at least the majority of them, were married, with Peter himself at the head of that list, and that they continued to live out their marriages after Easter.[25] This means that Jesus' call to follow him in no way called for "getting divorced." Jesus himself had explicitly rejected such an action. Most certainly, the follower who had left his family would not have had the freedom later on to enter into a new marriage. It is possible that the wives of the disciples were part of the larger circle that accompanied Jesus on his way to Jerusalem. John 19:25 mentions four woman at the foot of the cross: the mother of Jesus with her sister; Maria, the (wife) of Clopas, who was possibly a sister-in-law of the mother of Jesus;[26] and Mary Magdalene. Mark 15:40 speaks later of an indeterminate crowd of women and mentions only three names, without the mother of Jesus and in a different order. It is possible that Mark's generation, at the time when his gospel appeared shortly before A.D. 70, knew much more about the familial connections than we do today. According to the information from the ancient church, along with the presence of many Latinisms, we conclude that Mark wrote this in

24. Origen, *Comm. Matth.*, XV, 21 (GCS 40, ed. E. Klostermann and E. Benz, 411ff.).

25. Giving up possessions and connections with families takes place in Mark "for the sake of Jesus and the gospel" and in connection "with persecutions" (10:29, 30). The concrete experience of Nero's persecution may lie behind this passage for him, which would have happened a mere five or six years before. See also pp. 5-7 above.

26. Thus Hegesippus, according to Eusebius, *Hist. eccl.* 3.11; cf. 3.32.4; 4.22.4: Clopas, "an uncle of the Lord." On this, see R. Bauckham, *Gospel Women: Studies of the Named Women in the Gospels* (Grand Rapids, 2002), see index, p. 312, under the name Clopas (John 19:25).

Rome shortly before A.D. 70.[27] The Roman house churches were at the point of taking over the inheritance of the church in Jerusalem. The Jews of Rome were particularly closely tied to Jerusalem.[28] This would have applied as well to the Christian communities in Rome, which were established relatively early.[29]

The indirect reference to Peter as married is all the more surprising because the gospels by and large lack personal references of this type. Besides Peter, Mark mentions by name only the mother of Jesus and his four brothers, in connection with his failed debut in Nazareth. His sisters, who would have lived there, which means they were likely married,[30] are simply mentioned collectively; and a reference to Jesus' father Joseph is lacking altogether, likely because he was long since dead.[31] Even Mark's enigmatic brevity is possible only because more was known in the communities than what the evangelist reports.

Female disciples appear in Mark only in the Passion Narrative, which means at the point where the disciples fled and had made their denial. Thus in 15:40-41, at the crucifixion of Jesus, Mark mentions the women "who had followed him in Galilee and had served him," in contrast to the

---

27. On this, cf. Irenaeus, *Haer.* 3.1.1; Clement of Alexandria, according to Eusebius, *Hist. eccl.* 2.15, and, on this, see C.-J. Thornton, *Der Zeuge des Zeugen. Lukas als Historiker der Paulusreisen*, WUNT 56 (Tübingen, 1991), 20ff., 44-45, 64-65. The information stems from the Roman archive; cf. also M. Hengel, "Entstehungszeit," 43-45. See also p. 40 above.

28. In 15:21 Mark refers to two of the persons mentioned in the Roman community: Alexander and Rufus, the sons of Simon of Cyrene; cf. Rom. 16:13: "Rufus, the one chosen in the Lord, and his and my mother"; see also 16:7: Andronicus and Junia(s), "who are famous among the apostles, who were in the Lord before me," which means before Paul's conversion (ca. A.D. 33), and who supposedly belonged to the original Jerusalem community. On this, see R. Bauckham, *Gospel Women*, 165-81.

29. On this, see Hengel and Schwemer, *Paul*, 257ff., and n. 250 above.

30. Mark 6:3 = Matt. 13:56. In the dramatic narrative in Luke 4:16-30 there is no room for Jesus' family. It is only in the later apocryphal traditions, after the time of Epiphanius, *Pan.* 78.8.1 and 78.9.6, that the (half-)sisters have names, thus, e.g., Mary and Salome, the most common names for women in Palestinian Judaism. On this, see J. Blinzler, *Die Brüder und Schwestern Jesu*, SBS 21 (Stuttgart, 1967), 35-38; R. Bauckham, *Jude and the Relatives of Jesus in the Early Church* (Edinburgh, 1990), 37-44, 226-34. Bauckham wonders whether more ancient traditions are at work here, but that is highly unlikely.

31. It is only in the Matthean parallel, in 13:55, that the question of the Nazarenes: "Is this not the carpenter [ὁ τέκτων]?" is replaced by "Is this not the carpenter's son [ὁ τοῦ τέκτονος υἱός]?" With this adjustment, the occupation of Jesus, which stood in the way for many, disappears and, at the same time, the father who is missing is inserted. Only Mark reports about Jesus' occupation, which demonstrates once again his relative trustworthiness.

depiction in John 19:25, where it describes those "who looked on from afar." As in Mark 1:31, we find the key word διακονεῖν (serve) in the durative imperfect. In addition, there are "many other [women] who went up with him to Jerusalem." This means that the Jesus movement was *also* a women's movement, a point that fades too far into the background in the gospels over against the historical reality.[32] Mark names only three of the women in a sequence that at the same time presents a ranking: Mary Magdalene; the mysterious other Mary, mother of "lesser James" and of "Joses"; and Salome, who is changed in Matthew to become the "mother of the sons of Zebedee." It is likely that Matthew had a different tradition at his disposal, which is to be taken seriously.[33] Luke and John have further information about women at their disposal, but these are no longer connected with the circle of the Twelve. That Mark gives no further information about Salome is once again linked to the fact that his hearers and readers knew who these women were, and the same is true for the mysterious "Mary, the mother of the lesser James and of Joses."[34] Whether wives of the disciples would have been included among the "many others who had gone up with him to Jerusalem" must remain an open question, though it is not unlikely. He emphasizes the three names because they were known to have found the empty tomb on Easter morning.[35]

32. This is still most extensively accentuated by Luke; see M. Hengel, "Der Lukasprolog und seine Augenzeugen. Die Apostel, Petrus und die Frauen," in S. C. Barton, L. T. Stuckenbruck, and B. G. Wold (eds.), *Memory in the Bible and Antiquity*, WUNT 212 (Tübingen, 2007). On the problem, see R. Bauckham, *Gospel Women*.

33. Mark 15:40-41; cf., along with that, Matt. 27:56 and also 20:20, where the introduction of the mother of the two Zebedee family members serves to take the blame away from the sons.

34. Mary was far and away the most commonly used woman's name in Judea, with Salome second; on this, see T. Ilan, *Lexicon of Jewish Names in Late Antiquity*, vol. 1, TSAJ 91 (Tübingen, 2002), 9: Altogether, about 48 percent of the women mentioned have one of these two names. Altogether the woman are significantly underrepresented: "with 2509 named men against 317 named women, they constitute only 11.2% of all persons mentioned in the corpus"; see also tables 4 and 8, pp. 55 and 57; in addition, see pp. 242ff., 249ff. Concerning the various Salome traditions, see R. Bauckham, *Gospel Women*, index, 318.

35. Mark 16:1; cf. 15:47; cf. M. Hengel, "Maria Magdalena und die Frauen als Zeugen," in *Abraham unser Vater*, FS O. Michel, ed. O. Betz et al., AGSU 5 (Leiden, 1963), 243-56. Instead of Salome, Luke 24:10 mentions a Johanna; according to 8:3, she is the wife of a steward of Herod Antipas. Apparently there were various women who claimed that they participated in finding the empty tomb.

2. Paul and the Other Apostles

A completely new light on our problem is provided by a self-declaration of *the apostle Paul.* He himself calls it an "apology" over against his critics who, in Corinth, and likely in connection with the Petrine mission or else when Peter himself made a visit to the capital city of Achaia,[36] would not give his apostolate full recognition. Among other reasons, this happened because he and Barnabas took care of their living expenses as missionaries on their own and also because they were not married, which meant that they were not accompanied by wives on their journeys.[37] They did not have to ask the communities to care for them and their families. "Rejecting this apostolic right . . . is seen in Corinth as an admission that he held a lesser position: Paul did not dare to claim an apostolic right because he knew that he was no real apostle."[38] After the confrontation in Antioch that is recorded in Gal. 2:11ff., a long, enduring tension developed between Peter and Paul that spread into the region of Paul's missionary activity.[39] First Corinthians was written in Ephesus to the community that had become insubordinate in Corinth not all that long after this conflict broke wide open.

> That is my defense [ἀπολογία] against my critics: Do we not have the freedom to eat and to drink [i.e., to let ourselves be cared for by the communities]? *Do we not have the freedom* [ἐξουσία] *to bring along a sister as [marriage] partner, as is the practice of the rest of the apostles and the brothers of the Lord and Cephas?* Or is it I alone, and Barnabas, who do not have the freedom to forgo having to work with our hands [to get the necessities of life]? . . .[40] But we have not made any use of our freedom; instead, we bear everything so that no hindrance is placed in the way of the gospel of Jesus Christ.[41]

"The rest of the apostles" refers to the messengers of the Resurrected One in Jerusalem, Judea, and Galilee, and later in Syria as well; the circle might

---

36. On this, see pp. 66ff. above.

37. The extensive argumentation concerning this problem in 1 Cor. 9:1-23 shows how important this was for Paul.

38. H. Lietzmann and W. G. Kümmel, *An die Korinther,* 2 vols., HNT 9 (Tübingen, 1949⁴), 40.

39. See pp. 57ff. above.

40. First Cor. 9:3-6.

41. First Cor. 9:12b; cf. v. 18; Paul takes the problem up again in 2 Cor. 11:7ff. It must have been a significant issue for the Corinthians.

stretch wider than just the Twelve whom the earthly Jesus himself called, though it does include these as well and also the brothers of Jesus.[42] At the very least, the large majority of them would have been married, and all of them (1 Cor. 9:6) were provided care by the communities. *Cephas,* that is, Peter,[43] stands as the climax at the end of the list. Against the subsequent early-church explication, which can be found already in Clement of Alexandria,[44] these "apostolic" marriages were real marriages and not simply "spiritual" relationships, as we find practiced by the "Syneisakten"[45] from the second century on, in which ascetics lived with young women. Mentioning, in addition, ἀδελφήν (sister) along with γυναῖκα (wife) means that these apostolic marriage partners, among whom Cephas/Peter is given particular emphasis at the end, were without question connected by a common faith and undertook missionary journeys together.[46] "Among these women . . . one must understand that they were not just household workers or helpers with the mission activity. Paul is thinking of the actual wives of the apostles."[47] One cannot conclude from 1 Cor. 9:5 that all of the apostles and brothers of the Lord were married, but this likely holds true for the majority. Thus, unlike the way Luke handles it in Acts, Paul would have been thinking not only about the circle of the Twelve but of the expanded circle of 1 Cor. 15:7, which admittedly also includes a definitive group.[48] One can certainly assume thereby that the view of the original community, which is shown for example by the fact that they held all things in common, was that they were part of a large *familia Dei,* as the οἶκος θεοῦ (family of God).[49] In addition, it is possible that sending them out two by two, which we know al-

---

42. Cf. Mark 6:3 and, in a critical vein, 3:31ff., as well as John 7:5ff.

43. Concerning the form of the name, see above, pp. 16-26. The reference to the "foundation stone" Christ, 1 Cor. 3:10ff., is a Pauline polemic against the Petrine claim; see pp. 66ff. above.

44. See pp. 123ff. below.

45. On this, see S. Elm, "Syneisakten," *RGG*[4] 7:1956; A. Adam, *RGG*[3] 6:560-61. See also K. S. Frank, "Subintroductae," *The Encyclopedia of Christianity* 5:210-11. First Cor. 7:36 is not speaking about this issue; it may be an issue for prophets in the puzzling text *Did.* 11:11.

46. On περιάγειν + τινά, see BDAG, 798-99: "take someone about *or* along with oneself, have someone with oneself (constantly) *or* accompanying oneself."

47. W. Schrage, *Der erste Brief an die Korinther,* EKKNT 7/2 (Zurich, 1995), 292.

48. Ibid., 293.

49. On this, cf. O. Michel, "οἶκος," *TWNT* 5:122-37 [Engl: *TDNT* 5:119-35]. The community appears as the house of God, making use of the LXX, in the sense of the temple of God, but it can also serve to represent the "(large-) family" of God; see, with reference to Num. 12:7 (LXX), Heb. 3:6: οὗ [Χριστός] οἶκός ἐσμεν ἡμεῖς.

ready from the traditions about how they were sent out according to the gospels, would also have applied after Easter under certain circumstances for married couples going out on missionary trips. Unfortunately, though it is certainly an important aspect, nothing is said about this in 1 Cor. 9:5; it is completely lacking in the depiction of the early Christian mission according to Luke and in the letters of the unmarried Paul.

Paul would have certainly gotten to know the family of Cephas when Paul visited him personally in Jerusalem, since Paul stayed with him for fifteen days.[50] Apparently, then, the marriage of the leading apostle would later have been held up to the celibate Paul by Peter's associates in Corinth.[51] Cephas and his wife possibly even visited Corinth.

Jesus places marriage at a level of high importance in the creation because it had been ordained by God himself, as can be seen according to Mark when he discusses its establishment (Mark 10:6-9) and uses that to establish the commandment against divorce. According to God's will man and woman are "one flesh," from which comes the consequence: "What God has now joined together, a human being ought not to separate."[52] Is it just by chance that the *Pauline student Luke* does not make use of this text from Mark and transmits only the prohibition of remarriage, which certainly comes from the logia tradition, which Paul accentuates clearly as well for the community in Corinth?[53] Certainly for Mark, also with reference to Peter and the other apostles, the bond of marriage had a validity that was not to be broken, which was not even to be up for discussion if one was sent in the service of proclamation, whereas the unmarried Paul and — in his footsteps? — Luke represent a point of view here that one might term either more free or more rigorous.[54]

Does this have something to do with the experiences of the wide-ranging Pauline mission, in which the family of a missionary that traveled with him would have brought too heavy a burden? Paul himself not only had rejected a false asceticism in marriage but, with an almost unsettling,

---

50. Gal. 1:18; ca. three years after his conversion. Cf. Hengel and Schwemer, *Paul,* 76-89.

51. First Cor. 9:5; on this, see the emphasized phrase καὶ Κηφᾶς, at the end, and cf. Mark 16:7, the phrase καὶ τῷ Πέτρῳ, pp. 41-42 above; concerning the Cephas party, see pp. 66ff. above.

52. Mark 10:8-9, which is taken up word for word in Matt. 19:6. Cf. Gen. 2:24 (LXX).

53. Luke 16:18; cf., using a somewhat different phraseology, Matt. 5:32 and 1 Cor. 7:11.

54. Also in the words about following in the logia tradition, Luke 9:57-62 = Matt. 8:18-22 (on this, cf. M. Hengel, *Nachfolge,* 18-19); only in Luke 9:62 does Jesus prohibit saying good-bye to one's own (large-) family (οἶκος).

realistic justification, had directly encouraged getting married,[55] and in fact even permitted remarriage, admittedly with the limitation "only in the Lord" (μόνον ἐν κυρίῳ), which means only with those who were believers. Yet, by contrast, he depicts his own charisma (1 Cor. 7:7) by describing that the better way is not to marry, specifically because of the situation at the end of time, since the married couples with children would have it worse in the "eschatological woes" that were to be expected (7:28ff.), whereas those who were not married could direct all their "burdens" toward the Lord (7:32ff.). But above all else, it is the freedom for the service of proclaiming the gospel, particularly in pressure situations, which moves him time and again to give the advice that the unmarried are to stay in the same state in which they are now, "as also I."[56] At this point, however, he specifically states that this advice is no "commandment," only his "personal opinion"[57] that he wants to articulate.

But does Paul not indirectly, by sharing his opinion about being unmarried, reveal what he thinks about the married apostles and brothers of the Lord in Jerusalem, with Peter at the top?[58] Even the word of Jesus that is appended only by Matthew at the end of his parenesis about marriage, that some "have made themselves eunuchs [εὐνούχισαν ἑαυτούς] for the sake of the kingdom of God" (19:12), gives no command but is an indication concerning the free charisma of remaining unmarried. The passage closes with the observation: "Whoever can comprehend such things, comprehend them." Certainly it means that in the area where the unknown author was working (ca. A.D. 90-100), this was a relatively rare exception and not the rule. At the same time, 1 Corinthians 7 and Matt. 19:12 point to a touchy point that was under discussion in the communities, which could lead to controversies. This is shown by what came into existence at roughly the same time as Matthew, in *1 Clem.* 38:2,[59] and roughly fifteen years later,

---

55. First Cor. 7:1-6, 9, 36ff. Concerning remarriage, 7:39; cf. also the argumentation of Rom. 7:2-3.

56. First Cor. 7:7, 8, 40.

57. First Cor. 7:6; cf. vv. 35, 40.

58. First Cor. 9:5: One certainly gets the impression that in 1 Corinthians 5–12 — at least to some extent — problems are dealt with that were also up for discussion in Antioch and Jerusalem and that were connected with the ramifications of the criticism of the law by Paul and the activity of Peter's friends in Corinth.

59. Cf. *1 Clem.* 35:2; 64:2: It deals with a gift of God. In 38:2, at the culmination of a long list, there is a warning against pride with respect to sexual asceticism. It could certainly be a sarcastic remark against those in Corinth who are causing unrest.

in Ignatius, *Pol.* 5:2. In a Christian "admonition about marriage," the texts warn the ascetics, who are an exception to the rule, not to praise themselves and not to be arrogant.

We first discover the renunciation of getting married — indeed the emphatic forbidding of marriage on the dualistic basis of hating one's body — among those who practice Platonizing, dualistic gnosis and among the radical, ascetic Encratites of the second century. For this group the "materially" visible world no longer presents God's good creation and therefore is seen as basically inimical to the body. The Pastoral Letters, written in the first two decades of the second century[60] and directed against the danger of a type of "gnosis" that is just beginning but that, with respect to content, can hardly be clearly defined (1 Tim. 6:20), count among its errant teachings the prohibition of marrying (4:3). Over against such a notion, the unknown author, once again quite sensibly, encourages the younger widows that they would be better off to "marry and to have children and to properly take care of their household" (5:14). It is obvious that he assumes that the leaders of the Christian communities are normally married: the *episkopos* (overseer) should be "beyond accusation, married to *one* wife" — which means that it would be offensive for him, as the one who carries the weight of the office, to have a second marriage after the death of his first wife. In addition, he should "stand as head of his own house" and "have obedient children." If he is not in such circumstances, "how can he care for the community of God?" (3:2ff.). The Letter of Titus even places this demand upon the "elders." They should be "husbands of *one* wife" and should "have believing children" (Tit. 1:6). Corresponding to this for early Christian parenesis, with a definite connection to the Old Testament, Judaism, and the Stoic tradition, great importance is placed on an orderly life in the family, which is rooted in the love of Christ. These families, in whose "houses" people came together, constitute the centers for the Christian congregations in each community.

---

60. The Pastoral Letters are generally dated too early. I would date them roughly to the same time as the letters of Ignatius. They assume that the Pauline letters have been collected as a group, and they are aware of what is in the Acts of the Apostles. See nn. 174, 270 above. In my opinion, H. v. Campenhausen has demonstrated the material and theological closeness to Polycarp, in *Polykarp von Smyrna und die Pastoralbriefe*, SHAW.PH (Heidelberg, 1951), 5-51 = idem, *Aus der Frühzeit des Christentums* (Tübingen, 1963), 197-252; Polycarp is admittedly not the author of the Pastoral Letters, and they also do not belong to the disagreement with Marcion, but more likely to the early period of the bishop of Smyrna, which is the same time that his letter to the community in Philippi is to be dated.

We learn so few concrete details about the relationships within the families in the earliest Christian texts because such writings have very little concern for personal, biographical, and private details with individual specifics. Within the expansive corpus of Paul, we hear not a single word about Paul's parents and his family. The fact that he comes from Tarsus, is a Roman citizen, and that he has a nephew (a sister's son) in Jerusalem, which means at least that he had a sister living in Jerusalem, is related to us only by Luke.[61] The focus of the gospels, as in that of the letters, is not the individuals and their family circumstances but rather the saving work of Christ, the preaching of Jesus and the apostles; this means that the message centers on the gospel and the faith that flows from it, as well as on admonition to live a life that is appropriate for a Christian in the Spirit.

3. Later Information about Apostolic Families

We do have a few additional and scattered references that are related to the missionary activity of individual "families." Luke relates in Acts 21:8 that Paul, on his last trip to Jerusalem, together with numerous traveling companions, found a place to stay "in the house of the evangelist *Philip,* one of the Seven," who had four daughters who were virgins and prophetesses. This Philip is a mysterious figure, about whom we know a little more than we do about the other early Christian missionaries.[62] According to Acts 6:5 he holds the second position in the list of the seven "Hellenists" in Jerusa-

---

61. Acts 9:11; 21:39; 22:3; cf. 9:30; 11:25. Concerning the sister's son, see 23:16. This little note also gives insight into Phil. 3:5-6 and Acts 22:3. Paul comes from a Pharisaic family that had ties to Jerusalem, where he had studied; see M. Hengel, *Kleine Schriften III,* WUNT 141 (Tübingen, 2002), 68-192. Luke knows a lot more than what he happens to report. Without the references to Tarsus, according to the letters one would have to consider Paul to be a Greek-speaking Palestinian Jew. Such notations show the relative trustworthiness of the Lukan report in the second half of the Acts of the Apostles. Luke was an actual travel companion of Paul.

62. On the texts that are linked to Philip, see A. v. Dobbeler, *Der Evangelist Philippus in der Geschichte des Urchristentums. Eine prosographische Skizze,* TANZ 30 (Tübingen, 2000); concerning his prophetic daughters, see pp. 233-48. Dobbeler refers to the depiction of the four inspired daughters of Job in *T. Job* 46–53, and he admittedly considers the possibility that the comment about the four daughters of Philip could also be referring to "female students" (235); he thereby leaves the realm of what can be treated as historically likely. The historical descriptions of Luke, Papias, Polycrates of Ephesus, and Clement of Alexandria would speak against his purported scenario.

lem, right after Stephen, the first martyr. Having been chased out of Jerusalem, Philip carried out missionary activity, according to Acts 8, first in Samaria, and then he converts the Ethiopian finance minister, who is returning to his homeland. In addition, Philip appears as a missionary to the cities along the Palestinian coastal plain "until he came to Caesarea" (8:40). He disappears then from the Lukan narrative[63] until he surfaces once again as the father of four prophetically gifted daughters and as the one who entertains Paul in 21:8-9, shortly before the Feast of Weeks in A.D. 57. It could be that 23/24 years lie in between.[64] As a free, wandering missionary, he had apparently established his own home in Caesarea, the port city and official capital city of the Roman province of Judea. Luke says nary a word about his wife, only that in the meantime he had four girls, now grown, who were inspired. They were such a strange phenomenon that Luke, speaking at this point in the first person plural and as one who accompanied Paul on his journey, as an eyewitness,[65] did not want to pass over this in silence. Philip was apparently the head of the oldest house community in Caesarea and sympathetic toward Paul, in spite of the attacks against him by Jewish Christian circles. Luke specifically says that the traveling company turned in to the "house of the evangelist Philip . . . and remained with him." This means that Paul and those who accompanied him, Luke included, were guests of Philip for several days.

It is unique that we have late and yet relatively trustworthy information about Philip and his daughters from the second century. Apparently because of the severe unrest between Jews and "Greeks" in Caesarea, just before the outbreak of the Jewish War in A.D. 66 they emigrated to Hierapolis in Phrygia. There, at a later time, Papias, the bishop in this city, personally heard oral traditions about these sisters concerning unique miracles.[66] The most extensive report comes from Bishop Polycrates of

---

63. It is characteristic of his rigid, eclectic way of telling a story that Luke does not have Philip appear afterward, in connection with the conversion and baptism of the Roman centurion Cornelius by Peter.

64. The persecution and the banishment of the "Hellenists" take place about A.D. 32/33.

65. On this, see C.-J. Thornton, *Zeuge*, 275-76.

66. Cited by Eusebius, *Hist. eccl.* 3.39.9ff.; cf. also Proclos in Eusebius, *Hist. eccl.* 3.31.4. If these daughters were born roughly between A.D. 33 and 45, and if Paul met them on his trip to Jerusalem roughly in 57, they could certainly have lived until ca. 110. Papias would have been the bishop in Hierapolis ca. 110-140. According to Polycrates, the daughters were very aged. Concerning the entire topic, see T. Zahn, *FGNK* 6:158-75, concerning Philip in Hierapolis.

Ephesus, who had been a Christian for sixty-five years and who, in a letter to Bishop Victor of Rome,[67] speaks about Philip and his daughters and their later residency in Hierapolis. He does this in order to elevate the importance of the apostolic authority of the Asia Minor traditions over against that of the Roman bishop, in connection with the controversy about the celebration of the Passover.

> For also in Asia great luminaries have found their place of rest who will rise to life on the last day with the reappearance of the Lord. On this day the Lord will come with all majesty from heaven and will seek all the saints, namely, Philip, one of the twelve apostles, who fell asleep in Hierapolis, with his two aged daughters who remained in their virginal state, whereas another daughter, who went about in the Holy Spirit, rests in Ephesus, and John, who lay at the breast of the Lord, was a priest, a witness to the faith, and a teacher, and he went to rest in Ephesus.[68]

Philip is identified here as an apostle — against Luke, who distinguishes between the "evangelists" and one who is an "apostle"[69] — namely, the apostle who, already in the Fourth Gospel, as Philip of Bethsaida, is the most important disciple after Peter; this happens again with Papias, who reckons Philip as a member of the Johannine circle. An identity as both apostle and evangelist is thus not to be rejected as impossible. It is possible that he consciously left the circle of the Twelve to transfer into the "Seven."[70] The alternative would be that the residents of Asia Minor, by identifying their Philip as an apostle, sought to attribute to him importance over against the Roman claim to Peter and Paul. In any case, it is noteworthy that the Beloved Disciple John is positioned after him, in second place. In my opinion, this latter individual was not an "apostle" but was a "disciple of the Lord," and he is identical to the "aged" John in Papias and in Second and Third John. With respect to him, church tradition since the time of Tertullian and the *Acts of John* maintains that he remained un-

---

67. Eusebius, *Hist. eccl.* 5.24.1-8.

68. Eusebius, *Hist. eccl.* 5.24.2-3 = 3.31.3-4; cf., on that and on the following, M. Hengel, *Johanneische Frage*, 33-36, 79-82, 91-92.

69. Cf. Luke 6:13-14; Acts 1:13 and 6:5; 8:5; 21:8.

70. By his designation "the evangelist from the circle of the Seven," Luke from his vantage point would have highlighted his later distance with respect to the circle of the Twelve and circle of the apostles (no longer intact in the year 57), just as he also refrains from attributing to Paul the title of apostle (with the exception of Acts 14:4, 14) over against the Twelve.

married.[71] There is a similar tradition about Andrew, the brother of Peter, who, according to the *Acts of Andrew,* was a radical ascetic who busied himself trying to hinder marriages from taking place.

Polycrates, born about 125, came from an old Christian family that had produced seven bishops before him, whom he calls his relatives (συγγενεῖς). He himself is the eighth. One could assume that at least some of them were fathers in their families and that the son followed the father in the office.[72] Polycrates must have had traditions that related what Luke had discussed about 100 years earlier, and he must also have proceeded further with the notation by Papias and that of Proclos, a Montanist contemporary of Polycrates in Rome,[73] since he speaks then of only three daughters, two of whom are prophetesses who remained unmarried into their old age, as well as that their father died in Hierapolis and was buried there, and that the third was a citizen of Ephesus, supposedly because she was married and lived there. That she also "went about in the Holy Spirit" points to her faithfulness to the Christian faith.

Only with difficulty can we attempt to understand the liveliness of the worship services in the house church of Philip in Caesarea and later in Hierapolis, with four, or else three, prophetically inspired persons. The best commentary on such practices is provided for us by Paul, in his depiction of the enthusiastic worship services in the early period in 1 Cor. 14:26ff. The *mulier tacet in ecclesia* (women should be silent in the churches) in 14:34, unless it was inserted at a later time, serves to dampen the enthusiastic rapture. First Cor. 11:2-12 shows that spirit-filled women certainly did bring forth "prophetic speech" in the worship service. The decisive phrase in this difficult text stands as a summary at the end: "In any case, in the Lord a wife is not apart from the husband, nor is the husband apart from the wife" (11:11). This may apply to early Christian marriage in general. These four daughters of Philip — and thus indirectly the marriage of this important early Christian missionary — is mentioned only because of the special spiritual cha-

71. Cf. M. Hengel, *Johanneische Frage,* 116-17.

72. According to Hippolytus's lost *Syntagma,* Marcion was the son of a bishop from Sinope in the Asia Minor region of Pontus; cf. A. v. Harnack, *Marcion* (repr., Darmstadt, 1960), 23, 23*-28*. Marcion himself, corresponding to his dualistic-Gnostic view of the world, advocated a strict prohibition of marriage for the members of his community; cf. ibid., 148-49, 277*-278*: "He baptized only those who were not married or who were separated." This practice may go back to the practice of older "dualists," such as Cerdo, whom Irenaeus identifies as Marcion's teacher; see part I, n. 286.

73. Eusebius, *Hist. eccl.* 3.31.4.

risma of the four young girls, which served for the proclamation of the gospel and which — in this "family-related" form — served as an exception to the rule, which no one afterward ever forgot.[74] In the second half of the second century, Montanist prophets and prophetesses used them as examples.[75]

A completely different example of an "apostolic family" is presented by the married couple *Priscilla and Aquila*, whom Paul and Luke always mention only as a married couple. In this case the woman, who was certainly the more active member, is mentioned first, apart from two exceptions that are called for by the context. This all serves as another unique aspect in early Christendom.[76] Paul meets both of them in Corinth and attaches himself to them because he is a "tentmaker," as they are. One can assume that he found work in their place of business. As Jewish Christians, they had been driven out of Rome by Caesar Claudius just prior to this, in A.D. 49.[77] At the end of Paul's eighteen-month stay in Corinth, about 51, they accompanied him to Ephesus, where he left them behind so that they could prepare for the establishment of a house community. Among other tasks, they were to instruct Apollos, a Christian missionary who was born in Alexandria and a rhetorically well-trained teacher; "although he was on fire in the Spirit," he "needed to be taught more exactly in matters concerning the way of God" (Acts 18:25-26).

During Paul's later, roughly three-year stay in Ephesus, with a risk to their own lives, Priscilla and Aquila vouched for him in a threatening situation.[78] After the edict of Claudius was lifted[79] that had driven the Jewish

74. Their names first appear in a late, completely legendary Byzantine *Monologion:* Hermione, Charitine, Irais, and Eutychiane; cf. R. A. Lipsius, *Die apokryphen Apostelgeschichten und Apostellegenden,* vol. 2/2 (1884; repr., Amsterdam [1906]), 3n.

75. Cf. the anti-Montanistic *Anonymus* in Eusebius, *Hist. eccl.* 5.17.2-3: Mention is made here of another pro-Montanistic Christian prophetess, Ammia from Philadelphia. Cf. also Rev. 2:20 for the polemic against a "prophetess" who receives the insulting name Jezebel (1 Kgs. 16:31) because she is said to have led Christians astray to practice libertinism.

76. In the Letters of Paul they appear twice as "Prisca and Aquila," in Rom. 16:3 and in the deutero-Pauline 2 Tim. 4:19. Luke speaks of "Priscilla and Aquila" in Acts 18:18, 26. Only in 1 Cor. 16:19 and in Acts 18:2, when they are mentioned for the first time, is the husband mentioned first: "And he [Paul] found a Jew named Aquila, who came originally from Pontus, and who had just then arrived from Italy, and Priscilla, his wife."

77. Acts 18:2; cf. Suetonius, *Claud.* 25.3; on this, see R. Riesner, *Die Frühzeit des Apostels Paulus,* WUNT 71 (Tübingen, 1994), 199ff.; see also the index.

78. Rom. 16:4; cf. 2 Cor. 1:8 and Acts 19:23ff.

79. The suspension would have taken place soon after Nero took power on October 13, 54.

Christians from Rome, one can assume that they returned to Rome, not least because they would be there to support the apostle's long-planned trip to Rome and his further trip to Spain by establishing a house community.[80] In addition to all the other communities in the province of Asia, 1 Cor. 16:19 names only them and their "house community" in Ephesus by name and has the community in Corinth be especially greeted by them. In the chapter that includes Paul's greetings in the Letter to the Romans, which was written from Corinth in the winter of 56/57, Paul mentions Priscilla and Aquila first, and specifically by name as "my fellow workers in Christ Jesus, who risked their necks for my life [which means, went surety], and whom not only I but all the communities of the Gentiles owe thanks" (16:3-4). Then he greets the community "in their house" and a larger number of the community members known to him. Since the major city Rome, one would assume, did not know of the practice of closed communities within neighborhoods,[81] it is likely that the community in their house was the actual recipient of the letter. It would then have been passed on to the other house churches.

An additional "mission helper" of Paul, who would have been at the head of her own "house" and who also had substantial means, is "Phoebe," who delivered the Letter to the Romans; she held the office of "servant" (διάκονος) of the community in Cenchreae, the neighboring city to Corinth on the Aegean. She had been "of assistance to many, and to me as well."[82] One might consider her to be the first "interpreter" of the Letter to the Romans. She must have been in the position of being able to answer any questions the Roman Christians had about this difficult letter and would also have been able to provide personal information about Paul and his travel plans.

As for those who receive further greetings in Romans 16, the fourth

---

80. The establishment of a Pauline house community, with the support of a well-to-do woman who operated a business, is described in Acts 16:14-15. Lydia, a dealer in purple goods, "was baptized together with her entire household"; on this, see J.-P. Sterck-Degueldre, *Eine Frau namens Lydia*, WUNT 2/176 (Tübingen, 2004). In Col. 4:15 Paul greets "the brothers in Laodicea, and Nympha and the church in her house." Here also it involves a woman. Maybe Lydia and Nympha were widows. In the Pastoral Letters and early Christianity in general, widows played a significant role as those who gave support to the social work of the community; cf. 1 Tim. 5:3ff.

81. Cf., on this, the unique form of address in Rom. 1:7 "to those who are in Rome," which thus avoids using the word ἐκκλησία.

82. Rom. 16:2: προστάτις, literally "female protector, patroness"; see BDAG, 885.

place is held by still another married couple: "Greet Andronicus and Junia,[83] my relatives and my fellow prisoners, who are esteemed among the apostles and who became Christians before I did" (Rom. 16:7). This couple perhaps belongs to what is described in 1 Cor. 15:7 as the members of the larger apostolic circle that extended beyond the circle of the Twelve. An alternative view would be that they enjoyed great respect among the Jerusalem apostles. Even 1 Cor. 9:5 mentions that "the other apostles" were married. For our passage, if the first interpretation holds true, the wife would also be designated as an apostle.[84] "My relatives" certainly points to those who share a common Jewish heritage,[85] but it does not automatically eliminate the possibility that there was a blood relationship here as well. Paul had a nephew in Jerusalem (Acts.23:16). Though we do not know when, they seem at one time to have been "fellow prisoners"[86] with Paul. This "apostolic" couple, or at least this couple who was closely allied with the apostles, points back to the beginnings of the early community in Jerusalem and to the circle of the "Hellenists" that were there, or else to Tarsus and Antioch. It is possible that they belonged to the otherwise unknown original founders of the community in Rome,[87] which came into existence roughly during the time of Caligula (A.D. 37-41). From these widely scattered references we see how little we know about personal relationships, which means also about "apostolic families," in early Christianity. Only the Pauline letters, and at times Acts, enlighten our darkened knowledge a bit.

---

83. Concerning the feminine form of the name, cf. P. Lampe, *Die stadtrömischen Christen*, WUNT 2/18 (Tübingen, 1989²), 137-40, 147; idem, *From Paul to Valentinus: Christians in Rome in the First Two Centuries* (Minneapolis, 2003), 166-71, 176-77. The masculine form "Junia," as a short form of "Junianus," has not been found, whereas "Junia" as the name for a wife is used frequently.

84. The Greek church in later times designated individual women such as Mary Magdalene, Thecla (who accompanied Paul, according to the *Acts of Paul*), and Helena, the mother of the emperor, as ἰσαπόστολος, which means "like apostles"; cf. C. Du Cange, *Glossarium ad scriptores mediae et infimae Graecitatis* (1688; repr., Graz [1958]), cols. 521-22.

85. Cf. Rom. 9:3; 16:11, 21. The συγγενεῖς μου could have come originally from Jerusalem (cf. Acts 23:16ff.) or from Tarsus (Acts 9:30; 11:25). Paul certainly worked there as a missionary for many years; cf. Hengel and Schwemer, *Paul*, 80ff., 151ff., 178ff.

86. Rom. 16:7: συναιχμαλώτους μου; cf. 2 Cor. 11:23: ἐν φυλακαῖς περισσοτέρως (with far more imprisonments).

87. On this, see the extensive treatment in R. Bauckham, *Gospel Women*, 109-202 (197-98). In a bold way, he connects Junia with the Joanna mentioned in Luke 8:3; 24:10.

4. Clement of Alexandria and Encratism

An advantage for a married couple who were active in mission work was that the wife would have had better chances to connect with the women of the family among the more important households in society, who were women of luxury and thus hard to approach. This can be demonstrated in roughly 200 in the writings of *Clement of Alexandria,* who was the "most positive toward marriage" among the early Eastern church fathers and the "first Christian ethicist."[88] According to our way of thinking, his concept of marriage is ascetic, but he defends it as something that is right and its necessity as a divine order of creation, over against the radical dualistic-Encratic and Docetic heretics. He thus can wax eloquent in a positive way about producing children as a responsibility of the marriage, even though he places refraining from sexual activity in the marriage on a higher level. On a basic level, however, the "estate of the bachelor stands at a lower level than that of one who is married, insofar as there are fewer chances for a bachelor to be caught up in self-deception."[89] As an example, he points to "apostolic marriages." He falsely understands that γνήσιε σύζυγε, "beloved companion," in Phil. 4:3 means "wife" and concludes from this phrase that Paul ended up being married, in spite of 1 Corinthians 7, suggesting only that "he did not take her around with him for the convenience of his ministry."[90] But even the married apostles, "in conformity with their ministry concentrated on undistracted preaching,[91] and took their wives around as Christian sisters rather than spouses, to be their fellow-ministers in relation to housewives, through whom the Lord's teaching penetrated into women's quarters with-

---

88. A. Oepke, "Ehe I," *RAC* 4:662, with further references there. As happens already within New Testament parenesis, Old Testament and Stoic traditions blend together, though the philosophical influence is stronger. Clement of Alexandria's overwhelmingly positive statements about marriage are often supported by Pauline texts, though he interprets them in a Platonizing sense. Cf., for example, book 3 of the *Stromateis,* where, besides other texts, 1 Corinthians 7 and 1 Timothy are also in the background. At the same time, however, the man who is a true Christian Gnostic "achieves a greater service before God" if he "can increase the strictness of his life" and if he "has practiced pure and prudent abstinence." But this ought not to be done to such a great extent that it results in pride. For "marriage also [has] its own accomplishments of service and duties"; cf. *Strom.* 3.79.4-5 (German trans. by O. Stählin, in BKV 3.304; cf. English trans. by J. Ferguson, in FC 85). Clement was likely married and the father of a family. The same applies to his contemporary Tertullian in Carthage.

89. H. Chadwick, "Enkrateia," *RAC* 5:358.

90. Cf. 1 Cor. 9:5; see pp. 111ff. above; Clement of Alexandria, *Strom.* 3.53-54.

91. Cf. 1 Cor. 7:35.

out scandal."[92] And yet "refraining is the highest ideal" for him as well; corresponding to this, "the married apostles . . . no longer had any marital relations with their wives," since "the sensual passions [no longer] played a role in the love of a Christian for his wife." A husband and wife were no longer to be connected through the body, "but only through the beauty of the soul. . . . This situation is a foretaste of the angel-like [Luke 20:36] life in heaven" and "an imitation of the Lord." Clement sets forth the ideal of an "orthodox Encratite" who practices abstinence "out of love for the Lord and not because of disdain for created things."[93]

Behind Clement's conceptualization of the "apostolic marriages" stands not only the rejection of the radical ascetics, who rejected marriage in principle, but also the actual experiences of missionaries from the first roughly 150 years of the history of the Christian mission. Josephus already provides evidence that Gentile women demonstrated a particular interest in the Jewish synagogue worship service, with its attractive preaching about a living, ethical monotheism. Luke provides similar evidence with respect to the earliest Christian mission activity, reporting that Paul himself encountered women who were interested in hearing him in this milieu.[94] In particular circumstances the women could be more effective in the families who belonged to the upper level of society.

This aspect of their role progressed during the entire second and third centuries. But then, especially because of the appearance of Gnostic female teachers in the schools of Marcion and Valentinus and of prophetesses among the Montanists, the active teaching role of women was gradually suppressed, and these women increasingly were limited to the role of social care ministry — a really sad loss for the further development of the church.[95] But even in the *Acts of Paul,* strongly colored with Encratism and composed by a presbyter from Asia Minor toward the end of the second century, we read that Thecla, who honored Paul fervently, was sent by the apostle as a female missionary: "Go forth and teach the word of God."[96] This woman, who is de-

---

92. Clement of Alexandria, *Strom.* 3.53.3 (English trans. by J. Ferguson).

93. H. Chadwick, "Enkrateia," 358-59, replete with references.

94. Cf. Josephus, *B.J.* 2.560, on Damascus; *Ant.* 20.34; Acts 13:50-51. One notes how the women are mentioned prominently: 16:13-14, 17:4, 34: on this, cf. Hengel and Schwemer, *Paul,* 29-30.

95. Cf., on this, the brief, but as yet unparalleled, treatment by A. v. Harnack, *Die Mission und Ausbreitung des Christentums in den ersten drei Jahrhunderten* (Leipzig, 1924[4]), 2:589-611.

96. Tertullian, *Bapt.* 17; *Acts of Paul and Thecla,* chap. 41, *NTApocr*[5] 2:223 [Engl: 2:246].

scribed as one might portray a character in an early Christian novel, is said to have renounced marriage because of the preaching of Paul, remaining a strict ascetic to the end of her life. Christian literature, which grew by leaps and bounds during the second half of the second century with its apostolic stories and legends, includes a clear hostility toward marriage, with a radical Encratic tendency that no longer had any interest in "apostolic families." In such literature "the spiritual marriage or else the bride's refusal to marry is depicted as the consequent result of apostolic preaching."[97]

An exception is provided by *Peter* and to a limited extent by *Philip*. Concerning these, one cannot escape completely from the biblical narratives. Clement thus refers to "the righteous of past days," which means from the Old Testament, concerning whom "some married and produced children." Only with punishable pride can one "claim to be their superiors in lifestyle, but they will never remotely be able to match their praxis." But "are [these ascetics] not criticizing the apostles?" For even "Peter and Philip produced children, and Philip gave his daughters away in marriage."[98] In addition, Clement noted a unique, legendary tradition about Peter and his wife, who — as is true of much else about his information — might have come from oral, probably Roman tradition, since it is not preserved for us anywhere else afterward, not even in the later *Acts of Peter*. It describes the martyrdom of Peter's wife:

> So we are told [φασὶ γοῦν] that the blessed Peter, when he beheld his wife on her way to execution, rejoiced on account of her call and her homeward journey, and addressed her by name with words of exhortation and good cheer, bidding her "remember the Lord [μέμνησο, ὦ αὕτη, τοῦ κυρίου]."[99]

For Clement, she served as the example par excellence: "Such was the marriage of those blessed ones and such their perfect control over their feelings

---

97. A. Oepke, "Ehe I," 660; cf. H. Chadwick, "Enkrateia," 354-55, who maintains that these apostolic stories, with their negative view toward marriage, "are on the boundary between orthodoxy and heresy."

98. Clement of Alexandria, *Strom.* 3.52.1-2, 4; 3.52.5 = Eusebius, *Hist. eccl.* 3.30.1: Πέτρος μὲν γὰρ καὶ Φίλιππος ἐπαιδοποιήσαντο, Φίλιππος δὲ καὶ τὰς θυγατέρας ἀνδράσιν ἐξέδωκεν. With respect to Philip, Clement is not as well oriented as is his contemporary, Polycrates of Ephesus; see n. 68 above.

99. Clement of Alexandria, *Strom.* 7.63.3 (English trans. by J. E. L. Oulton and H. Chadwick, in LCC 2); cf. Eusebius, *Hist. eccl.* 3.30.2. We would certainly have many more comparable legendary traditions if the *Hypotyposes* of Clement had been preserved.

even in the dearest relaions of life," and he makes reference in this regard to Paul once again: "Whoever marries, it shall be as if he had not married [ὡς μὴ γαμῶν]." If this ὡς μή (1 Cor. 7:29, 31), *"as if not,"* was determined for Paul on the basis of the nearness to the Lord's return, the "perfect control" — about which Paul does not speak — was closer for Clement to the Stoic ideal, which the entire demeanor of the true Christian "Gnostic" is to present, who "uses God's creatures, when, and so far as, it is reasonable, in a spirit of thankfulness to the Creator."[100] The legends about the wife of Peter might have come into existence in Rome, where the tradition about the martyrdom of Peter had been strongly anchored since the time of Nero's persecution. Clement of Alexandria himself relates the story about the way the Gospel of Mark came into existence in Rome,[101] and Clement of Rome already mentions the martyrdom of Peter about A.D. 100.[102] A short time later, he alludes to women as martyrs in Nero's persecution.[103]

That Peter would have been accompanied by his wife on his missionary journeys is related to us, admittedly only marginally, another three times in the *Pseudo-Clementine Recognitiones* and *Homiliae*. The wife of the apostle accompanies him to Laodicea, along with Clement and his mother, who had been resurrected from the dead, and by means of an oath attests to a daylong fast of Clement before his baptism. In this regard, she might be playing the foil to Helena, the travel partner of Simon Magus.[104] In what is the original version of the anti-Pauline Pseudo-Clementines, which are Jewish Christian, where Peter stands far off to the side of James, no one is bothered by the marriage of the first disciple, nor that his wife accompanies him on journeys. In the later *Acts of Peter* that we have available, she is mentioned no longer, but Peter's daughter is mentioned, admittedly now with clear Encratic tendencies.

100. Clement of Alexandria, *Strom.* 7.62.3-4 and 7.62.1; cf. also Eusebius, *Hist. eccl.* 3.30.2.

101. Eusebius, *Hist. eccl.* 2.15.1-2 and 6.14.5ff., according to Clement, *Hypot.;* cf. Irenaeus, *Haer.* 3.1.1.

102. *First Clem.* 5:4 "The ones doing battle in the most recent time" (*1 Clem.* 5:1) refers naturally to the Roman martyrs. Cf. also, without place-names being mentioned, John 21:18; cf. 13:36 and Dionysius of Corinth in Eusebius, *Hist. eccl.* 2.25.8. Further examples are provided above, pp. 5-7 and 98-99.

103. *First Clem.* 6:2: "Through envy, those women, the Danaids and Dircae, being persecuted, after they had suffered terrible and unspeakable torments, finished the course of their faith with steadfastness" (ANF 1:6). On this, see Tacitus, *Ann.* 15.44 and part I, n. 11.

104. Pseudo-Clementines, *Recog.* 7.25.3; 7.36.1; 9.38; *Hom.* 13.1.1; 13.11.2; on Simon and Helena, *Hom.* 2.25.1.

4. Clement of Alexandria and Encratism

Clement of Alexandria also knew of a tradition about the children of Peter.[105] It is possible that he also knew the unique legend that is written in story form about the *"Daughter of the Apostle,"* which belongs to the *Acts of Peter* and is preserved in its most original form in a Coptic papyrus. It is also in the *Acts of Philip* and, according to Augustine, in the Manichaean *Acts of the Apostles.* The young girl had been lame on one side of her body since she was ten years old, and Peter refused to heal her because of God's will, since it was revealed to him at her birth: "Peter, a great test faces you this day; this one [your daughter] will do damage to many souls if her body stays healthy." Being lame thus protected the young girl from marrying someone rich, who would wish to take her as wife against the wishes of her parents.

> The *Acts of Peter* reports: "And a man with many possessions by the name of Ptolemy, when he saw the young girl bathing with her mother [2 Sam. 11:2], sent to her in order to take her as wife; [but] the mother did not allow herself to be talked into it." A gap follows, which plainly describes the abduction of the young girl. But through his prayer Peter makes it happen that his daughter becomes lame. Ptolemy subsequently has his people bring her back, and they "lay her before the door of the house. . . . But as I and her mother looked on . . . we noticed that one side of the young girl . . . was completely lame. We took her [into the house] and praised the Lord, who had kept his servant girl from being defiled, violated, and ruined." As a punishment, Ptolemy was struck with blindness, but by means of a vision he was converted and healed, and then he put it in his will that the young girl should receive a piece of land that would provide for her living costs, "because he had come to faith in God through her and had been saved."[106] In order to convince a critical questioner and the multitude that God is able to heal, at the very beginning of the story Peter allows her to become suddenly perfectly well and then once again to fall back into her sickness.

In the briefest form, the *Acts of Philip* tell about what happened in order to illustrate why "the illustrious Peter fled from the slightest glance of a

---

105. See n. 98 above.

106. Cf. *NTApocr*[5] 2:256; cf. also 251 [Engl: 2:286]; Coptic texts are found in J. Brashler and D. M. Parrott, *The Act of Peter,* BG 4:128.1–141.7, in: NHC V, 2-5 and VI, with Papyrus Berolinensis 8502, 1 and 4; NHS XI (Leiden, 1979), 473-93. See now also H. M. Schenke, in *Nag Hammadi Deutsch* (GCS, n.s., 12), 2:844-52, translation 851; parallels: *Acts Phil.* 36, see *AAAp* 2/2:81, with two versions; Augustine, *Contra Adimantum* 17.5 (CSEL 25.1.170).

woman." For, as the example of Eve already demonstrates, "that evil desire in the eyes is πορνεία [sexual immorality]." In the *Acts of Saints Nereus and Achilleus*, which dates to the fifth/sixth century, which is dependent in its chap. 15 on the *Acts of Peter*, the sentimental story is told in a quite different fictional version. There the daughter is healed after she had become strong within herself in her piety, but she dies anyway when she is sought after as wife by one Comes Flaccus because of her beauty, after a three-day fast and after receiving the Eucharist. Peter's daughter receives here the name *Petronilla*, whereas the mother remains nameless.[107] The name originally was connected with a Roman Christian girl who was martyred in the early era, and it was only secondarily transferred to Peter's daughter in the fifth/sixth century.[108]

The contradictory nature of the short notes found in the writings of someone like Clement of Alexandria, as well as in the legends of the *Acts of Peter*, is apparent. Clement, the first great Christian scholar, uses the references to Peter and Philip in defense of marriage as God's good gift in creation, by means of which the lives of the partners in marriage are sanctified in faith and love. He therefore further adds that Philip also had married off his daughters. This does not exclude the possibility that he viewed remaining unmarried, based on his reference to Paul, as still more preferable. At the same time, he contradicts the growing Encratic movement in the church, which was dualistic and thus inimical toward the body, and which generally had its roots in a Gnosticizing background. Typical of this view are the popular "Encratic" fictional novels about the apostles, with their legendary narratives that not only minimize the importance of marriage and bearing children but as a rule fully reject such behavior, honoring instead a contrived ascetic ideal that identifies the gospel with preaching about sexual abstinence. The story of Peter's wife and

107. Cf. H. Achelis, *Acta SS. Nerei et Achillei*, in TU 11/2 (Berlin, 1893), 14-15. Their grave in the Domitilla catacombs is mentioned in 17-18. For more on this, see R. A. Lipsius, *Apostelgeschichten*, 2/2:203-6. The esteemed Syrian teacher Bar Hebraeus (thirteenth century), in connection with 1 Pet. 5:13 and Acts 12:12-13, tells of a daughter of Peter with the name Rome or Rhode; see T. Zahn, *Einleitung in das Neue Testament* (Leipzig, 1924³), 2:16, n. 11, according to the publication by M. Klamroth, in *Act. apostolicas et epist. catholicas adnotationes* (Göttingen, 1878), 15, 29 (not available to me).

108. It deals with a Latin name that is derived from Petronius/ia, which has nothing to do with Peter (see part I, n. 63). E. Diehl, *ILCV* 1, no. 1995B note. The inscription on a sarcophagus that was lost: *Aur. Petronillae filiae dulcissimae* "points to belonging . . . to the family of the Aurelians"; on this, see G. Muschiol, "Petronilla," *LTK* 8:89. See more below, nn. 118-20.

the mother of the young girl, which one cannot completely reject on the basis of the gospels and 1 Cor. 9:5, thereby takes on only marginal significance. In contrast to the daughter, she remains nameless in every possible reference in any source.

There is no room here to go further into the exegesis of the Fathers with respect to our few New Testament texts about "apostolic marriages." Nevertheless, the eleventh-century bishop *Theophylact(us)*,[109] who assembled the exegesis of the Fathers in a massive Bible commentary, includes at Matt. 8:14 (= Mark 1:29-30) the observation that "marriage does not hinder virtue. For the head of the apostles had a mother-in-law." This means that he takes a similar position to that of Clement of Alexandria eight hundred years earlier. One wonders whether there is a little jab against the West at this point, which in that very eleventh century, in connection with the Cluniac reform, established the rule of priestly celibacy.[110]

The interpretation of 1 Cor. 9:5 is more difficult. Clement had already emphasized that the apostles had not really taken their wives along as true marriage partners but instead as missionary helpers in the mission to women, and he interprets the passage at the same time as being good Stoic teaching, as an expression of one's self-control.[111] *Severian of Gabala*[112] leaves the question open about whether this deals with actual "marriage partners or not." The word "sister," which is added by Paul to "wife," gives expression to "the seemly and self-controlled and pure one" and shows "that, with respect to Peter and the other [apostles], the women went along because of their interest in teaching." *Theodoret*[113] makes reference to an expansive interpretation that considered these women not as marriage partners but as "believing women who had followed the Lord[114] and who took care of the needs of the disciples to provide for the basics of life." So, at a later time, some of them followed the

109. Cf. PG 123, col. 221. Theophylact(us) was the bishop of Ochrida (modern Ohrid) in Macedonia, roughly 1050-1108.

110. See H. Chadwick, *East and West: The Making of a Rift in the Church* (Oxford, 2003), 220-21, 225: "but major issues were Western scorn for married priests."

111. Clement of Alexandria, *Strom.* 3.53.3 and *Paed.* 2.9.1.

112. Bishop of Gabala, toward the end of the fourth century, cited according to K. Staab, *Pauluskommentare aus der griechischen Kirche* (Münster, 1933), 256. For 1 Cor. 9:5 some Western manuscripts (F G a b; Tert Ambst Pel) read only the plural γυναῖκας (wives).

113. Bishop of Cyrrhus, first half of the fifth century, cited according to J. A. Cramer, *Catenae Graecorum Patrum in Novum Testamentum*, vol. 5, *Catenae in Sancti Pauli epist. ad Cor.* (1841; repr., Hildesheim, 1967), 166.

114. Cf. Mark 15:40-41 and Luke 8:2-3; see pp. 109-10 above.

apostles, thereby showing their fervent faith; they dedicated themselves to the teachings of the apostles and became their fellow workers in bringing the divine message. In Theodoret's view, the main point of the text is rooted completely in the idea that a marriage partnership is for following in a spiritual sense. Admittedly this interpretation also contains a *particula veri*. We cannot exclude the possibility that, among the Galilean wives who followed Jesus and his group of disciples, there were also wives and other family members of these disciples. Theophylact(us) simply follows this interpretation later, when he emphasizes that these were "well-to-do women" who took care of the basic sustenance needs for the apostles so that they could dedicate themselves, without concern, to the matters of proclamation.[115] In this way the original meaning of this text of Paul was turned in a different direction.

At the same time, the wife and family of Peter were included in legends in later Byzantine texts as well. One example will have to suffice. According to *Life of Andrew* by *Epiphanius Monachus*,[116] a poor man, Jonah from Bethsaida,[117] left two sons, Simon and Andrew, in abject poverty; the sons earned their keep as day workers (cf., against this view, Mark 1:20). Simon took the daughter of Aristobulus, a brother of the apostle Barnabas, as wife, and with her, as some say, he produced a son and a daughter, but then later after the death of his mother-in-law, he gave his wife to the mother of God. "Andrew dedicated himself to chastity."[118] It is surprising that, in all of these legends, the wife and the mother-in-law of Peter both remain anonymous, whereas for the legendary daughters — even though it takes place only in later traditions, supposedly because of some confusion — the name of a daughter Petronilla is preserved and becomes a supposed martyr and a Roman saint, whose grave was venerated in the Domitilla cata-

---

115. Cf. PG 124:665; cf. Luke 8:3.

116. From the Kallistratos monastery in Constantinople, written between 800 and 813; cf. H. G. Beck, *Kirche und theologische Literatur im Byzantinischen Reich*, Byzantinisches Handbuch 2/1 (Munich, 1977), 513; see PG 120:216-60. He also composed the first known story of the life of Mary. On this, cf. R. A. Lipsius, *Apostelgeschichten*, 1:570ff.

117. Concerning Jonah, cf. Matt. 16:17, and concerning Bethsaida, cf. John 1:44.

118. R. A. Lipsius, *Apostelgeschichten*, 1:575; cf. the reference to a Patriarch Sophronius of Jerusalem (d. 638), to whom is attributed a fragment preserved in Latin, "De laboribus, certaminibus et peregrinationibus SS. Petri et Pauli," and the Greek Menaia and Menologia, for example, the *Menologicum Basilii*, in PG 117:513-14, in which the legend recurs in a similar form. The Greek *Acts of Andrew* presents its hero as an outspoken enemy of marriage; on this, see *Acta Andreae*, ed. J.-M. Prieur, CCSA 5-6, 2 vols (Turnhout, 1989), index, 2:762; see under "Encratisme (rejet de la sexualité)" and "Mariage."

combs and was adorned with a basilica. A fresco there, from approximately 357, shows her as one who guided the souls into paradise. By order of Pope Paul I (757-67), her relics were transferred to St. Peter's, where they were placed in a chapel. She is depicted very realistically on a wall painting in the cathedral in St. Goar, in the fifteenth century, as the "manager of the household of Peter," with keys and a broom. Her popularity was also enhanced by her vita, which Jacob of Voragine included in his collection *The Golden Legend*.[119]

In spite of the ancient notation by Clement of Alexandria about the martyrdom of Peter's wife, which Jacob of Voragine discovered on the basis of his readings from Eusebius's church history,[120] as far as I know she remains nameless in all the apostolic legends and has been essentially forgotten. Only her father is remembered, in a late text, as the supposed brother of Barnabas, and he is given the good Jewish name Aristobulus,[121] based on knowledge of the name that Josephus provided. She herself therefore appears in the later lives of Peter as a niece of Barnabas, which means that she becomes thereby the equivalent of his nephew, John Mark (Acts 12:12, 25; 13:5, 13; 15:37; Col. 4:10), who is named as "my son" in 1 Pet. 5:13 and who, according to a trustworthy tradition, was the student and interpreter of Peter.[122] But even this passage, which has clear information, was changed in meaning because of a puzzling Oriental tradition that appears in the writings of the scholarly Nestorian exegete Isho'dad of Merv (ninth century).[123] In his introduction to the explanation of the Gospel of Mark, he writes:

---

119. See n. 108 above, and Jacob of Voragine, *Legenda aurea* (German trans. R. Benz [Jena, 1925]), 1:513-15; concerning the grave, 1:508; according to him, Saints Nereus and Achilleus, who were baptized by Peter, were buried with him. Cf. also 2:511, concerning their transfer to St. Peter's. Concerning their chapel, see F. Gregorovius, *Geschichte der Stadt Rom im Mittelalter* (Munich, 1978), 1/1:150 and 1/2:383-84 [Engl: *History of the City of Rome in the Middle Ages,* trans. G. W. Hamilton [New York, 2000], 1:324 and 2:318-19]. Concerning the Domatilla catacombs, cf. H. Leclercq, in *DACL* 4/2:1409-22; 1/1:1515, illus. 360; L. Schütz, *LCI* 8:157. Concerning the church in St. Goar, cf. J. Braun, *Tracht und Attribute der Heiligen in der deutschen Kunst* (Stuttgart, 1943; repr., 1964), 295, illus. 150; concerning the conveyance to St. Peter's, cf. W. Buchowiecki, *Handbuch der Kirchen Roms,* vol. 3 (Vienna, 1947), 354, cf. 362. Now see, as well, G. Muschiol, "Petronilla," 89.

120. Jacob of Voragine, *Legenda aurea,* 1:556-57.

121. These are the names of the three Hasmonean high priests and of the son of Herod and Mariamne, the father of King Herod Agrippa I.

122. See n. 1 above.

123. Concerning his person, see R. Peters, *BBKL* 2:1364-65.

But as Clement gives testimony, Mark is a son of Peter. For Clement says in that extensive letter that he wrote against those who wanted to cast off marriage ties, in which he provides a list of those apostles who were married in the world, but who later became disciples of the Lord, that they preserved purity and holiness, as did Moses and others who, after they had been treated as worthy of receiving divine revelation, kept distant from marital relations and preserved holiness. For this one [Clement] says: "Or did they also reject the apostles? For Peter and Philip indeed bore children; but Paul did not think it unfitting to greet his marriage partner in his letter;[124] but he did not carry on with her because of the holiness of the service."[125]

Theodore Zahn supposes that Isho'dad cites an early writing, now lost, that only Clement himself mentions.[126] Against this view, C. Heussi[127] offers the objection that it could be a relatively free citation from *Stromata*, book 3, which deals with the topic of marriage and abstinence and which agrees quite closely in §§ 52-53 with the text from Isho'dad, except for the unique reference at the beginning of the citation that Clement identifies Mark as the physical son of Peter. Since this peculiar interpretation of 1 Pet. 5:13 does not appear anywhere else in the works of Clement, and since it more probably contradicts his information about the Second Gospel coming into existence in Rome, in which Mark appears as a "follower" of Peter,[128] it is quite unlikely that the source of this information is Clement. Since, by contrast, it is just as unlikely that Isho'dad invented this himself, its source remains an open question. Whereas there is an easily understood consensus that 1 Pet. 5:13a — "the fellow elect [συνεκλεκτή] in Babylon greet you" — refers to the Christian congregation in Rome, some earlier

124. Phil. 4:3: γνήσιε σύζυγε (O loyal companion); on this, see n. 90 above.

125. German translation in T. Zahn, "Retractationes," *NKZ* 12 (1901): 744-45. Text and English translation: *The Commentaries of Isho'dad of Merv in Syriac and English*, ed. M. D. Gibson, HSem 5, vol. 1 (Cambridge, 1911), 123.

126. Clement of Alexandria, *Paed.* 2.94: περὶ ἐγκρατείας (on continence) or 3:41: λόγος γαμικός (treatise on married life) [English trans. by S. P. Wood, in FC 23], see *FGNK* 3:37; on this, see also O. Stählin, *Des Clemens von Alexandria ausgewählte Schriften. Aus dem Griechischen übersetzt*, BKV 2/7.1 (1934), Introduction, 39-40: "a special, not otherwise known, writing" (40).

127. C. Heussi, *ZWT*, n.s., 10 (1902): 480-87.

128. According to Clement of Alexandria, *Hypot.* 6, in Eusebius, *Hist. eccl.* 6.14.6; 2.15.1; *Adumbrationes ad 1 Petr.* 5:13; see K. Aland, *Synopsis* (Stuttgart, 1996^15), 555. See pp. 46-48 above.

interpreters were of the opinion that this reference was to the wife of Peter. The most well-known advocate of such an interpretation was Albrecht Bengel in his *Gnomon Novi Testamenti* (on 1 Pet. 5:13): "*Elected together with* — Thus he appears to speak of his wife; cf. ch. iii. 7; for she was a *sister*, 1 Cor. ix. 5; and the mention of his *son* Mark agrees with this."[129]

5. Concluding Considerations

We have followed a course that led from the house of the fisherman in Capernaum all the way to the fantasy-filled late legends, along with unique assumptions by individual interpreters, on a long and often complicated path. It shows, first of all, how little we know about the actual life accomplishments of the great figures who established the early church. Nevertheless, the way was richer, livelier, and, one could even say, more surprising and more inscrutable than we would like, taking into account our penchant for theological abstraction and schematization. With Jesus and the circle of disciples he called to accompany him, marriage and family apparently played a larger, but also contradictory, role already at the first beginning points than is generally taken into account. The problem begins with the criticism from Jesus' own family after he took up his public role in Galilee.[130] It expanded still further in his call for some to follow him, given the pressing nearness of the inbreaking reign of God, which called for a break with family connections and even brought Jesus himself into a crisis with his own family. This call first went out to Simon the fisherman, who was married, to whom Jesus gave the nickname "Rock," and to his brother Andrew, as well as to the sons of Zebedee, who were closely connected with them. And yet the family ties were not loosened forever. Just the very opposite. Connections with family members played a certain role already within the circle of those who were part of the larger following, who had accompanied the master to Jerusalem. To that group belonged apparently also women from the extended family of Jesus and the disciples.

After Easter the families, with their "houses," took on a new task as the

---

129. *John Albert Bengel's Gnomon of the New Testament*, trans. C. T. Lewis and M. R. Vincent (Philadelphia, 1864), 2:759. On this, see G. Wohlenberg, *Der erste und zweite Petrusbrief und der Judasbrief,* KNT 15 (Leipzig, 1915), 161n.; T. Zahn, *Einleitung in das Neue Testament,* 2:16, n. 11.

130. See the shocking texts Mark 3:21, 31-35 = Luke 8:19-21 = Matt. 12:46-50; Mark 6:1-6a par.; John 7:2-10.

home base for the network of the Jesus communities that were being formed. Even names such as Mary, Martha, and Lazarus are evidence of that. Without the "house communities" and the common missionary activity carried out by Christian married couples, the new message would not have been able to expand with such speed and endurance. From the very beginning there were two opposing forces at work. On the one hand, there was the nearness of the end and the freedom that this nearness called for in connection with service to the coming Lord; on the other hand, there was the necessity of the house community to exist as the kernel of the ongoing, progressing construction of the communities. Our theme — the family of Peter and the other apostolic families — is to be inscribed in this tension-filled parallelogram of forces. Peter and Paul seemingly stand as opponents against one another in this aspect as well. Missionary couples such as Prisca and Aquila provide balance; Paul and his missionary activity owed them untold thanks, but we also need to mention Andronicus and Junia in Rome, with their unknown previous history. Possibly one must consider the almost completely unknown missionary activity of the married man Peter and other married apostles from this point of view as well.

First Corinthians 7 negatively influenced the high view of marriage and family, which has its roots in the Old Testament–Jewish tradition, because of the way it was applied in later times. In the second century the workings of a Platonic type of ascetic-Encratic dualism gained strength as a movement that was inimical to the body and against marriage and that minimized having a family. In its most radical forms this movement essentially rejected marriage but still allowed for a compromise that remained unsettling, which can be seen for the first time in a relatively detailed form in Clement of Alexandria. This compromise, which had significant impact on the church's understanding of marriage in the future, was not a proper one when considered in light of the original reality of "apostolic families" in the earliest community.

Chronology

Tiberius	*September 17, A.D. 14–March 16, 37*
Appearance of John the Baptist	ca. 27
Call of Peter	ca. 28/29
Death of Jesus and the Easter event	Passover festival 30
Peter in Jerusalem	Pentecost festival 30
Death of Stephen and expulsion of Hellenists	ca. 32/33
Conversion of Paul	ca. 33
Paul's visit with Peter	ca. 36
Beginning of the mission to the Gentiles in Antioch	ca. 36/37
Paul in Tarsus	ca. 36-39/40
Conversion of Cornelius	ca. 37-38
Caligula	*March 18, 37–January 24, 41*
The first Christians in Rome	ca. 38-40
The threat to the temple by Caligula	ca. 39/41
Claudius	*January 25, 41–October 13, 54*
Agrippa I, king in Jerusalem	early 41
Arrest and flight of Peter	Passover festival 42/43
Death of Agrippa I; Judea once again a Roman province	early 44
Apostolic Council	ca. 48/49
Expulsion of the Jewish Christians from Rome	ca. 49
Paul in Corinth	ca. 50/51

Conflict in Antioch	ca. 52/53
Paul in Ephesus	ca. 53–early 56
Peter in Corinth	ca. 53/54
Nero	*October 13, 54–June 9, 68*
Return of the Jews (Jewish Christians) who had been expelled from Rome	from the end of 54
1 Corinthians	ca. 54/55
Galatians, 2 Corinthians	56
Paul in Corinth once again; Epistle to the Romans	winter 56/57
Arrest of Paul in Jerusalem	Pentecost 57
Imprisonment of Paul in Caesarea	57-59
Transport to Rome	winter 59/60
Imprisonment of Paul in Rome	ca. 60-62
Trip to Spain	ca. 62-64
Stoning of James and other Jewish Christian leaders in Jerusalem	62
Persecution by Nero	64ff.
Martyrdom of Peter and Paul	64/66
Outbreak of the Jewish War; flight of the community to Pella	summer 66
Vespasian	*July 1, 68–June 24, 79*
Siege and conquest of Jerusalem by Titus	April–September 70
Gospel according to Mark, in Rome	ca. 69/70
Two-volume work by Luke	ca. 75-85
Titus	*June 24, 79–September 13, 81*
Domitian	*September 14, 81–September 18, 96*
Gospel according to Matthew, in southern Syria	ca. 90-100
First Letter of Clement	soon after 96
First Letter of Peter	ca. 90-100
Nerva	*September 18, 96–January 98*
Trajan	*January 27, 98–August 8/9, 117*

Chronology

Collection of the Letters of Paul	ca. 90-100
Publication of the Gospel according to John	
and the Letters of John, in Ephesus	ca. 100-110
The Pastoral Letters	ca. 110
Letters of Ignatius	ca. 110-114
Hadrian	*August 11, 117–July 10, 138*
Second Letter of Peter	all ca. 120-140
Papias of Hierapolis	
Basilides in Alexandria	
Valentinus in Rome	
Phlegon of Tralles	
Antoninus Pius	*July 10, 138–March 7, 161*
Excommunication of Marcion	144
Justin Martyr	
Apology	after 150
Dialogue with Trypho	ca. 160
Martyrdom of Polycarp	156 (or 167)
Marcus Aurelius	*March 7, 161–March 17, 180*
Hegesippus	
Trip to Rome	ca. 160
Five books of *Hypomnēmata*	ca. 180
Dionysius of Corinth	ca. 160-170
Irenaeus of Lyon	ca. 180

Sources: R. Riesner, *Die Frühzeit des Apostels Paulus,* WUNT 71 (Tübingen, 1994); M. Hengel and A. M. Schwemer, *Paul between Damascus and Antioch: The Unknown Years* (Louisville, Ky., 1997), x-xiv; M. Hengel, *The Four Gospels and the One Gospel of Jesus Christ* (London, 2000), 208-9.

Index of Ancient Works

I. OLD TESTAMENT

Genesis
2:24 (LXX)   113
9:5   63

Exodus
19:6   19
32:28   34

Leviticus
17–18   62
17:11-12   63

Numbers
12:7 (LXX)   112
20:8-10   22
34:11   40

Judges
6:20   22
15:13   22

1 Samuel
13:6   22
23:25   22

2 Samuel
11:2   127

1 Kings
16:31   120
19:11   22

Job
30:6   21

Psalms
8:6   88
24:1   66
110:1   88
118:22   23

Proverbs
10:25   8

Isaiah
8:14   23
28:16   16, 18, 23
51:1-2   25
52:15   94
53   87
53:7-8   87
60:17   52

Jeremiah
4:29   21
9:23-24   68
23:29   22
48:28   22

Daniel
7:9-10   4
7:22   4
7:26   4

Joel
2:28-32   71

Amos
6:12   22

Habakkuk
2:4 (LXX)   59

Zechariah
6:12   16

II. APOCRYPHA AND PSEUDEPIGRAPHA OF THE OLD TESTAMENT

Assumption of Moses
1:12   8

4 Ezra
6:55-59   8
8:44   8

2 Maccabees
1:16 — 23
4:41 — 23

3 Maccabees
5:51 — 6

Psalms of Solomon
16:2 — 6
17:43 — 82

Sirach
40:15 — 21

Syriac Apocalypse of Baruch (2 Baruch)
14:18 — 8
15:7 — 8
21:24 — 8

Testament of Job
46–53 — 116

Wisdom of Solomon
16:13 — 6

III. QUMRANIC WRITINGS

Songs of Praise
1QH 14:23-24 — 16
1QH 14:26ff. — 16
1QH 15:8-9 — 16

Texts from Cave 4
4Q201, col. II.8 — 21
4Q204, frgs. 4, 5 — 21
4Q205, frg. 2, col. II.27 — 21
4Q206, frg. 5, col. III.19 — 21

Targum of Job
11Q10, col. 32.1 — 21
11Q10, col. 33.9 — 21

IV. FLAVIUS JOSEPHUS

Antiquitates judaicae
18.153 — 38
20.34 — 124
20.200ff. — 10, 65

Bellum judaicum
2.560 — 124
2.560-61 — 56
5.189 — 21
6.410 — 21
7.43 — 30

V. NEW TESTAMENT

Matthew
1:21 — 86
4:18 — 19, 26
4:18-22 — 107
4:19 — 55
4:24 — 40
5:10-12 — 7
5:13-20 — 28
5:17-19 — 31
5:18 — 31
5:32 — 113
5:44 — 7
6:12 — 86, 97
6:14-15 — 86
7:12 — 53, 62
7:13-14 — 5, 28
7:21-22 — 5
7:24ff. — 5
8:14 — 19, 105, 129
8:14-15 — 104
8:18-22 — 113
8:19-22 — 108
8:21-22 — 107
9:5-7 — 105
9:13 — 43, 53
10:2 — 19, 26, 28, 44, 81
10:4 — 20
10:10 — 68
10:20 — 34
10:23 — 7
10:37 — 107
11:25 — 15
11:27 — 15
12:7 — 53
12:46-50 — 10, 133
13:16-17 — 15
13:52 — 4, 51
13:55 — 10, 109
13:56 — 109
14:28-29 — 28
14:28-33 — 44
14:33 — 15
15:15 — 28
16 — 25
16:13-16 — 19
16:16 — 4
16:17 — 3, 8, 22, 105, 130
16:17-18 — 19
16:17-19 — 1ff., 13-15, 17, 19, 23, 27, 32, 36, 51, 96
16:18 — 1-2, 3, 16, 18-19, 21, 23-25, 31, 91
16:18-19 — 8, 99
16:19 — 3-4, 27
16:21-23 — 7
16:22 — 7
16:23 — 7-8, 28, 70
16:24 — 7
16:27-28 — 15
17:5 — 15
17:24ff. — 28
17:24-27 — 44
17:25 — 19, 22
18:17 — 3
18:18 — 4, 27
18:21-22 — 28
18:21-35 — 27, 86
19:6 — 113
19:12 — 114
19:16-26 — 107
19:27 — 108
19:28 — 4, 108
19:29 — 107-8

20:20	26, 110	1:34	39	9:33-37	93
22:44	88	1:36	41	9:38	26, 49
23	5	2:1	40	9:41	39
23:1-12	5	2:5ff.	86	10:6-9	113
23:13	5, 28	2:9-12	105	10:8-9	113
23:23	53	2:17	43, 86	10:17-27	107
23:34	4, 7, 51	2:23-28	53	10:29	104, 108
24:3	7	3:12	105	10:30	108
24:9ff.	7	3:14	41	10:32	43
24:21-22	7	3:16	19	10:35	26
24:21-29	7	3:16-17	103	10:45	86-87
24:27	7	3:17	22	10:46	19
24:37	7	3:18	19-20, 26	12:6ff.	39
24:39	7	3:21	10, 29, 133	12:35ff.	39
26:26-29	87	3:31	29	12:36	88
26:28	86	3:31ff.	112	12:42	40
26:33-35	28	3:31-35	10, 133	13:3	26, 41, 49
26:64	88	3:35	29	13:10	41, 95, 104
26:73	13	5:37	49	13:19-20	7
26:75	28, 44	6:1-6	133	14:1	37
27:16	19	6:3	10, 109, 112	14:9	41, 84, 95, 104
27:56	26, 110	6:7	76	14:12	37
28:16-20	72	6:12-13	76	14:22-25	87
28:18-20	32	6:45	40	14:24	86-87
28:20	7, 31	7:3	37, 40	14:26-72	40
		7:3-4	37	14:29-31	40
Mark		7:18-23	53	14:31	83
1:1	15, 39, 104	7:26	40	14:33	40, 49
1:4	86	7:31	38	14:36	87
1:11	39	8:17ff.	43	14:37	22, 40
1:14	104	8:22	40	14:51	42
1:16	26, 40-42, 103	8:27–9:8	40	14:54	40
1:16ff.	41	8:29	15, 39	14:61	39
1:16-20	107	8:31-33	7, 39	14:61-62	15
1:16-39	40	8:32-33	83	14:62	88
1:17	41, 55, 95	8:33	43, 70	14:66-72	40
1:19	41	8:34	7	14:71	83
1:20	130	9:2	49	14:72	44
1:21	13, 40	9:5-6	39	15:16	40
1:24	39	9:6	43	15:21	109
1:25	105	9:7	15, 39	15:40	26, 108
1:29	13, 26, 106	9:10	43	15:40-41	109-10, 129
1:29-30	129	9:10-13	39	15:41	105
1:29ff.	106	9:19	43	15:47	110
1:29-31	41, 104	9:25	105	16:1	110
1:31	110	9:33	40	16:7	41, 103, 113

141

16:9-20	45
secondary ending	41

Luke

1:1	80
1:2	80
1:77	86
3:3	86
4:16-30	109
4:35	105
4:38	105
4:38-39	104
4:39	105
5:1-2	40
5:7	41
5:8	43-44, 86
5:10	55
5:11	107
5:23-25	105
6:13-14	118
6:14	19, 26
6:15	20
6:20	81
6:31	53, 62
6:40	81
7:18	81
7:48-49	86
8:2-3	129
8:3	105, 110, 122, 130
8:19-21	10, 133
8:22-23	40
8:33	40
8:45	41
9:14	34
9:20	15
9:22	7
9:35	15
9:42	105
9:49	49
9:57-62	108, 113
9:62	113
10:7	68
10:21	15
10:22	15
10:40	105
11:4	97
11:49	4
11:52	5, 28
12:12	34
13:24	28
14:26	81, 107
15	86
16:18	113
18:9-14	86
18:11	44
18:18-27	107
18;29	107
19:1-10	86
20:36	124
20:42-43	88
21:12-19	79
22:8	49
22:19-20	87
22:27	87
22:30	4
22:31	22
22:31-32	44, 86, 99
22:32	44, 87, 96
22:37	87
22:62	28, 44
22:69	88
23:43	86
24:10	110, 122
24:25-26	43
24:31-32	43
24:34	22, 29, 44
24:37	14
24:39	14
24:47	43, 86

John

1:35-40	19
1:35-42	29
1:40	26
1:42	20, 22, 105
1:42-43	19
1:44	13, 20, 26, 105, 130
6:8	26
6:60-61	31
6:66-69	8, 31
7:2-10	133
7:3-10	29
7:5	10
7:5ff.	112
10:12	12
12:2	105
12:20ff.	20
12:22	26, 77
13:23ff.	82
13:36	5, 31, 126
16:2	12, 31
19:25	108, 110
19:26-27	82
19:35ff.	82
20:8	82
20:20	14
20:23	27
20:27	14
20:28	8
20:31	15
21	29, 31, 39
21:5	14
21:7	82
21:12	14
21:15	23
21:15-17	8, 20, 30-31, 44, 97
21:15-18	99
21:15-19	8, 49
21:17	22
21:18	7, 126
21:18-19	5, 31

Acts of the Apostles

1–5	85
1:8	79
1:13	26, 49, 118
1:15	34
1:23	19
2	71
2–5	55
2:9-11	30
2:17-21	71
2:22-36	84
2:29	34
2:32	80
2:34-35	88

2:38	43, 86-87	10:14	53	15:13-21	10, 54, 77
2:41	34	10:14ff.	84	15:14	20, 22
2:42	85	10:38-39	80	15:19	63
3–4	87	10:41	14	15:19-20	74
3:13	87	10:43	43, 87	15:19-21	62
3:15	80	10:44	71	15:20	63, 66
3:19	87	11:1	53	15:22	64
3:26	87	11:1-3	58	15:22-23	78
4:4	34	11:2-3	53	15:23-29	62
4:6	12	11:8ff.	84	15:27	64
4:8	34	11:15	71, 122	15:28	63, 65
4:13	12, 34	11:20	57	15:28-29	74
4:20	80	11:25	116	15:29	63, 66
4:27	87	12:1ff.	77	15:37	46, 97, 131
4:29	34	12:2	49	15:37-38	98
4:30	87	12:12	46, 97, 131	15:37-39	58, 98
4:31	34, 71	12:12-13	128	15:39	46, 58, 97
4:36	19	12:17	10, 46, 48-49, 79	15:40	64
5:3ff.	83	12:25	46, 97, 131	15:40-41	74
5:15-16	76	13:1	59	16–28	78
5:31	43, 87	13:1ff.	57	16:1	98
5:32	80	13:5	131	16:1-3	61
5:41	79	13:6	19	16:4	62, 74, 78
6:1	58	13:7ff.	57	16:7	49
6:1ff.	84	13:13	97-98, 131	16:13-14	124
6:5	116, 118	13:14	97	16:14-15	121
6:14	53	13:31	80	17:4	124
7:59-60	87	13:38	43, 84, 87	17:16	58
8	117	13:43-48	57	17:34	124
8:5	118	13:50-51	124	18:2	49, 95, 120
8:14ff.	91	13:51	97	18:3	68
8:14-25	79	14:1	97	18:18	120
8:20ff.	83	14:4	77, 118	18:22-23	58, 74
8:32-33	87	14:6	97	18:23	62
8:40	91, 117	14:8	97	18:24	50, 67
9:4	75	14:14	77, 118	18:25-26	120
9:11	116	14:19	79, 97	18:26	120
9:19-22	56	15	78	19:8	67
9:26-28	35	15:1	77	19:10	67
9:29	35	15:1ff.	64, 84	19:21-22	67
9:30	116, 122	15:5	66, 77	19:23ff.	67, 120
9:32ff.	91	15:7	58, 77, 83	20:1-3	93
9:32-43	55, 76	15:7-9	84	20:18 D	67
9:32–11:18	79	15:7-11	53, 77, 83	20:24	84, 98
9:36ff.	91	15:11	84	20:29	98
10:1–11:18	49, 53, 84	15:13	10	20:29-30	79

20:29ff.	85	1:16	56, 82	15:30-32	55
20:31	67	2:16	45	15:31	64-65
21:8	116, 118	3:5-8	73	16	121
21:8-9	117	3:8	55, 70-71, 73	16:1-23	73
21:8ff.	91	3:20-31	60	16:2	121
21:10-16	73	3:28	59	16:3	74, 120
21:18	10, 78	6	70	16:3-4	121
21:18ff.	58	6:1	73	16:3-5	95
21:18-26	73	7:2-3	114	16:4	120
21:20	34	7:7	73	16:7	55, 73, 109, 122
21:21	84	8:3ff.	60	16:11	122
21:21-25	54	8:15-16	87	16:13	109
21:23ff.	58	8:34	88	16:17-20	73, 93
21:25	62-63, 74	9–11	95	16:21	122
21:27ff.	65	9:3	122	16:25	45
21:28	84	9:5	76		
21:28ff.	65	11:1	73	**1 Corinthians**	
21:39	116	11:13	56, 73	1–3	25
22:1	98	11:14	56	1:10–3:4	24
22:3	116	11:17-24	95	1:11-12	66
22:7	75	12–13	76	1:12	30, 49, 67
22:15	77	12:1ff.	70	1:12-13	35
22:17-21	56, 73	13	6	1:13	66, 97
23:16	116, 122	13:11-12	83	1:31	68
23:16ff.	122	14	66	2:2	75
24:17	58, 65	14:1	75	2:10	15
24:23	58, 73	14:15-23	75	3:4-9	67
26:14	75	14:17	75	3:9	17
26:16	77	14:22-23	75	3:10	16, 94
26:16-18	56	15	93	3:10ff.	16-18, 67, 92, 112
27:3	58	15:8	76	3:10-15	15
28:14-16	78	15:17-21	68	3:10-17	17
28:15	73	15:18-19	93	3:11	16-17, 24, 67, 78
28:30	6	15:19	64, 73, 76, 94	3:12-15	73
28:31	79	15:19-20	78	3:15	73
		15:20	16, 24, 67, 94	3:16-17	17
Romans		15:22	74, 78, 94-95	3:21-22	68
1:1	73	15:22-24	94	3:21-23	68, 70
1:1-15	78	15:23ff.	94	3:22	30, 49, 67
1:3-4	76	15:24	6, 92	5–12	114
1:7	121	15:25-26	64	5:1-5	63
1:10-13	94	15:25ff.	65	5:9	63
1:11-15	95	15:25-31	74	5:9-13	63
1:13	74	15:26	11	6:2-3	4
1:13-14	94	15:28	6, 92	6:9-13	70
1:14	56	15:30-31	65	6:12ff.	70

7	114, 123, 134	9:22	61	3:1ff.	91
7:1-6	114	10:4	17, 24	3:1-3	71
7:6	114	10:21	62	3:6-7	69
7:7	114	10:23	70	3:6-11	54
7:8	114	10:25-26	66	4:2	91
7:9	114	10:25-29	75	5:12	91
7:10	76	11:2-12	119	5:14-15	60
7:11	113	11:11	119	5:16	44, 72, 76
7:18	69	11:16	70	5:16-17	75
7:18ff.	61	11:19	66	5:20	60
7:19	69-70	11:23	76	6:4	91
7:25	76	11:23ff.	75	7:5	93
7:28ff.	114	13:5	58	7:11	91
7:29	83, 126	14:26ff.	119	8–9	65, 69
7:31	126	14:34	119	8:1	93
7:32ff.	114	15:1ff.	68, 92	8:4	74
7:35	114, 123	15:3	34, 87	8:9	75-76
7:36	112	15:3ff.	75	9:1	74
7:36ff.	114	15:3-5	44	9:12	74
7:39	114	15:5	22, 30, 66	10–13	72, 93
7:40	114	15:6	34	10–12	35, 102
8–10	63, 66	15:7	10, 67, 112, 122	10–11	69, 72
8:1	63	15:9	44	10:1-6	67
8:1-13	75	15:9-10	66, 68	10:2	71-72, 91
8:7	75	15:10	34	10:7-11	71
8:10	75	15:11	66, 68	10:12	71
8:12	75	15:25ff.	88	10:12-18	92
9:1ff.	67, 72	15:50	15	10:13	72, 92
9:1-5	66	15:56	54	10:14	92
9:1-7	49, 67	16:1	69, 74	10:15	92
9:1-23	111	16:1ff.	65	10:16	92, 94
9:2-3	24	16:3	64	10:17	68
9:3-6	111	16:12	67	10:18	91
9:3-18	68	16:15	74	11:2	72
9:4ff.	67	16:19	120-21	11:4	71
9:5	24, 30, 42, 67-68, 70, 106-7, 112-14, 122-23, 129, 133	16:22	72, 87, 93	11:5	67, 70, 77
				11:7ff.	68, 111
9:6	112	**2 Corinthians**		11:9-10	93
9:12	111	1	67	11:10	83
9:14	68, 76	1:8	120	11:12-15	70
9:15ff.	93	1:14	92	11:13	70
9:18	111	1:17	72	11:14	70
9:19-23	61	1:19	64	11:15	73
9:20-21	61	2:3	93	11:16-33	93
9:20ff.	56	2:13	93	11:22-23	70
		3:1	71	11:23	77, 122

11:29	72	2:11-21	57	**Colossians**	
12:11	70, 91	2:12	10, 53, 59, 63, 69,	2:7	18
12:11-12	67		71, 84	4:10	30, 46, 97, 104,
12:11ff.	76	2:13	58-59		131
12:13	68	2:14	24, 30, 60, 64,	4:14	81, 97, 105
13:3	93		83-84	4:15	121
13:4	72	2:14-21	83		
13:8	83	2:16	59, 83	**1 Thessalonians**	
		2:17	60	1:1	64
Galatians		2:18	60	2:14-15	61
1:1	67	2:19	60	2:15	72
1:6	72	3:1	75	2:19-20	92
1:7	71	3:13-14	60	4:14-17	34
1:8-9	60	4:4	75	4:15	76
1:11-12	45, 82-83	4:4-5	60	5:2	76
1:12	16	4:5-6	87	5:2-3	34
1:13-14	44	4:25-26	64		
1:15-16	16	4:26	18	**1 Timothy**	
1:15ff.	56	4:29	61	1:15	43
1:15-23	73	5:3-4	63	1:15-16	44
1:15-24	94	5:6	61, 70	3:2ff.	115
1:16	15	5:11	61, 72	4:3	115
1:17	56, 68, 76	5:13ff.	70	5:3ff.	121
1:17-18	64	5:25	70	5:14	115
1:18	24, 30, 35, 88, 113	6:11-17	93	6:20	115
1:19	10	6:12-15	61		
2:1	64			**2 Timothy**	
2:1ff.	84	**Ephesians**		1:3ff.	97
2:1-10	69	1:20-22	88	2:8	45
2:2	64, 68	2:20	16, 19	3:11	97
2:3-5	60	2:20-21	18	3:15	98
2:5	64, 83	3:5	15	4:3	98
2:6	74, 77	3:8	44	4:6-8	98
2:7	30, 41			4:7	98
2:7-8	24, 55, 84	**Philippians**		4:11	46, 97-98
2:7-9	55, 57	1:14-17	49, 68	4:12	98
2:8	30, 55	1:15	71	4:16	98
2:9	9, 10, 24, 30, 50-	1:15-16	78	4:16-18	98
	51, 54-55, 77-78,	2:16	92	4:19	120
	82	3:2	72	4:20	98
2:10	11, 65, 74	3:2-11	54		
2:11	24, 30, 59, 64	3:5	71	**Titus**	
2:11-12	11, 55	3:5-6	116	1:6	115
2:11ff.	24, 52, 58-59, 62,	3:6	44		
	111	4:3	123, 132	**Philemon**	
2:11-14	66	4:12-18	68	24	46, 97

Hebrews

2:3	80
3:6	112
6:1	16
10:38	59

James

1:1	10
2:20-26	92
2:24	59
4:13ff.	92

1 Peter

1:1	11, 49-50
1:5	15
2:4	18
2:4-8	18
2:6	18
2:9	19
2:13ff.	6
2:22-25	87
3:22	88
4:17	84
5:1	5, 98
5:12	64
5:13	5, 46-47, 98, 103, 128, 131-33

2 Peter

1:1	11, 20, 22
1:13-15	5
3:15-16	98

1 John

1:1	14

Jude

1:1	10

Revelation

2:20	120
14:6	84
20:4	4
20:10	7
20:14	7
21:2	18
21:14	18
22:20	87

VI. NEW TESTAMENT APOCRYPHA

Apocryphal Acts of the Apostles

Acts of Andrew

10:80-81	7, 50

Acts of Peter (Actus Vercellenses)

1:1	6
37–41	5
37–38	7

Acts of Philip

36	127

Ascension of Isaiah

4:2-3	5

Gospel of the Hebrews

Fragment 7	9

Pseudo-Clementine Literature

Epistle of Clement

1:1	9
1:2-3	17

Epistle of Peter

1:1	9

Homiliae

2.25.1	126
7.8.1	62
8.19.1	62
13.1.1	126
13.11.2	126

Recognitiones

1.43.3	51
7.25.3	126
7.36.1	126
9.38	126

VII. APOSTOLIC FATHERS

Epistle of Barnabas

5:9	43

1 Clement

1:3	52
5–6	6, 35
5	99
5:1	126
5:1-4	49
5:4	14, 126
5:7	6
6:1	6
6:2	126
21:6	52
35:2	114
38:2	114
42:4-5	52
44:5	52
59–61	95
64:2	114

Didache

10:6	87
11:11	112

Ignatius of Antioch

Letter to the Ephesians

12:2	99

Letter to Polycarp

5:2	115

Letter to the Romans

2:2	5
4:3	14, 35, 49, 99

Letter to the Smyrnaeans

3:1ff.	14
3:2	41, 99
5:3	71
7:2	71

Polycarp of Smyrna

Letter to the Philippians

9:1-2	6

Shepherd of Hermas
Similitudes
9.14.6 (= 91.6) 16

VIII. WRITINGS FROM
NAG HAMMADI

Apocryphon of James
NHC 1:2 10

Gospel of Thomas
Logion 12 8, 82
Logion 13 82
Logion 39:1-2 5
Logion 114 82

*(Second) Apocalypse of
James*
NHC V, 4 10

*Acts of Peter and the
Twelve Apostles*
NHC VI, 1 26

Apocalypse of Peter
NHC VII, 3 26

Letter of Peter to Philip
NHC VIII, 2 26

Acts of Peter
BG 8502, 4 26

IX. CHURCH
FATHERS, CHRISTIAN
AUTHORS AND
WRITINGS

*Acts of Saints Nerii and
Achillei*
14–15 128
17–18 128

Augustine
Contra Adimantum
17:5 127

Muratorian Canon
37ff. 6

Clement of Alexandria
*Adumbrationes in
epistolas canonicas*
On 1 Peter 5:13 47, 132

Paedagogus
2.91 129
2.94 132
3.41 132

Stromata
3 123
3.52.1-2 125
3.52.4 125
3.52.5 125
3.53-54 123
3.53.3 124, 129
3.79.4-5 123
7.62.1 126
7.62.3-4 126
7.63.3 125
7.106.4 33

Epiphanius of Salamis
*Panarion (Adversus
haereses)*
78.8.1 109
78.9.6 109
78.14 10

Eusebius of Caesarea
*Hieronymi
chronicon* 6, 50

Historia ecclesiastica
2.1.3 9, 51
2.1.4 9
2.1.5 10, 109
2.14.6 50, 55
2.15 103
2.15.1 132

2.15.1-2 47, 126
2.16.24 50
2.23.4 9
2.23.4-18 10
2.23.8-18 82
2.25.8 6, 35, 67, 126
3.1.1-2 50
3.1.2 7
3.5.3 65
3.11 108
3.22 50
3.30.1 125
3.30.2 125-26
3.31.3-4 118
3.31.4 117, 119
3.32.4 108
3.39.4 29, 104
3.39.7 46
3.39.9ff. 117
3.39.14-15 46
3.39.15 12, 33, 36, 103
3.39.16 13, 32, 47
4.11.1 85
4.11.2 85
4.22.4 108
5.8.3 47
5.17.2-3 120
5.23.1 37
5.24.1-8 118
5.24.2-3 118
5.24.6 37
6.14.5-6 126
6.14.5-7 47
6.14.6 132
6.25.6 48
8.6.1-4 31

Irenaeus of Lyon
Adversus haereses
1.26.2 11
1.27.1 85
3.1.1 6, 35, 47, 103, 109, 126
3.3.2 35
3.4.3 85
3.12.15 9, 51

Index of Ancient Works

Jerome
De viris illustribus
1   50, 55
2   9
8   48

Justin
Apologia I
67   95
67.3   45

Dialogus cum Tryphone
47   11
103.8   45
106.3   44, 103

Origen
*Commentarium in
evangelium Matthaei* 48
XV.21   108

Contra Celsum
1.63   43
2.14   33

Homiliae in Lucam
VI   50

Tertullian
Adversus Marcionem
4.5.3   44

4.13.6   17
De baptismo
17   124

*De praescriptione
haereticorum*
22.44   17

De pudicitia
22.9   17, 19

Scorpiace
15.3   7

X. RABBINIC WRITINGS

Babylonian Talmud
b. Ḥag. 12b   8

Midrash Qohelet
1.8   106

Yalqut Shimoni
I §766   25

Targums
Onkelos
Num. 20:8-10   22

Yerushalmi I
Num. 20:8-10   22

XI. PAGAN ANCIENT SOURCES

Livy
39.13.14   6

Porphyry
"Against the Christians"
III.22   58

Suetonius
Divus Claudius
25.3   120

Nero
16.2.38   6

Tacitus
Annales
15.44   126
15.44.2-5   6
15.44.4   6-7

Index of Modern Authors

Achelis, H., 128
Achtemeier, P., 42-43
Adam, A., 112
Ådna, J., 16
Aland, B., 45
Aland, K., 8, 132
Allison, D. C., 1, 4, 25
Arnold, C. E., 62

Baldwin, M. C., 27, 30
Barrett, C. K., 62, 67
Bauckham, R., 6, 7, 32, 108-10, 122
Bauer, W., 6, 98-99
Baur, F. C., 42, 52, 69
Beck, H. G., 130
Becker, H.-J., 5
Bengel, A., 133
Berger, K., 27
Bernheim, P.-A., 9, 11, 51
Betz, O., 16
Beyer, W., 92
Billerbeck, P., 4, 13, 15, 62
Blinzler, J., 109
Böcher, O., 1, 34, 36
Bockmuehl, M., 13-14, 20, 25, 30, 44
Böttrich, C., 21
Brashler, J., 127
Braun, J., 131
Brun, L., 34
Buchowiecki, W., 131

Burchard, C., 77
Byrskog, S., 80

Campenhausen, H. v., 49, 115
Caragounis, C. C., 21
Chadwick, H., 123-25, 129
Claudel, G., 2
Conzelmann, H., 34, 38
Cook, J. G., 33, 58
Cramer, J. A., 129
Cullmann, O., 1, 6, 60, 106

Davies, W. D., 1, 4, 25
Deines, R., 28, 31, 63
Dell, A., 21
Dibelius, M., 18
Diehl, E., 128
Dobbeler, A. v., 116
Dschulnigg, P., 2, 40, 44
Du Cange, C., 122

Elm, S., 112

Feldmeier, R., 28-29, 36-37, 39, 103
Ferguson, J., 123
Fitzmyer, J. A., 21
Ford, J. M., 21
Frank, K. S., 112
Froelich, K., 50

Gäckle, V., 63, 66, 75
Gnilka, J., 2, 46
Grappe, C., 1, 6-7, 16-17
Grässer, E., 72, 76
Gregorovius, F., 131
Günther, M., 46

Haenchen, E., 34, 46
Harnack, A. v., 6, 45, 58, 77, 85, 105, 119, 124
Heckel, T. K., 45, 47
Heckel, U., 8, 72
Herzer, J., 54
Heussi, C., 98, 132
Hezser, C., 12
Hommel, H., 6
Horbury, W., 84
Hurtado, L., 86

Ilan, T., 20, 110

Jeremias, J., 23
Jülicher, A., 4
Jüngel, E., 84-85

Kammler, H.-C., 24
Klamroth, M., 128
Karrer, M., 66, 71
Kelhoffer, J. A., 45
Klauck, H.-J., 27
Klijn, A. F. J., 21
Klostermann, E., 44
Knoch, O., 30
Köhler, W.-D., 14, 32
Körtner, U. H. J., 46
Kümmel, W. G., 43, 62, 93, 111

Lagrange, P. M.-J., 1
Lampe, P., 21, 31, 38, 51, 86, 122
Lang, G., 38
Leclercq, H., 131
Lietzmann, H., 62, 66-67, 69, 70, 93, 111
Lindemann, A., 38
Lipsius, R. A., 120, 128, 130
Löhr, H., 95
Löhr, W. A., 33

Luz, U., 1, 3, 14, 21, 25, 30, 34

Mach, R., 9
Markschies, C., 33
Martínez, F. G., 16, 21
Metzger, B. M., 62
Meyer, E., 38, 67, 70
Michel, O., 112
Mimouni, S. C., 11
Mitchell, M. M., 32
Mittmann-Richert, U., 43, 87
Morgenthaler, R., 29
Muschiol, G., 128, 131
Mutschler, B., 47

Nau, A. J., 2, 28

Oepke, A., 123, 125

Paget, J. C., 11
Parrott, D. M., 127
Pesch, R., 1, 21-22, 107
Peters, R., 131
Philonenko, M., 87
Pratscher, W., 9
Prieur, J.-M., 7, 130

Rahmani, L. Y., 20
Regul, J., 48
Riesner, R., 77, 95, 106, 120, 137
Rüger, H.-P., 22, 37

Schenk, W., 31
Schenke, H. M., 127
Schlatter, A., 1, 21-22, 26, 93
Schlier, H., 18
Schnelle, U., 12, 38, 46
Schrage, W., 66, 112
Schürer, E., 30, 78
Schütz, L., 131
Schwemer, A. M., 10, 29, 61, 67
Shanks, H., 106
Smith, T. V., 42, 70
Sokoloff, M., 21
Staab, K., 129
Stählin, O., 123

Sterck-Degueldre, J.-P., 121
Strange, J. F., 106
Strobel, A., 57
Stuhlmacher, P., 25, 84

Testa, E., 106
Thornton, C.-J., 47, 109, 117
Thrall, M. E., 70, 72, 92
Thümmel, H. G., 6
Tigchelaar, E. J. C., 16, 21
Trebilco, P., 47

Vielhauer, P., 4, 18, 46, 67, 96

Wehr, L., 2-3, 21, 23, 25, 46, 50
Wellhausen, J., 38
Wenham, D., 76
Wiarda, T., 2
Wilckens, U., 34-35
Windisch, H., 92
Wohlenberg, G., 133
Wrede, W., 43

Zahn, T., 42, 50-51, 117, 128, 132-33
Zuntz, G., 12

Index of Subjects

Abba/Abba cry, 87
Abraham, 25
Achaia, 50, 92
Acts of Andrew, 50, 119, 130
Acts of the Apostles, 55, 77-79, 97-98
   historical reliability, 116-17
Agrippa I, 46, 53, 65, 90, 131
Agrippa's persecution, 10, 29, 46, 48, 55,
   77, 90, 100
Alexander and Rufus, 109
Alexandria, 50, 120
Ananias and Sapphira, 89
Andrew
   the brother of Peter, 13, 19-20, 26, 29,
      40-41, 49, 77, 105, 119, 130, 133
   a radical ascetic, 119
Andronicus and Junia, 55, 73, 109, 122,
   134
Anicetus, 51
Antinomians, 5, 28, 67
Antioch in Pisidia, 84, 97
Antioch in Syria, 30, 48-50, 54, 56-57,
   63-64, 74ff., 77-78, 83, 90-91, 122
   conflict between Peter and Paul, 24,
      50, 52, 55, 57ff., 66, 74-75, 79, 84-85,
      90, 96, 100
   dating, 57
   establishment of the community, 50,
      76
   Gentile Christians, 59, 60-61, 64, 74

Jewish Christians, 57ff., 64, 74
Apollos, 24, 50, 67, 120
Apostles: acts/novels, 26, 120, 124-25,
   127-28
Apostolic Council, 10, 24, 48, 50, 52ff.,
   60ff., 69, 75, 77, 83, 96, 100-101
Apostolic Decree, 50, 62ff., 74, 78, 85
   dating, 75
Apostolic tradition/witness, 33, 89, 99,
   102
Aquila. *See* Prisc(ill)a and Aquila
Asia (Roman province), 49, 121
Asia Minor, 49, 52, 74
Ascetics/asceticism, 112-15, 119, 123, 125,
   128
Augustus, 13

Babylon, 106
Barnabas, 9, 30, 55, 57-62, 64, 73-74, 111,
   130-31
   break with Paul, 58-59, 98
Barnabas, Letter of, 85
Basilides, 33
Benedict XVI, 84
Bethsaida, 13, 40, 105, 118, 130
Binding and loosing, power of, 4

Caesar, cult of the, 88
Caesarea, 49, 56, 73, 78, 91, 117
Caligula, 53-54, 65, 76, 122

Capernaum, 13, 40, 49, 104-6
Celibacy, 129
Celsus, 33
Cenchreae, 121
Cephas. *See* Peter
Cephas party. *See under* Corinth
Cerdo, 85, 119
Charismatic gifts, 72
Christ. *See* Jesus Christ
Christology, 34, 40, 54, 85, 87-88, 98, 101,
  116
  development, 34, 101
Church unity, 65, 68-69, 74, 84, 90-91,
  97
Cilicia, 78
Circle of the Twelve, the "Twelve," 18-19,
  26, 70, 77-78, 89, 100, 110, 112, 118
  crises/disagreements, 8, 26, 31, 93
  full authority to carry out discipline,
    4, 27
  miracles, 77
  witnesses to the resurrection, 68
Circumcision, 55, 60-62, 69
Claudius, 50, 54-55, 95, 120
Claudius, Edict of, 95, 120
Clement of Alexandria, 9-10, 23, 27, 33,
  47, 51, 103, 112, 116, 123-29, 134
  understanding of marriage, 123-29
Clement of Rome, 12, 17, 48, 126
Colossians, Letter to, 97
Community
  as (eschatological) temple, 16-18, 112
  as the house of God, 112
  as a priestly community, 19
  social care, 121, 124
Community of goods, 112
Conflict in Antioch. *See* Antioch in
  Syria
Continuity between Jesus and the
  church, 76, 87
Corinth, 24, 35, 49, 63ff., 66ff., 81, 83, 91-
  93, 111, 120
  Cephas party, 24, 35, 66-68, 78, 96,
    101, 114
  founding of the community, 17, 66-
    68, 92

visit by Peter, 66ff.
Corinthians, Letters to, 33, 66ff., 69, 73,
  101
1 Corinthians, 111
  dating, 73, 111
2 Corinthians, 69ff., 93
  dating, 73, 93
  hypotheses about dividing them, 93
Cornelius, 57, 79-80, 84, 90-91, 117
Corpus Johanneum, 99, 102

Damascus, 35, 38, 56, 84, 124
Denying oneself, 129
Diaspora, 30, 50, 55, 61, 95
Dionysius of Corinth, 6, 35, 67, 126
Disciple, Beloved, 8, 19, 26, 29-30, 82,
  118
  competition with Peter, 8
Disciples of Jesus
  call, 19, 107
  lack of understanding, 43-44
  as "walk-ons," 25, 29, 82
  wives/marriage, 108, 112
  See also Circle of the Twelve
Disciples of Jesus, female, 108-9, 130, 133
Docetists/Docetism, 70, 123
Domitian, 7, 12
Domitilla-catacombs, 128, 130-31

Earliest community, 22-23, 30, 43, 44,
  59, 61, 65-66, 75, 77, 86-88, 95, 109,
  122, 134
  commonality of goods, 112
  as the *familia Dei,* 112
  leadership. *See* James, brother of the
    Lord; Peter
  spiritual enthusiasm, 87
Ebionites, 11, 51
Egypt, 21, 47, 50
Elders, 10, 54, 78, 115
Election, 15, 26, 83
Encratites/Encratism, 115, 123ff., 128, 134
Enoch Fragments, 21
Enthusiasm, 34, 87, 119
Ephesians, Letter to
  coming into existence/dating, 18

Ephesus, 49, 67
Ethos, Christian, 88, 101, 123
Eucharist, 9, 59, 63, 84, 100, 128

Families, apostolic, 104ff., 115ff., 122, 134
Fisher(s) of human beings, 41, 55, 107
Flesh offered to idols, 57, 63, 66
Forgiveness, 27, 43-44, 86, 97
Form-history, 88

Galatia, 24, 49, 62, 64, 66, 69
Galatians, Letter to, 33, 69, 85, 101
   coming into existence/dating, 66
Gentile Christians/Christendom, 32, 52, 57ff., 61, 64, 65, 74
Glaucias, 33
Gnostics/Gnosticism, 70, 72, 85, 115
Godfearers, 56, 60, 91, 100
God's reign, 4, 25, 27, 82
Golden Legend, The, 131
Golden Rule, 62
Gospel of the Hebrews, 9
Gospels, 29
   addressees, 32-33, 45
   references to authors, 37, 45, 104
   relationship as they come into existence, 3, 33, 45, 48, 88
   Synoptic tradition, 89
Grace, 26, 68, 84

Hadrian, 33, 46
Hegesippus, 10, 82, 108
Hellenists, 22, 53-54, 56, 90, 100, 116, 122
Herod Antipas, 110
Hierapolis, 118
House community(ies), 115, 117, 119, 133-34
   in Ephesus, 121
   in Rome, 73, 90, 95, 109, 121

Iconium, 97
Identity, Jewish, 61, 63
Ignatius of Antioch, 14, 49-51, 54, 99, 115
Illyricum, 78, 94
Irenaeus, 11, 32, 35, 45, 47, 85, 103, 119
Isho'dad from Merv, 131-32

James, brother of the Lord, 8ff., 22, 29-30, 32, 35, 53-55, 62, 67, 69, 96
   bishop of Jerusalem, 9-10
   claim to be leader, 8-9, 51
   community leader in Jerusalem, 42, 48, 51-52, 78, 100
   frequency in the New Testament, 10-11
   "The Just," 8-9, 82
   martyrdom, 10, 51-52, 65, 82
   messengers from, 54, 59, 65, 84
   recipient of a revelation, 9
   relationship with Peter, 9
   witness to the Resurrection, 68
James, son of Zebedee, 26, 49
James, Letter of, 54, 92
Jerusalem, 17, 55-56, 61, 64, 73-74, 100
   destruction after A.D. 70, 4, 11, 85, 105
   end-time, 18
Jerusalem, collection for, 55, 58, 65, 69, 74
Jesus Christ
   brothers of Jesus, 10, 29, 67, 109, 112, 114
   as cornerstone, 18
   crucifixion/death, 31, 33, 44, 60, 64, 66, 68, 72, 82, 108-9
   following, 31, 107ff., 133
   as foundation, 16-17, 112
   miracles, 72, 104-5
   occupation, 109
   predictions of suffering, 7, 39
   relatives of Jesus, 10, 108-9
   resurrection, 68, 77, 84, 87, 110
   as "Rock," 17
   servant of God, 3, 87
   sisters of Jesus, 109
   Son of God, 4, 15, 25, 75, 82
   turning toward sinners, 86
   understanding of marriage, 107ff., 113
Jewish Christians/Christianity 9, 11, 25, 31, 52, 54, 61-62, 69, 70, 74, 95, 106
   accusation of apostasy, 54, 65
   in Antioch, 64, 66, 75
   in Capernaum, 106
   in Jerusalem, 65, 69, 74, 100

missionaries, 70-71, 92, 95
oppression/persecution in Jerusalem,
  61, 65, 84, 100-101
  role as leaders, 57, 90, 95
  zealous for the law, 65, 70
Jewish War, 6, 52, 65, 78, 117
Jews, 23, 55
  in Anatolia, 62
  in Caesarea, 78
  in Palestine, 4-5, 30, 37, 53, 65, 76, 107,
    109
  in Rome, 6, 76
  in Syria, 30
Jo(h)anna, wife of Chuza, 110, 122
Johannine school, 47, 49
John, Acts of, 118
John, Apocalypse of, 7
John, the Elder/Presbyter, 13, 32-33, 37,
  46, 103, 118
John, Gospel of, 8, 12, 39
John, son of Zebedee, 5, 10, 12, 26, 30-31,
  80, 90
John the Baptist, 86
Joppa, 90-91
Joseph, father of Jesus, 109
Josephus, 10, 13, 21, 30, 56, 124, 131
Julia (city), 13
Julian the Apostate, 33, 58
Justin, 32, 44, 47, 103
Just/Righteous, the, 8-9, 43, 125

Laodicea, 121, 126
Last Supper description, 44, 75, 87
Law, Jewish, 11, 31, 54, 59, 62, 65, 70, 73,
  75
  meaning for salvation, 60, 70
Letters of (re)commendation, 71, 91
Libertinists/libertinism, 5, 28, 70, 73, 120
Logia tradition (Q), 38, 81-82, 107-8
Luke, evangelist, 44, 79ff.
  call, 80, 105
  coming into existence/dating, 79-80
  harmonization/transmission, 11, 53,
    57-58, 66, 70-71, 77-79, 85-86, 102
  Jesus tradition, 80
  Pauline influence, 44, 86, 113

travel partner of Paul, 80-81, 116-17
two-volume work, 33, 79, 90
visit to Jerusalem, 80
Luke, Gospel of, 80
  author, 44
  date, 80
  depiction of Peter, 80, 90
Lydda, 90-91
Lydia, 121
Lystra, 61, 97

Macedonia, 50, 93, 129
Maranatha, 87
Marcion, 17, 45, 85, 115, 119, 124
Marcionism before Marcion, 85
Maria, wife of Clopas, 108
Mark, evangelist, 36ff., 42, 97-98, 103-5
  disciple of Peter, 36ff., 80, 86, 98, 101,
    103
  interpreter of Peter, 12, 37, 46, 103
  nephew of Barnabas, 46, 97, 104
  recognized authority, 46, 104
  secondary name: John, 42, 97, 104, 131
  son of Peter, 132
  theology, 86
Mark, Gospel of
  anti-Peter tendencies? 42
  author, 38, 43-44, 46
  coming into existence, 36-37, 40
  dating, 39, 104, 108
  depiction of Peter, 14, 41, 101
  historical reliability, 86, 105, 109
  inclusio for Peter, 41-42, 103
  language/vocabulary, 37, 40, 104
  Petrine tradition/authority, 38-39, 40,
    44-47, 103ff.
  redaction, 39
Marriage, 113ff., 123ff.
  apostolic marriages, 112, 123
  bishops' marriages, 115
  divorce, 108, 113
  high regard for marriage, 134
  remaining unmarried, 114ff.
  remarriage, 113-15
  renunciation of marriage, 125, 128-29
  "spiritual marriage," 125, 130

Married couples, missionary, 113, 123, 134

Married wives, apostolic, 68, 107, 111-12, 123

Martyrs, female, 126

Mary, mother of James and Joses, 110

Mary, mother of Jesus, 108-9

Mary, mother of John Mark, 46

Mary and Martha, 134

Mary Magdalene, 108, 110

Matthew, evangelist, 4-5, 14
    collection of logia of Jesus, 13, 32, 47
    Jewish-Christian scholar of the law, 4, 31
    toll collector, 13
    understanding of marriage, 114

Matthew, Gospel of
    author, 3, 31, 43-44, 114
    coming into existence/dating, 5, 51
    depiction of Peter, 28, 30-31, 91
    redaction of the evangelist, 3
    situation, 5, 12, 28, 31
    vocabulary/theology, 5
    "word about the Rock" (Matt. 16:17-19), 1ff., 14, 19, 23, 96

Messianic secret, 43

Minor agreements, 107

Mission, 49ff., 66ff., 78-79, 90ff., 95
    battle concerning missional territories, 78, 92
    competition, 92-94
    demarcation of the Jewish and Gentile missions, 54-57, 60-61
    missionaries, female, 121, 124, 129
    mission to the Gentiles, 31, 56, 101
    Pauline areas of missional activity, 49-50, 61, 69, 78, 91, 113
    Petrine areas of missional activity, 49, 54
    worldwide mission, 72, 95

Mixed marriage, 61

Monarchical office of bishop, 9, 51, 98
    development, 51-52

Montanists, 120, 124

Nag Hammadi, 10, 26, 127

Nearness of end, expectation of, 34

Nero, 6ff., 33, 95, 120

Origen, 1, 7, 33, 43, 107-8

Palestine, Jewish, 4, 30, 57, 79, 90, 92

Papias, 12-13, 29, 32, 37, 46-47, 103-4, 116-18

Parenesis, 76, 88, 115-16, 123

Parousia of Christ, 7, 12, 15, 92, 118

Pastoral Letters, 12, 97, 115, 121
    author, 115
    dating, 52
    understanding of marriage, 115

Paul, 5-6, 32, 57ff., 64, 67, 111ff., 120
    autobiographical witness, 15, 56, 111
    apostolic office. *See below,* contested apostolate
    break with Antioch, 64
    contested apostleship, 66ff., 72, 77, 91ff., 111
    conversion, 35, 109
    familial relationships, 116, 122
        Pharisaic background, 13, 96, 116
        vocation, 68, 120
    frequency of mention in the New Testament, 11
    imprisonment, 67-68, 122
    irony, 72, 91
    Jesus tradition/Words of the Lord, 75-76, 81
    martyr/martyrdom, 6, 40, 47, 98
    miracles/acts of power, 76-77
    mission, 49, 56, 68, 75, 80, 90
        "first missionary journey," 56
        "second missionary journey," 57, 61, 64, 74, 98
        "third nissionary journey," 57-58, 62, 64, 95
        trip to Spain, 6, 92, 94, 121
    opponents/accusations, 11, 35, 58, 66, 69-70, 72, 76, 91, 100
    persecutor of Christ, 44, 53, 68, 75
    polemic, 17, 59, 66-67, 72, 112
    relationship to Peter
        basic consensus, 68, 83, 97, 102

conflict. *See* Antioch in Syria
  opponent/rival, 32, 53, 89, 134
  reconciliation, 97ff.
  visit to Peter, 35, 88, 113
  self-praise, 66, 72, 93
  theology, 5, 83
    conceptualization of the law, 54, 70
    ethic, 70
    justification, 44, 59, 72, 83
    theologia crucis, 70
    theological testament, 72
    understanding of marriage, 113-14
    the "thirteenth witness," 77, 82
    weakness/deficit, 72, 92
Paul, Acts of, 124
Pauline Letters, 33, 38, 53, 71, 83
  collection of letters, 12, 18, 46, 115
  mention of Peter, 23-24, 30
Pauline school, 97
Pella, flight to, 65
Persecution, eschatological, 7
Persecution, Neronic, 5-7, 48, 71, 97-98,
  108, 126
Petronilla, daughter of Peter, 21, 128, 130
Peter
  authority, 4-5, 13, 36, 95, 96
    authoritative disciple, 42, 82, 85
    bishop in Rome, 50
    central apostolic figure, 28, 30-31,
      36
    eyewitness, 80
    foundation stone, 14, 16-18
    founder of the mission to the
      Gentiles? 57
    full power as leader, 4
    guarantor of tradition, 42
    leading role in the Gospels, 42, 45,
      48, 90
    primacy, 96
    protophany (first appearance), 29,
      34, 42, 44, 66, 68, 100
    receiver of revelation, 15ff.
    speaker for the disciples, 13, 29, 35,
      71, 82, 100-101
    teacher, 4, 89
    "typical disciple"? 25

  unique importance, 3, 5, 13, 89
in Corinth, 66ff.
delegation from Peter, 24, 35, 49-50,
  56, 63, 69, 71, 76-77, 81, 91-92
family, 106
  children, 125, 130
  daughter, 126-30
  father, 105
  marriage, 125-26
  married state, 104, 107
  mother-in-law, 41, 104-5, 129-30
  occupation, 12-13, 19, 29, 40, 68, 96,
    106, 133
  wife, 105, 111-13, 125-27, 130, 133
    martyrdom of, 106, 125-26, 131
flight from Jerusalem, 48, 55, 95, 100
frequency in New Testament, 10-11,
  28-29, 39
giving of the name, 17, 19ff., 36, 100
  "Man of Rock," 7, 14ff., 34, 90
  name of honor, 23, 89
  "Simon Bar Jonah," 3, 19, 105
  Rock, 16-17, 22ff., 25
  rock or stone? 21-22
knowledge of Greek, 12-13, 101
leader of earliest community, 29, 34,
  48, 75, 89, 100
martyrdom/martyr, 5-7, 16, 31, 36, 40,
  50, 83, 89, 96-97, 126
  doubt about martyrdom, 89, 99
miracles, 76-77, 90, 93, 127-28
mission, 13, 17, 41, 50, 54, 66-68, 70,
  75-78, 89, 92, 95, 100ff.
  establishing communities, 50, 90-
    91
  missionary to the Gentiles, 34, 52,
    56-57, 101
  missionary to the Jews, 34, 55, 101
  mission strategy/organizer, 89, 95,
    101-2
  preaching, 34, 85-89
relationship with James, 9-10, 52
relationship with Jesus
  beatitude, 8, 25
  call, 29

confession about the Messiah, 3-4,
14ff., 39
denial of Jesus, 40, 44, 86
function as intermediary, 82
Jesus tradition, 14, 34, 53, 75, 88, 101
relationship with Mark, 45ff.
inclusio in Mark, 42, 103
relationship with Paul
basic consensus, 68, 83, 97, 102
conflict. *See* Antioch in Syria
opponent/rival, 32, 52-53, 83, 89,
134
reconciliation, 97ff.
in Rome, 50, 55, 70, 94-95
theology, 35, 38, 40, 79, 83, 85-86, 96,
102
bridging function, 79-80
concept of the law, 53
early kerygma, 88
Judaist? 69
theological mediator? 35
underestimation, 32, 34, 37, 85, 96
Peter, Office of. *See* Primacy, claim of
Petrine Literature, 5, 12, 14, 26-27, 30, 35,
126-28
Gospel of Peter, 31
Letters of Peter, 12
1 Peter, 46, 54, 86, 98, 103; Author
of, 48, 103
2 Peter, 12
Petrine school, 35, 89
Philemon, Letter to, 97
Philip, Acts of, 127
Philip, apostle and evangelist, 20, 26,
90-91, 116ff., 125
house community, 119
identity, 118
marriage, family, 125
prophetic daughters, 116ff., 125
Philippi, 51
Philippians, Letter to, 101
coming into existence, 49, 67
Philo of Alexandria, 23
Phlegon of Tralles, 33
Phoebe, 121
Polycarp, 98, 115

Polycarp, Letter of, 51
Polycrates, bishop of Ephesus, 37, 116-
17, 119, 125
Porphyry, 58
Power to teach and discipline, 4, 27
Primacy, claim of, 96, 99
Prisc(ill)a and Aquila, 49, 73, 95, 120,
134
Prohibition about eating, 75
Pseudo-Clementine Literature, 9, 11, 17,
27, 126
Purity, understanding of, 57ff.

Q-Hypothesis, 81-82, 107
Qumran, 16, 21, 71

Rabbis, 4-5, 20, 25, 81, 106
Rock, 17ff., 20ff.
Romans, Letter to, 55, 73, 78, 101, 121
dating, 93, 121
Rome, 1, 6, 30, 37, 40, 48-49, 55, 73, 78,
83, 90, 94-95, 99, 109, 121-22
"Babylon," 46, 103, 132
bishop of, 1, 50
community archive, 47, 109
concept of presbyters/elders, 51
founding of the community, 54, 73,
76, 78, 94
St. Peter's Basilica, 1, 99, 131

Sadducees, 65
Samaria, 90-91, 117
Scribes, 4-5, 27
Septuagint, 15, 88, 94, 112
Severian, bishop of Gabala, 129
Sidon, 58
Silvanus/Silas, 64, 74, 98
Simon Magus, 50, 85, 90, 126
Simon of Cyrene, 109
Simon Peter. *See* Peter
Spain, 6, 92, 94, 121
Spirit, gifting of, 72, 120
Stephen, 87, 117
Super-apostle, 76
Synagogue(s), 11, 56, 61, 67, 100, 124
Syneisakten (Subintroductae), 112

Syria, 30, 40, 49, 55, 70, 74, 78, 91-92, 95, 111

Table fellowship, 53, 57, 60, 63, 65, 74, 84
Tarsus, 13, 116, 122
Tertullian, 1, 17, 19, 48, 118, 125
Thecla, 124
Theodoret, bishop of Cyrrhus, 129
Theodotus, 33
Theophilus, 8, 45, 58, 79
Theophylactus, 129-30
Thomas, 8, 26
Thomas, Gospel of, 8, 82
Timothy, 61
Titus, 60
Trajan, 12, 21

Truth of the gospel, 63-64, 68, 83-84, 99

Valentinus, 33, 124
Victor, bishop of Rome, 118

Wandering in the wilderness by Israel, 24
Women's mission, 129
Women's movement, 109, 110

Zealots, 65, 84
Zebedee, sons of, James and John, 26, 40, 49, 107, 133
    frequency in the New Testament, 26, 49

Greek Terms

ἀκρογωνιαῖος, 18
ἀπομνημονεύματα τῶν ἀποστόλων, 32
(οἱ) ἀπόστολοι, 11, 73

Βαριωνᾶ, 3

γράμμα, 69

Ἑβραῖοι, 70-71
ἐκκλησία, 3, 17, 19, 95, 121
ἐκ πίστεως, 59
ἐπίσκοπος, 51
εὐαγγελίζεσθαι, 88
εὐαγγέλιον, 83, 88
εὐαγγέλιον τετράμορφον, 45

ζῆλος, 72

θεμέλιος/-ον, 16-18, 23-24, 67, 78, 94

ἰουδαΐζειν, 62
ἰσαπόστολος, 122

καταγιγνώσκειν, 58
καύχησις, 92
Κηφᾶς, 22, 42, 113

λίθος, 23

οἱ δώδεκα, 11
οἱ μαθηταί, 11, 82

παροξυσμός, 58
παρρησία, 34
περιτομή, 55, 69
πέτρα, 20-21, 100
πέτρος, 21, 23, 100
Πέτρος, 18-20, 23, 25, 28, 41-42, 67
πίστις, 75
πνευματικὴ πέτρα, 24
πορνεία, 63, 128
πρεσβύτερος, 52
προσήλυτος, 62
πτωχοί, 11
πύλαι ᾅδου, 6

Συμεών, 20, 22
συνείδησις, 75
συνεσθίειν, 62-63, 75
Συροφοινίκισσα, 40

τέκτων, 109
τέρμα τῆς δύσεως, 6

υἱὸς θεοῦ, 15
ὑπερλίαν ἀπόστολοι, 70, 77
ὑποστέλλειν, 9

Χριστός, 15, 24, 59, 77, 112

ψευδαπόστολοι, 70

ὡς μή, 126